Additional Praise for
The Global Expatriate's Guide to Investing

"This book is a must-read for expatriates or anyone thinking of becoming one. Whether you're an investor from Canada, the U.S., South America, Asia, Europe, Great Britain, Australia or New Zealand, you'll find the advice well-researched, useful, and easy to understand. Thanks to Andrew's wry sense of humor, it's surprisingly easy to digest too. "
Duncan Hood, Editor-in-Chief, *MoneySense* **magazine**

"A brilliantly written uncommon common sense guide to protecting your nest egg from both predators and yourself."
Allan Roth, author of *How a Second Grader Beat Wall Street*

"Millionaire Teacher resonated with so many investors because Andrew Hallam lives what he teaches. This new book has that same credibility, and it fills a huge gap in the marketplace. Expats don't just need to overcome the usual investment hurdles: they also face an extra logistical and tax burden when building their portfolios. Hallam is the ideal guide, because he's been there, and he's already cleared the trail."
Dan Bortolotti, Investment advisor with PWL Capital (Toronto), author Canadian Couch Potato blog

"This book is a must read by expats and their human resources departments if they hope to get on the path for a successful retirement. It covers all the bases including the egregious costs of the offshore pension schemes, country specific information on how to set up a low cost index investment approach and pitfalls expats need to avoid."
Robert Wasilewski, RW Investment Strategies, author of *DIY Investor* **Blog**

"Employers of expatriates, whether they're businesses or international schools, should give their employees a copy of this book. Hallam's investment strategies are aligned with academic evidence, and not the sales driven rhetoric to which so many naïve investors fall victim."
Larry Swedroe, Author of *Think, Act and Invest Like Warren Buffett,* **principal and Director of Research for Buckingham Asset Management Alliance**

"While Andrew Hallam's book is aimed at Expats, it's for anyone. It's a wonderful and breezy how-to book which will help Expats and home-bodies alike to avoid the myriad financial landmines that can derail our plans. It is, of course, must-read material for anyone thinking of moving or retiring in a foreign land. One thing I love about the book is the way that Andrew gleefully eviscerates sacred cows, whether they are widely accepted dogma or powerful interest blocs. It's fun to read truth that's not wrapped in caution."

Rob Arnott, Chairman and CEO, Research Affiliates; co-author, *The Fundamental Index*

"A good follow up book by Andrew Hallam, extoling the need to be self-reliant in our investing for our retirement. Andrew writes with a clear and logical thought process"

Jenny Chiam, Senior Vice President, Head of Securities—Singapore Exchange

"This is a great book for expatriates looking to grow and protect their hard-earned money. This book will help you avoid many costly and risky pitfalls with your life savings."

Craig Rowland, co-author *The Permanent Portfolio, Harry Browne's Long-Term Investment Strategy*

"In the opening lines of his book *The Global Expatriate's Guide to Investing,* Andrew Hallam reveals that at the tender age of nineteen, "I planned how much money I wanted to save, and why." If you gain nothing else from this book—and you will glean a great deal more—Hallam's reminder that saving is a critical part of the long-term wealth creation equation is priceless. And, the best part? Andrew will keep you laughing while you are learning–the mark of a great teacher who knows the material cold. This book is a must-read part of your investing library!"

Nancy Tengler, Author *The Women's Guide to Successful Investing,* **investing columnist for** *The Arizona Republic,* **former Chief Executive Officer and Chief Investment Officer, Fremont Investment Advisors**

The Global
Expatriate's Guide
to Investing

The Global Expatriate's Guide to Investing

From Millionaire Teacher to Millionaire Expat

Andrew Hallam

WILEY

Copyright © 2015 by Andrew Hallam. All rights reserved.

Published by John Wiley & Sons, Inc., Hoboken, New Jersey.
Published simultaneously in Canada.

For general information on our other products and services or for technical support, please contact our Customer Care Department within the United States at (800) 762-2974, outside the United States at (317) 572-3993 or fax (317) 572-4002.

Wiley publishes in a variety of print and electronic formats and by print-on-demand. Some material included with standard print versions of this book may not be included in e-books or in print-on-demand. If this book refers to media such as a CD or DVD that is not included in the version you purchased, you may download this material at http://booksupport.wiley.com. For more information about Wiley products, visit www.wiley.com.

Library of Congress Cataloging-in-Publication Data:

Hallam, Andrew (Teacher)
   The global expatriate's guide to investing : from millionaire teacher to millionaire expat/ Andrew Hallam.
     pages cm
   Includes bibliographical references and index.
   ISBN 978-1-119-02098-1 (cloth); ISBN 978-1-119-02100-1 (ebk); ISBN 978-1-119-02099-8 (ebk)
   1. Finance, Personal.   2. Investments.   3. Retirement income—Planning.   I. Title.
   HG179.H238 2015
   332.6—dc23

                                                                          2014030762

Printed in the United States of America
10 9 8 7 6 5 4 3 2 1

This book is dedicated to the millions of people who have taken the global road less traveled.
And to those who have purchased inflexible, expensive offshore pensions: May the cold calls stop ringing. And may global employers get wise to the investment foxes so many have invited into their own henhouses.

Contents

Foreword *Scott Burns*   xiii
Acknowledgments   xvii
Introduction   xix

Chapter 1: Setting Your Bull's-Eye   1

What's This Ailment Expatitis?   3
Cheating Conventional Retirement Rules   3
Cooking Up the Road Less Traveled   5
The Earthquake and the Epiphany   6
Jujitsu Junkie Taps Out for Home   8
Now It's Your Turn   9
Notes   10

Chapter 2: Building Your Pension   13

How to Never Run Out of Money   14
The Man with Nothing But a Backpack   16
The Couple with Swedish-American Dreams   18
A Front-End-Loaded Tale of Success   22
Notes   24

Chapter 3: The Truth about Stocks and Bonds   25

Halloween Grab Bag Treats Investors   26
Why Average Returns Aren't Normal   29

Stocks Pound Inflation 29
What Has the Stock Market Done for You Lately? 31
Undressing Stocks with 50 Shades of Gray 32
The Stock Market Stars as the Great Humiliator 35
Fast-Growing Economies Can Produce Weak Returns 37
Bonds Are Protective Nets for Jumpers 38
Can You Lose Money With Bonds? 41
Notes 43

Chapter 4: Don't Start a Fight with an Escalator 45
Yes, the Financial District Loves You! 46
Global Investors Getting Fleeced 47
Notes 50

Chapter 5: Where Are the Customers' Yachts? 51
Global Investors Bleed by the Same Sword 52
American Expatriates Run Naked 53
Why Brokers Want to Muzzle Warren Buffett 54
Financial Advisors Touting "The World Is Flat!" 56
Hedge Fund Money Spanked for Its Con 58
Why Most Investors Underperform Their Funds 62
Notes 65

Chapter 6: Don't Climb into Bed with a Silver-Tongued Player 69
Featuring the Rip-Offers 71
The Ten Habits of Successful Financial Advisors . . . Really? 72
When Your Advisor Is a Sales Commando 73
Welcoming Sharks into the Seal Pool 74
Misled Investors Pay the Price 75
A Canadian Investor Gets Bled 75
Would You Like a Band-Aid for That Bleeding Gash? 77
Masters of the Insured Death Benefit Illusion 77
Free Fund Switching Isn't a Perk 78
Making Millions off the General Public 79
Fooling the Masses with Numbers 79
Regulators Making an Effort 80
Can Squeaky Wheels Gain Redemption? 83
If Investors Can't Reclaim Their Losses 84
When High Fees Meet Gunslingers 86
A Son's Inheritance Gets Plundered 86
British Teacher Learns a Costly Lesson 90
Playing Soccer Like Wasps around Honey 90
Most Investors Are Crazy 92
Notes 93

Chapter 7:   Self-Appointed Gurus and Neanderthal Brains   95

Why Most Investors Should Hope for Falling Markets   96
It's Not Timing the Market That Matters; It's Time in
   the Market   97
High Unemployment and High Stock Returns   98
What Can You Miss by Guessing Wrong?   100
When Investors and Advisors Sabotage Their Rides   102
Popular Stocks Underperform   104
How About the Next Big Thing?   105
When Genius Fails   107
Notes   107

Chapter 8:   An Employer's Greatest Challenge   111

Fees—How Much Is Too Much?   113
So What's the Solution for Global Employers?   115
Notes   118

Chapter 9:   Couch Potato Investing   119

Don't Bonds Tie You Down?   120
Is It More of a Fling Than a Real Relationship?   120
Potatoes Growing Globally   122
Bonds Relative to Age and Risk   124
What If You're Falling Behind?   125
Profiting from Panic—Stock Market Crash 2008–2009   125
Owning the World   126
Where Do You Plan to Retire?   127
Are You Retiring in an Emerging Market Country?   129
Does This Sound Too Good to Be True?   130

Chapter 10: The Permanent Portfolio: Growth
                 without Risk   131

Gold in Isolation Is a Total Loser   132
A Disco-Era Brainchild from a
   Twentieth-Century Socrates   132
This Great Portfolio Will Never Be Popular
   (But It Should Be!)   133
Why Does It Work?   137
What Has It Done for Me Lately?   138
Notes   139

Chapter 11: Fundamental Indexing:
                 Can We Build a Better Index Portfolio?   141

Like Top Basketball Players Getting the Most Court Time   142

Index Funds That Appear to Beat the Market   144
Investment Legend Likens Them to Witchcraft   144
Global Fundamental Indexes Might Shelter
    Us from Bubbles   146
Emerging Markets Show the Greatest Difference   146
Aren't These Just Actively Managed Products?   147
Notes   148

Chapter 12: Capable Investment Advisors with a Conscience   149

Do You Have a Ninja's Discipline?   151
Qualities of a Great Financial Advisor   151
Investment Professionals worth Considering   153
Notes   170

Chapter 13: Choosing Your Offshore Brokerage—
For Non-Americans   173

DBS Vickers Securities Opens the Door
    to Everyone   174
Why You Should Avoid E★Trade Financial   176
TD Direct Investing International   176
Saxo Capital Markets—A Jewel with Distractions   177
Comparing Fees with International Brokerages   179
Is Interactive Brokers the Dark Horse Winner?   184
Notes   184

Chapter 14: The 16 Questions Do-It-Yourself
Investors Ask   187

What's the Difference between an Exchange-Traded
    Index Fund (ETF) and an Index Fund?   187
Do Non-Americans Have to Pay U.S. Estate Taxes
    upon Death If They Own U.S. Index Shares?   188
What's a Sector-Specific ETF?   188
Should I Buy an Index That's Currency Hedged?   189
What's the Scoop on Withholding Taxes?
    (For Non-Americans)   191
Will You Have to Pay Currency Conversions?   192
Should I Be Concerned about Currency Risks?   193
Do the Unit Prices of ETFs Show Which Are
    Expensive or Cheap?   194
If I Have a Lump Sum, Should I Invest It All at Once?   194
I'm in Some Expensive Products, but They're Currently
    Down in Value. Should I Sell Now or Wait?   195
How Do I Open a Brokerage Account and Make
    Purchases? (For Non-Americans)   195

What If I Find a Higher-Performing Bond Index? 200
What If I Find a Cheaper ETF? 201
Should I Be Most Concerned about Commissions,
  Annual Account Fees, Fund Costs or
  Exchange Rate Fees? 201
How Little Can I Invest Each Month? 201
Stock Markets Are High. Should I Really Start Investing? 202
Let's Go! 203
Notes 203

Chapter 15: Investing for American Expats* 205
Do You Currently Invest with Vanguard? 206
Couch Potato Investing with Vanguard 207
Couch Potato Investing with a Vanguard Stick Shift 209
When Investors Binge on Speculation 210
Charles Schwab Offers a Great Deal 212
Doing the Couch Potato with Schwab 212
Permanent Portfolio Investing with Schwab 214
Fundamental Indexing Magic in the Works 214
Don't Contribute Illegally to Your IRA 215
What Exactly Is an IRA? 216
Roth IRAs Are Different 216
Notes 217

Chapter 16: Investing for Canadian Expats 219
Canadian Funds Earn an "F" for Costs 220
Brokerage Options for Expatriate Canadians 221
Brokerages for Canadians in
  Capital-Gains-Free Jurisdictions 222
Building a Canadian Couch Potato Portfolio 223
ETF Canadian Price War 227
The Permanent Portfolio, Canadian Style 227
Fundamental Indexing Portfolios 229
What About RRSPs and TFSAs? 230
Swap-Based ETFs, the Ultimate Legal Tax Dodge 231
Notes 232

Chapter 17: Investing for British Expats 235
Expensive Firms Performing Like a Virgin 236
Couch Potato Investing for British Expatriates 237
British Investors and the Permanent Portfolio 240
Fundamental Indexing for the British 241
Notes 243

Chapter 18: Investing for Australian Expats   245

    Fancy an Australian Couch Potato?   247
    How About an Australian Permanent Portfolio?   248
    Fundamental Indexing for Australians   249
    Notes   251

Chapter 19: Investing for New Zealand Expats   253

    Kiwis Chilling Out With The Couch Potato   254
    Permanent Portfolio for Kiwis   255
    Fundamental Indexing for New Zealanders   255
    Notes   257

Chapter 20: Investing for South African and
             South American Expats   259

    South African Investors   259
    South Africans Fry Up the Couch Potato   260
    South African Writer Likes the Permanent Portfolio   261
    South Africans Preferring Fundamental Platforms   263
    South American Investors   263
    Brazilian Investing Models   264
    Notes   267

Chapter 21: Investing for European Expats   269

    Country-Specific European ETFs   269
    European Indexes That Investors Will Like   271
    Why Not Choose the Simpler Option?   274
    Calling Italians and the Swiss   275
    The European's Permanent Portfolio   276
    Fundamental Indexing for Europeans   277
    So What's It Going to Be—Couch Potato,
       Permanent, or Fundamentally Indexed?   279
    Notes   279

Chapter 22: Investing for Asian Expats   281

    An Indian National Divulges Her Plan   282
    Asians Embracing the Couch Potato   284
    Asians Choosing the Permanent Portfolio   287
    Fundamental Portfolio for Asians   288
    Notes   289

Conclusion   291
About the Author   293
Index   295

Foreword

Scott Burns

Investing: Now Anyone Can Do It, Anywhere

Some people like investing. Most people don't. They would rather do something else. Almost anything else, in fact. People clean their ovens, sweep the garage and clean out old files to avoid it. Others will fold socks, return used printer cartridges or visit their in-laws. They will do all this to avoid thinking about saving and investing.

That's just the way it is.

But Andrew Hallam has opened a door. Here, people who don't like investing can mix with people who do. And both can benefit. The people who like investing can benefit: These pages are a passport to investing anywhere in the world. Here, you can learn to be a free agent, in charge of your life, now and later.

The people who don't like investing can benefit because this book is an easy read. It tells you how to invest at the lowest possible cost. The result is more money growing for you. The book does the telling in step-by-step detail. And when it has a calculation, which is rare, it shows you how. Wherever you are from, and wherever you are, the Millionaire Teacher tells you how to invest your savings. He does this using a variety of funds, all focused on low costs, simplicity and diversification. And, yes, there can be a "tilt" toward where you expect your retirement home base to be.

Absolutely, positively don't want to do this on your own? Not to worry. Andrew introduces you to some low cost investment managers. These firms will build and track your portfolio at a fraction of conventional costs. Better still, the number and variety of these firms is growing.

So if you are an expat, working or living in a country that isn't the same as your native country, this is your cornerstone book.

If the mere mention of a calculation makes you nervous, don't worry. Andrew is a teacher, a good one. He assumes you know nothing and takes you through it step-by-step. Making it simple is important because the best way to achieve your goals is by being a low cost do-it-yourself investor.

Here's why. Most people worry about the taxman and the damage taxes can do to their savings. But the person likely to do the most damage is the one who wants to sell you an investment program. The offer is that your sage advisor will make brilliant and wise investment decisions for you.

Sorry, this doesn't happen. Instead, your money helps a salesperson make a pressing Mercedes payment. It may also help his boss buy a house in Aspen or the Hamptons.

The damage that person does isn't obvious. The financial services industry does its best to disguise the burden of its "customary and normal" fees. The problem starts with how financial expenses are expressed. Universally, they state expenses as a percent of assets managed. So if we commit $1,000 and the expenses are one percent, it's only $10 a year.

It's hard to complain about that, right?

But the functional burden is much larger. You have to measure by what counts: the actual return on your money. Managing your investment costs for a "modest" 1 percent of assets is one thing. But if the gross return on your money is 8 percent, the manager is taking 12.5 percent of your return. Raise the fees to 3 percent of assets and the manager's take is 37.5 percent of your return. Yet charges of 3 percent of assets are common in most of the world outside of the United States.

That's more than the taxman takes from most people. We have also made the benign assumption that the manager will actually deliver such a return. Most don't. As a multitude of research studies have shown, about 70 percent of all managed money fails to beat its appointed index.

But even that measure understates the true burden people saving for their retirements face. In the Journal of Portfolio Management industry guru Charles Ellis tells us the truth.[1] An "informed realist," he says, would measure the cost of active management as "the *incremental* fee as a percentage of *incremental* returns."

Sorry about that.

Here's his example, in plain arithmetic. Suppose you buy a managed fund that has expenses of 1.5 percent a year. Suppose it outperforms its benchmark index by 0.5 percent a year. Since the manager had to outperform the index by 2.0 percent to deliver the extra 0.5 percent, the true cost of management takes 75 percent of the gain. You won't find many taxmen, anywhere on the planet extracting that big a toll. But money managers around the world do it routinely.

Indeed, a management expense of 1.5 percent is low in most of the world outside of the United States. Check the examples provided in these pages. You'll see that expat investors often encounter fee levels of 3 percent and more.

Brokerage houses, insurance companies and banks would love to continue taking their gigantic fees. But the world has changed around them. Where once they were the only ways to distribute investment funds, today they are just the most expensive ways to invest.

Today, we have alternatives. The new institutions have fees so low that it can be 20 years, sometimes more, before their costs exceed what the old guard institutions collect in a single year. Today it is possible to put together a well-diversified global portfolio and do it for well under 0.20 percent a year.

When I introduced the first Couch Potato portfolio in 1991 index mutual funds were in their infancy. There were a handful of low-cost index funds in the United States. Of necessity the original portfolio was dirt simple: a 50/50 mix of US large stocks and US bonds. That simple solution has served thousands of people very well.

---

[1] Charles D. Ellis, "The Rise and Fall of Performance Investing," Journal of Portfolio Management, July/August 2014

Today there are thousands of Exchange Traded Funds providing low-cost choices. And they are available almost anywhere in the world. So you can do this wherever you are, tailored to wherever you are or wherever you go.

The good news doesn't end there. Intense competition among the lower-cost distribution companies has eliminated commissions on many ETF purchases. It has also brought down annual expenses on many of the most important index funds to own. *At long last, next to nothing stands between you and the return on your money.* This is a buyer's market.

And Andrew Hallam is here to guide you.

—Scott Burns

Acknowledgments

No book on low-cost investing should be written without a nod to John Bogle. Referred to by many as Saint Jack, he created the first low-cost index fund. The firm he founded, Vanguard, is now the largest mutual fund provider in the world. What's especially cool is that he didn't profit from its growth. Run much like a nonprofit firm, it's testimony to altruistic goodness gone positively viral.

I hope this book does justice to his low-cost, diversified mantra for investors.

I would also like to acknowledge investment writers Ian McGugan and Scott Burns. They're the best personal finance writers I know. And they continue to coach my writing. If this book reads clearly, with a dash of humor, it's largely thanks to them.

The expats profiled within these pages also deserve my heartfelt thanks. You let me pry into the good, bad, and ugly aspects of your personal financial lives. And this book is far more instructive (and, I hope, entertaining) because of your generosity.

Saintly financial advisor Tony Noto also helped greatly with my section on American individual retirement accounts (IRAs). I'm not sure if your clients know, Tony, how fortunate they truly are.

My agent, Sam Fleishman (the man who appears never to sleep) worked tirelessly to ensure I was given a strong publishing contract. Thank you, Sam. Now get to bed.

Finally, to my lovely wife Pele: You tolerated my mission, working as my editor and time manager—pulling me away from the manuscript when life needed living.

Introduction

On U.S. television, when law enforcement closes in on a white-collar heister, the fugitive often flees to a foreign country. He might steal a yacht headed for the Dominican Republic or fly a Learjet to the Caymans.

The 67 percent of Americans without passports might gasp at the ballsy border-bounding foolishness.[1] Doesn't the crook realize that by leaving the country, he risks being buried in an Afghan cave by Al Qaeda?

Smile if you're among the world's 230 million expatriates.[2] Such risks aren't likely. One genuine pitfall for expats, however, could be poverty in retirement.

Many on cushy foreign packages may scoff at my suggestion. After all, there's a large league of expats in Southeast Asia and the Middle East for which international living and working provide a fast track to Millionairesville. Teaching at international schools are couples with children, for instance, *saving* more than $100,000 (U.S. dollars) a year.

And the parents of the kids they teach? Most make the teachers seem like paupers by comparison. They left their home countries to work abroad in industries such as banking, information technology, oil, cosmetics, pharmaceuticals, and shipping. Many work for firms like Coca-Cola, American Express, Johnson & Johnson, Google, Microsoft, Exxon Mobil—the list goes on.

But not all expats (including millions in Europe) make buckets of money. And even those who do face financial risks.

In 2003, when I left Canada to teach in Singapore, I kissed goodbye to a defined benefit pension. Had I continued with my former job, I could have paid off a home, contributed modestly to investments, and received income for life.

Few expats have that luxury. What's worse, most don't realize they would need millions of dollars in the stock market or multiple mortgage-free rental properties just to equal, for example, the retirement benefits earned by most public-sector workers in Great Britain, Australia, or Canada.

Such benefits are globally waning. But they're still a reality, and most governments offer additional monthly cash. Social Security (for Americans), Canadian Pension Plan (for Canadians), and their equivalents for Brits, Australians, Germans, New Zealanders, and others provide income for non-expatriates. But without maximizing contributions to these plans, we can't fully open mouths to such morsels.

Most countries determine payments based on the amount of income employees earned coupled by the numbers of years they contributed to their home countries' respective social plans. Maximum Social Security payments for Americans, for example, exceeded $28,000 a year in 2012.[3] Expats seeking such income from an insurance company would have to invest nearly half a million dollars in an annuity. Those retiring in 10 or 20 years would need a lot more. Inflation is greedy.

Other countries also pay cash benefits to contributors of their respective social systems. Here's a snapshot.

Maximum Annual State Pension Payouts per Country

Country	Maximum Annual State Pension (Country Currency)	Maximum Annual State Pension (U.S. Dollars)
Germany	30,651 (euros)	39,374
United States	28,159 (U.S. dollars)	28,159
France	18,380 (euros)	23,612
Brazil	50,734 (Brazilian reals)	22,354
Australia	20,694 (Australian dollars)	18,862
Canada	12,295 (Canadian dollars)	11,704
United Kingdom	7,488 (British pounds)	11,174

Currencies converted: July 7, 2013.

SOURCE: Complementary and Private Pensions Database, "Private Pensions—OECD." Accessed April 29, 2014. www.oecd.org/finance/private-pensions/issaiopsoecdcomplementaryandprivatepensionsdatabase.htm.

Departing your homeland for a long-term contract or overseas adventure can leave you hungry—especially if your adopted country doesn't offer pensionable benefits. As a result, most expats need to save more and invest more effectively than their home-based contemporaries do.

Not all geriatric globe-trotters, however, get forced to a street corner with a busker's banjo. According to HSBC Bank's International Expat Explorer Survey, 68 percent of expats report saving more money than they could in their home countries.[4] So there's hope for prosperity.

But hope on its own is a lousy strategy. You need a plan. Start by asking the following questions:

- How much money will I need to retire?
- How much should I be saving and investing each month?
- How am I going to invest?

This book provides a game plan to answer such questions, whether you're aspiring to keep up with the Kardashians or live like a Buddhist monk.

One method to create or augment future retirement income is through the stock and bond markets. But many expats get rooked. Silver-tongued investment salespeople peddle dodgy products. Expats are easy targets.

Offshore investment schemes are often slippery pitfalls, rewarding financial advisors with massive commissions, hemorrhaging their clients' profits through high hidden fees and kickbacks. Many expat advisors sell them exclusively, locking unwary folks into 10-, 20-, even 25-year schemes.

Once an investor catches on to the fee-burdened riptide, it's often too late. Those scrambling out of the water face redemption penalties up to 80 percent of their accounts' proceeds. What's worse, many overseas employers welcome financial sharks into their company seal pools. With the best of intentions, they endorse offshore pension sellers, most of whom have a single purpose: reaping the highest possible commissions from unwary workers.

Whether you find a scrupulous financial advisor or manage your own investments, you should understand how the stock and bond markets work. I'll describe how money is made in the markets, answering many of the questions you may have been too embarrassed to ask. The stock market, you'll learn, represents a collection of real businesses. Investing in them doesn't have to be risky, time-consuming, or complicated—if you do it right.

I'll show how to spend just 90 minutes a year on your investments, while thumping the performance of most professional money managers. Best of all, you won't have to watch the stock market, follow the economy, or read the dull financial pages of the *Wall Street Journal*.

Sound too good to be true? It isn't. Use the Internet while reading this book. Doing so will allow you to verify my warnings about specific investment products. You'll find mountains of academic support for this book's investment strategies.

If you've invested poorly in the past, you have plenty of company. Dan Weil, writing for Moneynews.com, reported that a 20-year study by Chicago-based Dalbar proves most investors are like drowning ducks. While the average U.S. stock earned 384 percent (8.21 percent annually) between 1992 and 2012, the average American investor earned just 130 percent (4.25 percent annually) on stock market investments.[5]

Such poor investment performance might make the difference between eating cat food and caviar during retirement. I'll guide you toward something palatable.

Once you're armed with investment history and theory, the book's next sections get more specific. I'll show where you can open your investment account, while describing how to make your investment purchases.

As easy, however, as this investment strategy is, some people may still prefer an advisor. I profile some well-trained, ethical guides. Once you understand their philosophy, you'll know what to look for when picking an advisor.

Many people are also concerned with the practicalities of repatriating financial assets. Although this book doesn't cover such concepts, I continue to add articles and useful links pertaining to this subject for those of different nationalities at www.andrewhallam.com.

As an expatriate, you can live better, earn more, and provide for a generous retirement. But you'll need a plan. Fortunately, you're reading it.

Notes

1. Andrew Bender, "Record Number of Americans Now Hold Passports," *Forbes*, January 30, 2012. Accessed April 29, 2014. www.forbes.com/sites/andrew bender/2012/01/30/record-number-of-americans-now-hold-passports/.
2. "World Expat Population—The Numbers," Resources for Expats, International Moving Companies Moving Overseas, World Expat Population—The Numbers, Comments. Accessed April 29, 2014. www.feedbacq.com/blog/world-expat-population-the-numbers/.
3. "Private Pensions—OECD." Accessed April 29, 2014. www.oecd.org/finance/private-pensions/issaiopsoecdcomplementaryandprivatepensionsdatabase.htm.
4. "HSBC Bank International Expat Explorer Survey." Accessed April 29, 2014. www.expatexplorer.hsbc.com/files/pdfs/overall-reports/2009/economics.pdf.
5. Dan Weil, "Dalbar's Harvey: Individual Investors Brilliant at Mistiming Markets," Moneynews.com, March 11, 2013. Accessed May 12, 2014. www.moneynews.com/InvestingAnalysis/Dalbar-Harvey-individual-investors/2013/03/11/id/494045/.

The Global
Expatriate's Guide
to Investing

Chapter 1

Setting Your Bull's-Eye

When I first started investing, I wanted to retire at 40. I was 19 years old and saving like a lunatic. I won't confess the screwy things I did to pinch pennies. Instead, I want to share what I did right: the part you'll find helpful. I planned how much money I wanted to save, and why. Such planning, even more than the hyperactive saving, made my life a heck of a lot easier.

In 2014, shortly after my 44th birthday, my wife and I retired from our Singapore-based teaching jobs. That doesn't mean we live like trust-funded hedonists. Nor does it mean we'll never work again. It does mean, however, that our private parts aren't sitting in somebody else's vise. A few years back, if our boss had gone on a firing spree, sacking skinny bald guys and bilingual blondes, we would have been fine. We had enough money to survive without working.

When you're financially free, you might choose to keep working, take a long-term leave, or retire. Financial freedom provides options.

If you're not financially free today, set a target.

Begin with the following question:

If you were retired today, how much do you think you would spend each year?

For now, ignore inflation. Everything from a back wax to cornflakes will cost more in the future. But we'll make adjustments for that later. Just consider how much you would need annually if you retired today. It's silly to suggest a specific number of dollars needed by every retiree. If you're retiring in London, England, for example, costs will be higher than in Chiang Mai, Thailand.

Big spenders also require more. Five-star holiday junkies have pricier tastes than those who reserve luxury for special occasions. Some experts suggest you should budget retirement expenses totaling 70 to 80 percent of your working household income. But such cookie-cutter solutions make little sense. Even among those in the same income bracket, some people consume like gas-guzzling Mack trucks; others sip like a Smart car. Your future expenses depend on your personal needs, wants, and chosen retirement location.

To estimate future costs of living, figure out what you're spending right now. Record every penny you spend for at least six months. It's easy to do with an app on your phone, or with a pencil and notebook. Then make adjustments for predicted retirement lifestyle changes. Without a job, you won't be maintaining a professional wardrobe. Nor will you be saving for your kids' college or your retirement. Do you plan to be somewhere cheaper or more expensive than where you currently live? In either case, make adjustments. Costs of living in the world's major cities are available at www.numbeo.com.

This isn't about keeping up with Mr. and Mrs. Jones. But if you want to know how much the typical (non-expat) retired household spends, here's a peek.

According to the University of Michigan's Health and Retirement Study, total costs for the typical American retired household were $31,365 in 2012.[1]

Canadian Business magazine reported that on average a Canadian retiree spent $39,400 (Canadian dollars) in 2009.[2]

MGM Advantage estimates that British retirement expenses averaged £23,107 per year in 2013.[3]

Australian households, according to the ASFA Retirement Standard Benchmark, need $32,603 (Australian dollars) for a "modest" retirement.[4]

Your needs depend on you: your lifestyle, your retirement location, and your financial obligations. Unfortunately, those afflicted by expatitis crave more than the average Dick or Jane.

What's This Ailment Expatitis?

Expatitis isn't a common medical term. But if you're an expatriate, chances are either you or someone you know is infected. It's easily diagnosed. Symptoms get posted on Facebook. Fortunately, it doesn't hurt—at least not in its early stages.

Unlike bronchitis, arthritis, appendicitis, or colitis, expatitis is rather pleasant. Afflicted individuals get addicted to five-star holidays, manicures, pedicures, massages, expensive dining, and entertainment. But expatitis creates delusions. It's much like drinking champagne underwater without checking your air supply.

Symptoms creep up. The better the expat's financial package, the greater the risk of contracting the condition.

I've been giving financial seminars to expatriates for a decade. When I ask people to estimate their retirement expenses, their needs vary. And I expect that. But here's the irony. Those reporting they need the most money are usually saving the least.

Fortunately, such spendthrifts can eke out the final laugh.

Whether you're suffering from expatitis or hoping for a more luxurious retirement than you could afford in your home country, retiring overseas offers a creative solution.

Cheating Conventional Retirement Rules

Meet Billy and Akaisha Kaderli. They live better than the typical American retiree. But they also spend less.

If you struck up a midweek conversation with them, you might peg them as early retirees. The energetic 61-year-olds share the glow of a couple freed from the rat race. But a few things make them different.

They spend long-term stints (sometimes years) in low-cost countries. They also retired when they were just 38, and will mark their 25th year of retirement in 2016.

Previously, they owned a restaurant in the United States. Akaisha ran it. Billy worked at an investment firm. But in 1991, they quit. While most of their friends were acquiring large houses, new cars, and filling their homes with fine furnishings, the Kaderlis downsized. "We sold most of our possessions," says Akaisha, "including our house and our car." For a quarter of a century, they've lived off their investment portfolio. Today, it's worth more than it was the day they retired.

To stretch their income, they moved to Lake Chapala, Mexico. But they enjoy bouncing around, renting homes in new locations for months at a time. Some of their favorite hubs include Thailand and Guatemala. They commit to community projects, meeting people, embracing different cultures, and learning different languages. They have a mortgage-free apartment in the United States, where they stay when they visit family.

The Kaderlis have also discovered how to bask in luxury on a shoestring. Through TrustedHousesitters.com, they found a luxurious home overlooking Lake Chapala in 2013. They stayed four months without paying rent. "We may do more of that in the future," says Akaisha, "if the right opportunity arises."

Their living costs may be low, but the Kaderlis don't scrimp. "We have a great deal of fun," Akaisha says, "living on $30,000 a year." In 2013, they spent roughly $3,900 on housing, $5,400 on transportation, $6,600 on food and entertainment, $6,900 on medical expenses, and the rest on miscellaneous costs.[5]

The Kaderlis are the authors of *The Adventurer's Guide to Early Retirement* (CD-ROM, 2005). They also maintain a helpful blog, Retire Early Lifestyle, at www.retireearlylifestyle.com, where they share their stories and tips for living well on less.

Suzan Haskins and Dan Prescher, authors of *The International Living Guide to Retiring Overseas on a Budget* (John Wiley & Sons, 2014), live much like the Kaderlis. Located in a small town in Ecuador, they spend roughly $25,000 a year. "We live well. . . . We go out to lunch and dinner once a week . . . we enjoy the occasional martini or scotch, and every evening with dinner we polish off a bottle of wine." Their costs include at least one annual trip to the United States, occasional fine dining, and a worldwide health care policy that costs roughly $5,800 a year, with a $5,000 deductible.[6]

Cooking Up the Road Less Traveled

Forty-eight-year-old chef Shane Brierly desires a more upscale retirement than he could afford in his home country. The New Zealand native left Australia in 2004 to work in Dubai. He explains, "I thought it would give me an edge, giving me a more comfortable financial position than previously."

But instead of moving back to Australia, Shane moved to Vietnam, where he works as a chef at the Pullman Hotel in Ho Chi Minh City. Now he's planning to retire overseas. "The respect and community values in Asia really inspire me," says Shane. "Not so many criminals, a culture of nonviolence and respect, plus awesome food.

"Costs of living are also lower," he adds, "and these countries are far less materialistic." Shane's views on materialism were altered by misfortune. "But it was a blessing in disguise," he says.

A shipping company lost all of his household goods when he moved from Dubai to Vietnam. Initially forced to live with less, he warmed to its simplicity. "Owning a whole lot of stuff means maintaining, repairing, replacing, or running it." He no longer buys what he doesn't need, preferring to spend his money on traveling instead. Gaining experiences, Shane explains, is more fulfilling than acquiring possessions. "The Western economy runs on unneeded goods and services, and everyone lives to consume. You need half your income just to sustain impulse buys and comfort purchases. The rest disappears on essentials and tax."

Shane doesn't live like a monk. He lives simply, but doesn't mind paying a premium for quality. In a country where you can survive on a relative shoestring, he claims you can live well on $3,000 per month ($36,000 annually). "I love exploring. It's inexpensive to travel locally in Southeast Asia or in Vietnam, and you can splash out quite affordably and have a comfortable life." He plans to retire in central Vietnam,

Laos, Cambodia, or Chile. But he'll be keeping his hands in the hospitality business. "I'll probably set up a restaurant or guesthouse to run. To be financially free at 60 would rock, but retiring at age 65 is more likely."[7]

If Shane wants to retire with an income of $36,000 a year, he'll need to make adjustments. Inflation is greedy, sometimes frighteningly so.

Inflation.eu compiles country inflation figures. In 1981, Canada's inflation rate recorded 12.12 percent; in 1975 Great Britain's peaked at 24.89 percent; and in 1979 the cost of living in the United States rose 13.29 percent.[8] Those lamenting the good old days of the late 1970s and early 1980s, when savings accounts paid 10 percent a year, may have forgotten inflation's gluttony.

Lately, inflation's appetite has slowed. The decade ending 2012 saw Canada's annual inflation average 1.83 percent, Great Britain recorded 2.64 percent, and the United States averaged 2.41 percent per year.[9]

But past decade levels are rarely repeated in the future. Caution is prudent. In this case, let's assume inflation will average 3.5 percent each year—which is slightly higher than the developed world's 100-year average.

Shane plans to retire in 17 years, when he turns 65. If inflation averages 3.5 percent, he'll spend $64,608 annually 17 years from now to give himself and his wife the same buying power that $36,000 would provide today. In other words, if $36,000 can buy a certain number of goods and services now, it would require $64,608 to purchase those same goods and services in 17 years.

To make the postinflation adjustment, Shane went to www.money chimp.com and clicked Calculator. Figure 1.1 shows how he used the website to estimate his postinflation income equivalency.

The Earthquake and the Epiphany

When figuring out how much money you'll need, focus on your own lifestyle and needs, not somebody else's. Thirty-five-year-old Ben Shearon, a British professor living in Sendai, Japan, shares his retirement expense projections.

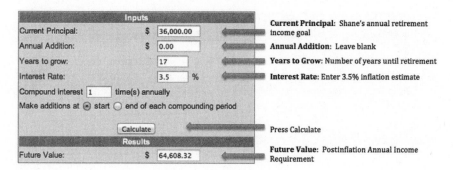

Figure 1.1 Shane Brierly's Postinflation Adjustment
SOURCE: www.moneychimp.com.

He and his wife, Chiho, lost their home to the Japanese earthquake in 2011. "That turned me into a pretty hardcore minimalist," Ben says. "I have seen how fragile life can be." The experience strengthened his desire for earlier financial freedom. Rather than working, he'd rather travel, read, keep fit, and spend time with his wife.

Ben and Chiho seek financial freedom when Ben turns 45. They save 50 percent of their household income, now that their three children are "mostly grown up and more or less independent." Ben hopes that he and Chiho can live off dividend and interest income from their stock and bond market portfolio. They're considering retiring in Malaysia or Thailand where the weather is better and the costs of living lower.

Working full-time as a teacher trainer at a university in Sendai, Ben also consults on English as a foreign language (EFL) textbooks and writes a blog. Chiho runs a small private school, which also absorbs a lot of Ben's time. "Right now it's all work, work, work, but we are hoping to gradually scale that back as we hire more people to help us with the school."[10]

Currently, they don't own property.

Ben and Chiho estimate their annual retirement costs at $47,100 (U.S. dollars). Because they're hoping to retire in 10 years, this sum will need to be adjusted for inflation. If inflation averages 3.5 percent, they'll require $66,439 each year (a decade from now) to give them the equivalent buying power of $47,100 today.

Figure 1.2 illustrates how their numbers look when plugged into the compound interest calculator at www.moneychimp.com.

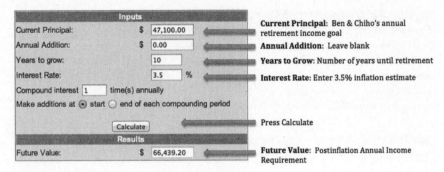

Figure 1.2   Ben and Chiho's Postinflation Adjustment
SOURCE: www.moneychimp.com.

Jujitsu Junkie Taps Out for Home

Despite his 44 years, school psychologist Jeff Devens strikes an imposing figure against younger fighters on the jujitsu mat. A wrestler in college, he took a break from grappling until he was 40, when the Brazilian jujitsu bug bit him. Today, he battles opponents half his age. But that doesn't mean the Singapore-based American lives in a youthful Neverland. Jeff and his wife Nanette know the years creep up. Consequently, they are prepared for their retirement. They plan to be based in the United States.

The typical American retiree spent $31,365 in 2012. But Jeff and Nanette don't want to be average. By sidestepping expatitis, the Devenses are realistically poised to retire on $93,300 per year.

They started their expat careers in 1995, teaching at the International School of Beijing, China. "We came overseas after two years of marriage," says Jeff, "with $25,000 of student loan debt. During our first year, we paid off our school loans and had enough money left over to put a down payment on a home in North Dakota."

Jeff and Nanette are now mortgage free. Each June, they fly from Singapore to the United States to spend time at their lakeside home with their two children. "Purchasing the house was a lifestyle decision," says Jeff. "It gives our family a place to spend seven weeks each summer. Paying off the mortgage also gave us peace of mind."

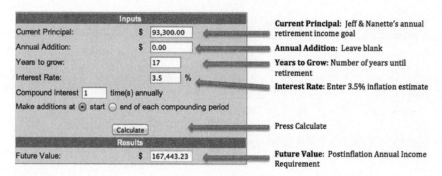

Figure 1.3 Jeff and Nanette's Postinflation Adjustment
SOURCE: www.moneychimp.com.

The Devenses figure they'll spend most of their retirement time in North Dakota. "When we get closer to retirement, we'll likely buy or rent a second home in a warmer climate, giving us an escape from North Dakota's winter months."

After researching medical insurance, Jeff realized it will cost them much more than it will for most stateside Americans. "We would have a high deductible because we haven't had enough years vested in any stateside school district, nor have we paid enough into Social Security to qualify for Medicare."[11]

Americans are required to pay 10 years or 40 quarters in Medicare taxes to qualify.[12] Career expatriates, like the Devenses, will pay higher insurance premiums if they can't accumulate the minimum requirements toward Social Security while living overseas.

Jeff and Nanette figure they can retire in 17 years. But if they want the equivalent buying power of $93,300 today, they'll need more money. If inflation averages 3.5 percent over the next 17 years, the Devenses will require $167,443 per year (see Figure 1.3).

Now It's Your Turn

The first step toward planning your retirement is realizing what you spend today. Every healthy business documents its income and expenditures. Those not doing so head for bankruptcy. Government

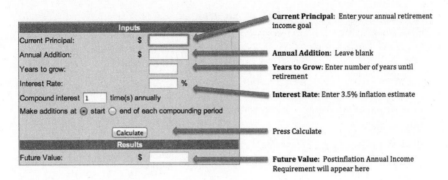

Figure 1.4   Your Postinflation Adjustment
SOURCE: www.moneychimp.com.

assistance doesn't intervene to save the grocery store or restaurant with the unbalanced budget. But many expatriate family households come to expect just that. Unfortunately, no such crutch exists for social pension noncontributors. Many expatriates sink or swim based on their own strokes.

After figuring out what you spend each year, determine how many years from now you want financial freedom. Estimate your postinflation cost of living with the calculator at www.moneychimp.com. Retirement is a journey to a foreign city. You've never been there, so you'll need a map—and knowledge of the number of steps ahead.

Take the first step now. Plug your numbers into Figure 1.4.

Notes

1. "Growing Older in America," University of Michigan Health and Retirement Study. Accessed April 30, 2014. http://hrsonline.isr.umich.edu/sitedocs/brochure/HRS-brochure.pdf.
2. "How Much Do You Need to Retire Well?" *Canadian Business*. Accessed April 30, 2014. www.canadianbusiness.com/investing/how-much-do-you-need-to-retire-well/.
3. "Couples Must Budget £600,000 for Retirement," *The Telegraph*, April 26, 2010. Accessed April 30, 2014. www.telegraph.co.uk/finance/personalfinance/7635532/Couples-must-budget-600000-for-retirement.html.

4. "Resources," ASFA Retirement Standard. Accessed April 30, 2014. www
   .superannuation.asn.au/resources/retirement-standard.
5. Interview with Billy and Akaisha Kaderli. Telephone interview by author, February 2, 2014.
6. Suzan Haskins and Dan Prescher, *The International Living Guide to Retiring Overseas on a Budget: How to Live Well on $25,000 a Year* (Hoboken, NJ: John Wiley & Sons, 2014).
7. Interview with Shane Brierly. E-mail interview by author, June 30, 2013.
8. "Inflation—Current and Historic Inflation by Country," Inflation.eu. Accessed April 30, 2014. www.inflation.eu/.
9. Ibid.
10. Interview with Ben Shearon. E-mail interview by author, June 20, 2014.
11. Interview with Jeff Devens. Interview by author, September 15, 2013.
12. Medicare.gov: Official U.S. Government Site for Medicare. Accessed April 28, 2014. www.medicare.gov/.

Chapter 2

Building Your Pension

Whether you expect to retire on $25,000 or $125,000 per year, you'll need a way to generate that income. Some will earn money from real estate rentals; others will rely on the stock and bond markets. Many will depend on both. Retirees may also receive some kind of pensionable benefit to augment their investment income.

Rental real estate is a great inflation fighter. If a retiree collects enough rental revenue to cover life's expenses today, it won't be undermined by the rising cost of living. Over time, rental income and inflation ride the same chair lift.

Those paying off investment mortgages before retirement can reap much from the rental proceeds.

Stock and bond market investments work a bit differently. If a retiree has a $500,000 investment portfolio, she'll need to know how much of her portfolio she can afford to sell each year. Those selling too much could end up broke—especially if they live longer than expected.

World Health Organization director Ties Boerma suggests a typical 60-year-old in a high-income country could expect to live to 84. But you could live even longer—perhaps much longer.[1]

Costs of living also increase. So what percentage of your retirement portfolio can you afford to sell each year, to provide high odds you'll never run out of money?

How to Never Run Out of Money

Respected financial planner and researcher Bill Bengen suggests that retirees should be able to sell roughly 4 percent of their investment portfolios each year. He back-tested a variety of historical scenarios, reporting results in a 1994 *Journal of Financial Planning* issue.[2]

As such, 4 percent of $500,000 would be $20,000; 4 percent of a million dollars would be $40,000. If you retired today with one million dollars, you could withdraw $40,000 in the first year of retirement. In the second year, you could sell a bit more to cover rising costs of living. The 4 percent withdrawal rate considers inflation.

If inflation averaged 3.5 percent per year, Table 2.1 is how withdrawals would look for the first 15 years of retirement.

Some say withdrawing 4 percent after inflation may prove to be too much. Skeptics of the 4 percent rule include Michael S. Finke, Wade D. Pfau, and David M. Blanchett. In a 2013 Social Science Research Network paper, they recommend sustainable postinflation withdrawal rates closer to 3 percent (see Table 2.2). Their rationale? Interest rates for bonds and savings accounts are currently lower than usual.[3]

Don't, however, let that spook you. Interest rates might not perpetually scrape along the sea floor. Researchers supporting the sustainability of a 4 percent withdrawal rate considered a variety of back-tested conditions: double-digit inflation in the late 1970s and early 1980s, stock market returns that went essentially nowhere (for the U.S. market) between 1965 and 1982, and a series of American-led wars.

That said, there's nothing wrong with a 3 percent withdrawal rate. When it comes to money, caution is cool.

Table 2.1 Four Percent Withdrawal Rate for $1 Million Portfolio with Inflation at 3.5 Percent per Year

How Much Would You Sell Each Year?

Year of Retirement	Maximum Amount You Can Sell
Retirement Year 1	$40,000
Retirement Year 2	$41,400
Retirement Year 3	$42,849
Retirement Year 4	$44,348
Retirement Year 5	$45,900
Retirement Year 6	$47,507
Retirement Year 7	$49,170
Retirement Year 8	$50,891
Retirement Year 9	$52,672
Retirement Year 10	$54,515
Retirement Year 11	$56,423
Retirement Year 12	$58,398
Retirement Year 13	$60,442
Retirement Year 14	$62,558
Retirement Year 15	$64,747

Table 2.2 Three Percent Withdrawal Rate for $1 Million Portfolio with Inflation at 3.5 Percent per Year

How Much Would You Sell Each Year?

Year of Retirement	Maximum Amount You Can Sell
Retirement Year 1	$30,000
Retirement Year 2	$31,050
Retirement Year 3	$32,136
Retirement Year 4	$33,261
Retirement Year 5	$34,425
Retirement Year 6	$35,630
Retirement Year 7	$36,877
Retirement Year 8	$38,168
Retirement Year 9	$39,504
Retirement Year 10	$40,886
Retirement Year 11	$42,317
Retirement Year 12	$43,799
Retirement Year 13	$45,332
Retirement Year 14	$46,918
Retirement Year 15	$48,560

By the end of this chapter you'll be able to determine how much money you'll need to retire. You'll also know how much money you should be investing each year to reach your goal. Meet some expats who figured it out.

The Man with Nothing But a Backpack

Profile 1: Lindell Lucy
Nationality: American
Residency: Hong Kong
Current Age: 29
Plans to Retire in: 41 years (at age 70)
Retirement Income Goal: $40,000 (U.S. dollars) per year
Postinflation Retirement Income Goal: $163,917 per year
Combined Investments in Stock/Bond Markets: $18,500
Current Real Estate Income: $0

Twenty-nine-year-old Lindell Lucy claims to own nothing but a backpack. The Arkansas-raised American went to Stanford University before catching wanderlust. "After leaving university, there was one six-month period," he says, "when I lived on the streets in five different countries—Japan, South Korea, China, Hong Kong, and Taiwan." He taught part-time while traveling, earning just enough money for food and shelter.

His entrepreneurial spirit led to a few additional work projects. One was spawned by his trouble finding adequately priced gyms to use while traveling. "Day passes are outrageously expensive," he says. He created Gymsurfer.com, a social network and marketplace for gyms. "I wanted to make it easy for people to find gyms and compare prices, which I hoped would spur competition and drive down prices [for day passes]. I also wanted to make it possible for people to meet at gyms, socialize, and stay in touch."

He also started a few writing projects before settling into his current job as a kindergarten teacher. "I ran out of money a few times on my travels and had to get bailed out by family. That was part of the reason I decided to get a full-time job in Hong Kong."

Lindell says he could live on $6,000 (U.S.) a year in rural China. But a couple of years ago, he was bit by something stronger than his lust to wander. He met his girlfriend Yan, who worked as a music teacher. She changed schools shortly after they met and Lindell followed her. He jokes about never retiring. "My body will wear out long before then." But he admits, "Retirement planning is a good thing."

Lindell figures he could retire at 70 on a shoestring, but that wouldn't please Yan. "She'll want some money to enjoy a more comfortable lifestyle than I could tolerate," he says, "so we'll probably need about $40,000 a year."[4] Based on calculations described in Chapter 1, Lindell would be spending $163,913 per year upon retirement, if he wants the same buying power that $40,000 would purchase today—assuming annual inflation of 3.5 percent.

Lindell won't be eligible for a defined benefit pension or U.S. Social Security if he remains overseas. Nor does he plan to purchase real estate for income purposes. So determining how much money he needs in a retirement portfolio is simple. The $163,913 he hopes to spend each year upon retirement must be 4 percent of a much larger sum. Studies suggest retirees can sell 4 percent of their portfolio each year without running out of money. In Lindell's case, $163,913 is 4 percent of $4,097,825.

To figure that out, he could do one of two things: multiply $163,913 by 25 or divide $163,913 by 0.04.

$$\$163,913 \times 25 = \$4,097,825$$

$$\$163,913/0.04 = \$4,097,825$$

It looks like a massive sum. But Lindell and Yan can reach it.

So far, they've accumulated $18,500 (U.S.) in an investment account. If they work 41 more years, they could reach their retirement portfolio goal size by investing $16,555 per year in the account, if their investments average 7 percent (see Figure 2.1).

Lindell and Yan can't control the stock market's return. It could earn more than 7 percent or it could earn less. Using the same Moneychimp. com compound interest calculator, Table 2.3 shows how much they would need to invest per year and per month, based on different stock and bond market scenarios.

So what investment return should Lindell and Yan bank on? Nobody knows. Historically, stock and bond market combinations have exceeded

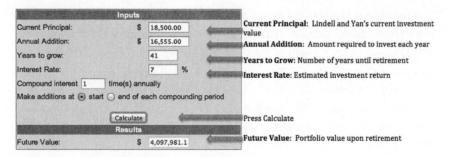

Figure 2.1 Determining How Much Lindell and Yan Need to Save
SOURCE: www.moneychimp.com.

8 percent annually: not every year, but during most 30-year durations. Prudence suggests it's better to expect lower than average returns.

But what if real estate were part of your investment plan? And what if (unlike Lindell) you'll receive some kind of government retirement payment or a defined benefit pension? How do such calculations apply then? Meet Keith Ferrell and Annika Dahlgren-Ferrell.

The Couple with Swedish-American Dreams

Profile 2: Keith Ferrell and Annika Dahlgren-Ferrell
Nationality: American/Swedish-American
Plan to Retire in: 10 years
Retirement Income Goal: $75,000 (U.S. dollars) per year
Postinflation Retirement Income Goal: $105,794 per year

Table 2.3 How Much Would Lindell and Yan Need to Save?

Investment Return	Savings Required per Year	Savings Required per Month
6%	$22,270	$1,855
7%	$16,555	$1,379
8%	$12,082	$1,006
9%	$8,610	$717
10%	$5,920	$493

Combined Investments in Stock/Bond Markets: $300,000
Current Real Estate Income (not including future primary residence): $25,000 per year

Keith and Annika met in 1994 while attending San Diego State University. They married in 1999, after teaching a handful of years in the United States. Seeking adventure and more disposable income, they moved to Venezuela, where they taught for two years. "When we first arrived," says Annika, "the school administrator handed us an envelope with a large lump of cash as a 'settling in' allowance. It reminded us of a Mafia payment."

"We've always been careful with money," says Keith. By the time they were in their early 30s, they had a completely paid off home in California. Moving to Singapore juiced their savings. Today Keith, aged 42, and Annika, 39, own three California homes. Two are completely paid off, and the third has $78,000 owed on the mortgage. "We'll definitely have the third house paid off before we retire," says Annika. They each enjoy their Singapore teaching jobs, but would like the option of retiring in 10 years. "We'll probably keep working," says Keith, "but if we decide to quit in a decade, we want the resources to do that."[5]

Besides his teaching salary, Keith plans to tutor. He'll file the additional money as self-employed income reportable to the U.S. Internal Revenue Service (IRS). Doing so allows him to earn Social Security credits, ensuring he's eligible for a smidge of government retirement income. He's not counting on it, however, preferring that he and Annika be fully self-sustaining.

From 2006 to 2013, they lived in Singapore on a single salary. Annika gave birth to their two children, Kaidan and Kiana (ages 6 and 8), after which Annika stayed home to raise them. Even on a single salary, the couple still saved for their retirement. They also started a healthy college fund for their kids.

With Annika working full-time again in 2013, they've been able to ramp up their savings. They're investing $88,000 per year, not including savings toward their kids' college educations. Nor does such savings include the cash they've been putting aside for a home they hope to buy soon in Sweden.

Will they be financially free in a decade?

Once their third U.S. property is mortgage free, they'll have $33,600 a year in free cash flow from rentals after property tax, maintenance, and property management costs. But they won't collect rent from one of the homes when they retire, keeping it for themselves when they're in California. "We plan to split our time between California, Sweden, and a tropical destination." After expenses they expect their two remaining properties to provide roughly $25,000 a year in income.

Keith will qualify for a small teacher's pension from his time in California. But he isn't counting on it. The real estate income of $25,000 a year should keep pace with inflation. But Keith and Annika will still have a $50,000 annual shortfall. Ten years from now, assuming inflation of 3.5 percent, this sum would need to be $70,529 for the equivalent buying power.

So their investment portfolio would need to generate $70,529 per year. Based on a sustainable withdrawal rate of 4 percent per year, $70,529 would need to represent 4 percent of the investment portfolio's total size. To figure that out, we would either multiply by 25 or divide by 0.04.

$$\$70,529 \times 25 = \$1,763,225$$

$$\$70,529/0.04 = \$1,763,225$$

Keith and Annika's portfolio goal size, in this case, would need to be $1,763,225 in 10 years.

Because they currently have $300,000 in stock and bond market investments, they could reach their goal in a decade under two circumstances:

1. They would need to continue investing $88,000 a year.
2. Their investments would need to average at least 6 percent per year.

Under those circumstances, the future value would be $1,766,758, surpassing their goal of $1,763,225 (see Figure 2.2).

For many expatriates, thoughts of saving $88,000 a year are daunting, if not impossible. But Keith and Annika have three things going for them: high salaries, low income taxes in Singapore, and the fact that they're frugal.

If they retired in 23 years, when Keith turns 65, the financial numbers change dramatically.

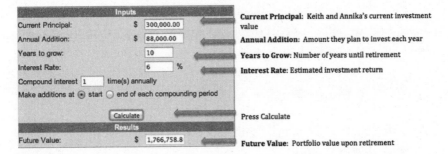

Figure 2.2   Calculating Annual Return Required for Keith and Annika to
Reach Their Goal
SOURCE: www.moneychimp.com.

Here's the alternative scenario: Keith and Annika would like to live on $75,000 a year in today's dollars. Real estate would provide them $25,000, which would increase with inflation. The $50,000 shortfall, compounded 23 years at 3.5 percent inflation, would now need to be $110,305 to provide equivalent buying power.

As such, the portfolio goal size would need to be $2,757,625 in 23 years. How much would they need to save? Instead of saving $88,000, they would need to invest roughly $22,300 annually if they earned a 7 percent return, $15,150 if they earned 8 percent, $7,650 at 9 percent, or less than $1,000 a year if they earned a 10 percent return.

A couple of things should jump out at you. Different investment returns dramatically change the game. If we pay investment fees that are 2 percent or 3 percent more than necessary, it can scuttle retirement boats. I'll expand on this in later chapters.

For now, consider your own financial scenario. Unlike Keith and Annika, you might qualify for government pensionable benefits. Many countries offer online calculators allowing citizens to estimate such payments. For Americans, it's the official website of the U.S. Social Security Administration.[6]

Canadians can use the Canadian government's online calculator to estimate future Canada Pension Plan and Old Age Security payments.[7]

UK citizens can use a State Pension calculator at GOV.UK.[8]

If your home country offers a state or government pension, you might find an online calculator online to estimate future payments. Jeff and Cheryl Smith have done just that.

A Front-End-Loaded Tale of Success

Profile 3: Jeff and Cheryl Smith (not their real names)
Nationality: American
Plan to Retire in: 13 years
Retirement Income Goal: $80,000 (U.S. dollars) per year
Postinflation Retirement Income Goal: $125,116
Combined Investments in Stock/Bond Markets: $1,500,000
Current Real Estate Income (not including future primary residence): $0

Jeff and Cheryl Smith have been expatriates for roughly nine years. Currently residing in Hong Kong, Cheryl worked as a lawyer for an international nonprofit organization for her first three years abroad. Jeff is an engineer, working in management for a large international corporation.

Five years ago, Cheryl quit her job to spend time with the couple's two young children. She's considering a career switch when her kids are a bit older. "I'm ready to work again, but the travel schedule I was keeping before is unworkable with kids."

Jeff and Cheryl have also moved around. "We've been in Hong Kong for two years, but we're likely moving to the Netherlands this summer," says Cheryl. "Before this, we were in England for three years and Zhuhai, China, for four years."

Jeff and Cheryl, 49 and 38 years old respectively, are great savers. They own a $650,000 home in the United States, with $235,000 owed on the mortgage. It's currently rented out. The couple's stock and bond market investments total $1.5 million.

They'll also be entitled to Social Security benefits. Jeff made U.S. payroll contributions from 1985 to 2006; his maximum salary was $110,000 a year. Cheryl contributed to Social Security from 1994 to 2009. Her highest U.S.-based salary was $72,000 a year.

Social Security projections from the U.S. government online calculator suggest Jeff should receive $1,250 a month when he turns 62. By deferring payments until age 65, he would receive $1,538 per month. Cheryl would receive $778 per month if she collected payments at 65.

They would like to retire in 2027; however, they're among many Americans questioning whether the U.S. government will have the resources to fulfill such pension promises. So Jeff and Cheryl lowered their Social Security expectations, banking on total payments of $1,200 per month in 2027, or $14,400 per year.

The couple would like to retire in 13 years, spending today's equivalent of $80,000 a year. If inflation averages 3.5 percent, they would be spending $125,116. We can subtract what they expect from Social Security ($14,400 per year) to determine how much they would need their stock and bond market investments to generate: $110,716 per year.

Considering a 4 percent withdrawal rate, $110,716 would need to be 4 percent of the portfolio's value. Either multiplying by 25 or dividing by 0.4 provides the answer. Jeff and Cheryl's portfolio goal size would be $2,767,900.

As shown in Figure 2.3, their portfolio is currently worth $1,500,000. If their current investment returns averaged 4.9 percent per year for 13 years, they wouldn't need to add another penny. Their portfolio would grow to $2,793,653.

Jeff and Cheryl are obviously in great financial shape. But not everyone is so fortunate. Expatriates in Europe, Africa, or South America often make far less money than their counterparts in the Middle East and Asia.

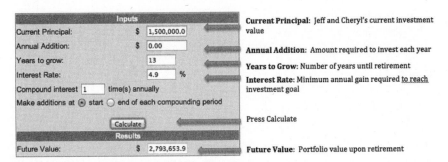

Figure 2.3 Jeff and Cheryl May Not Need to Invest Anything Else to Reach Their Retirement Goal
SOURCE: www.moneychimp.com.

Consequently, many will require strong returns from the stock market just to equal their most conservative retirement goals. Fortunately, global stock markets have easily exceeded 7 percent growth on average. But now for the bad news: Most investors haven't come close to making such a return. In the chapters ahead, I'll explain why they haven't, while showing how to maximize stock and bond market profits.

Notes

1. "Global Life Expectancy: Life Spans Continue to Lengthen around the World, WHO Says," *Huffington Post*/Reuters, May 15, 2013. Accessed April 30, 2014. www.huffingtonpost.com/2013/05/15/global-life-expectancy-span-world_n_3281211.html.

2. William P. Barrett, "The Retirement Spending Solution," *Forbes*, April 5, 2011. Accessed April 30, 2014. www.forbes.com/forbes/2011/0523/investing-retirement-bill-bengen-savings-spending-solution.html.

3. Michael S. Finke, Wade D. Pfau, and David M. Blanchett, "The 4 Percent Rule Is Not Safe in a Low-Yield World," *Journal of Financial Planning* 26(6): 46–55; Social Science Research Network. Accessed April 30, 2014. http://papers.ssrn.com/sol3/papers.cfm?abstract_id=2201323.

4. Interview with Lindell Lucy. E-mail interview by author, June 20, 2013.

5. Interview with Keith Ferrell and Annika Dahlgren-Ferrell. Telephone interview by author, April 30, 2014.

6. "Social Security," Official Social Security Website of the U.S. Social Security Administration. Accessed April 30, 2014. https://secure.ssa.gov/acu/ACU_KBA/main.jsp?URL=/apps8z/ARPI/main.jsp?locale=en&LVL=4.

7. "Canadian Retirement Income Calculator," Government of Canada, Service Canada. Accessed April 30, 2014. www.servicecanada.gc.ca/eng/services/pensions/cric.shtml.

8. "Get a State Pension Statement," GOV.UK. Accessed April 30, 2014. https://www.gov.uk/state-pension-statement.

Chapter 3

The Truth about Stocks and Bonds

I n 1992, the Canadian rock group Barenaked Ladies sang, "If I had a million dollars." The lead singer listed the crazy stuff he could buy with a seven-figure bank account, including a monkey, a special green dress, and John Merrick's creepy elephant bones.

Most global expats have better taste. But they're mistaken if they think a million dollars in a low-interest savings account will keep them from a retirement of dumpster diving. I'm not suggesting a million bucks isn't a nice chunk of change. But retirees withdrawing $40,000 per year from such an account (while slowly increasing withdrawals to combat inflation) will likely be broke after 15 years.

Most expats can't afford such risks. Whether trying to preserve wealth or grow it, the stock and bond markets offer a far more effective option. However, before getting into specific, purchasable investment products, let's see how the stock and bond markets tick.

Between 1926 and 2013, the world's largest stock market (the U.S. market) averaged a 9.92 percent annual return.[1]

I'll use the Standard & Poor's (S&P) 500 index to demonstrate the performance of the typical U.S. stock. Each year, this index represents the average growth or decline (including dividends) of 500 large American companies. You could purchase a product tracking this index, so it's not a hypothetical example.

Halloween Grab Bag Treats Investors

First available to investors on September 30, 1976, Vanguard's S&P 500 index was (and still is) like a Halloween grab bag of goodies. The treats inside include exposure to stocks such as Coca-Cola, Exxon Mobil, Apple, Wal-Mart, and Microsoft—along with 495 other companies. In other words, anyone buying an S&P 500 index fund becomes part owner in 500 of the largest U.S. companies. No financial wizard reshuffles the stocks, dumping poor performers for the latest highfliers. The composition of this index barely changes, year over year. So it's a naked measurement of how the U.S. market has performed.

If you had invested $10,000 in September 1976, it would have grown to $487,321 by January 2014. That's an overall gain of 4,873 percent (see Figure 3.1).

I'm not showing past performance of a single hot stock. Instead, the S&P 500 closely mirrors what the *average* U.S. large-cap stock earned between 1976 and 2014. The average global stock performed nearly as well.

Sometimes the U.S. stock market scintillated investors' palates, exceeding 11 percent growth; other times it poisoned investors like a bad seafood meal. But over investment lifetimes spanning 30 years or longer, U.S. and global stocks averaged 9 to 11 percent annually. Patient investors were rewarded—but only if they paid low fees on their investment products, and didn't play speculative games with their money.

Few regular people, however, had $10,000 to lump into the stock market in 1976. So here's a more pragmatic example.

Assume you had invested $1,600 in Vanguard's S&P 500 index fund at the beginning of 1978 (see Table 3.1). If you had added $100 per month, come hell or high water, you would have practiced something called dollar

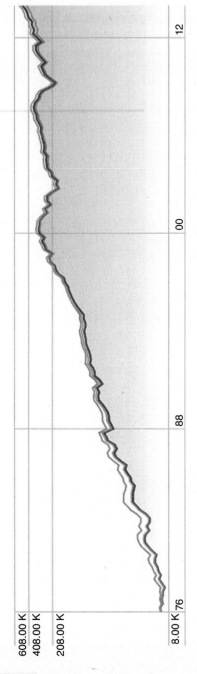

Figure 3.1 Vanguard's S&P 500 Index Performance: $10,000 Invested in September 1976 Grew to $487,321 by 2014
SOURCE: Morningstar.com.

Table 3.1   Dollar Cost Averaging with Vanguard's S&P 500 Index Fund

Starting with $1,600, and Adding $100 per Month

Year Ended December 31	Total Cost of Cumulative Investments	Total Value after Growth
1978	$1,600	$1,699
1979	$2,800	$3,273
1980	$4,000	$5,755
1981	$5,200	$6,630
1982	$6,400	$9,487
1983	$7,600	$12,783
1984	$8,800	$14,863
1985	$10,000	$20,905
1986	$11,200	$25,934
1987	$12,400	$28,221
1988	$13,600	$34,079
1989	$14,800	$46,126
1990	$16,000	$45,803
1991	$17,200	$61,009
1992	$18,400	$66,816
1993	$19,600	$74,687
1994	$20,800	$76,779
1995	$22,000	$106,944
1996	$23,200	$132,767
1997	$24,400	$178,217
1998	$25,600	$230,619
1999	$26,800	$280,564
2000	$28,000	$256,271
2001	$29,200	$226,622
2002	$30,400	$177,503
2003	$31,600	$229,523
2004	$32,800	$255,479
2005	$34,000	$268,932
2006	$35,200	$312,317
2007	$36,400	$330,350
2008	$37,600	$208,940
2009	$38,800	$265,756
2010	$40,000	$301,098
2011	$41,200	$302,298
2012	$42,400	$344,459
2013	$43,600	$403,514

SOURCES: Burton G. Malkiel, *A Random Walk Down Wall Street*, 11th ed. (New York: W.W. Norton, 2012); Morningstar.com.

cost averaging. Instead of speculating whether it was a good time or bad time to invest, you would have put your money on autopilot. Here's how that money would have grown in a tax-free account, if you had added $100 per month to the initial $1,600 investment between 1978 and 2013.

Between 1978 and 2013, the investor would have added just $43,600. But the money would have grown to $403,514.

Why Average Returns Aren't Normal

Although global stock markets have averaged 9 to 11 percent, there's a paradox. Returns landing precisely within this range aren't *normal*. If you're looking for a smooth 9 percent annual return from the stock market (plus or minus a percentage or two), you won't find it. Between 1926 and 2013, U.S. stocks gained between 9 and 11 percent just three times. In 1968, they gained 11 percent; in 1993, they gained 10.1 percent; and in 2004, they earned 10.9 percent. The rest of the time, stocks soared, sank, or sputtered.

U.S. stocks averaged 9.92 percent between 1926 and 2013, but single-year performances were schizophrenic. On 24 occasions, U.S. stocks recorded annual losses. On the flip side, stocks gained 25 percent or more during 24 other calendar years. Note the year-by-year performances in Table 3.2. Stock market volatility is normal. And it always will be.

International stocks prove the same paradox. Over long time periods they too averaged returns between 9 and 11 percent per year. But few individual years recorded profits within this range. During my lifetime, it has happened twice. Global stocks gained 10 percent in 2005 and 9.6 percent in 2007.[2]

But have the meteoric rises, crashes, and rises resulted in stocks outpacing inflation? As mentioned in Chapter 1, currency-buying power diminishes over time.

Stocks Pound Inflation

In Table 3.3, I've listed a dozen countries. You can see how much their stock market growth exceeded inflation, on average, between 1900 and 2012. For example, if inflation had averaged 4 percent per year in

Table 3.2   S&P 500 Annual Returns, 1926–2013

Percentages in Parentheses Show Losses

Return	Year	Return	Year	Return	Year
11.62%	1926	(35.03%)	1937	5.50%	1948
37.49%	1927	31.12%	1938	18.79%	1949
43.61%	1928	(0.41%)	1939	31.71%	1950
(8.42%)	1929	(9.78%)	1940	24.02%	1951
(24.90%)	1930	(11.59%)	1941	18.37%	1952
(43.34%)	1931	20.34%	1942	(0.99%)	1953
(8.19%)	1932	25.90%	1943	52.62%	1954
53.99%	1933	19.75%	1944	31.56%	1955
(1.44%)	1934	36.44%	1945	6.56%	1956
47.67%	1935	(8.07%)	1946	(10.78%)	1957
33.92%	1936	5.71%	1947	43.36%	1958
11.96%	1959	6.56%	1978	33.36%	1997
0.47%	1960	18.44%	1979	28.58%	1998
26.89%	1961	32.42%	1980	21.04%	1999
(8.73%)	1962	(4.91%)	1981	(9.10%)	2000
22.80%	1963	21.55%	1982	(11.89%)	2001
16.48%	1964	22.56%	1983	(22.10%)	2002
12.45%	1965	6.27%	1984	26.68%	2003
(10.06%)	1966	31.73%	1985	10.88%	2004
23.98%	1967	18.67%	1986	4.91%	2005
11.06%	1968	5.25%	1987	15.79%	2006
(8.50%)	1969	16.61%	1988	5.49%	2007
4.01%	1970	31.69%	1989	(37.00%)	2008
14.31%	1971	(3.10%)	1990	26.46%	2009
18.98%	1972	30.47%	1991	15.06%	2010
(14.66%)	1973	7.62%	1992	2.11%	2011
(26.47%)	1974	10.08%	1993	16.00%	2012
37.20%	1975	1.32%	1994	32.39%	2013
23.84%	1976	37.58%	1995	9.92%	**Average**
(7.18%)	1977	22.96%	1996		**Return**

SOURCE: Bogleheads.org.

Table 3.3   Postinflation Stock Market (Real) Returns, 1900–2012

Country	Inflation Beaten By
Australia	7.2%
Canada	5.7%
Denmark	4.9%
Finland	5.0%
Ireland	3.7%
Japan	3.6%
Netherlands	4.8%
New Zealand	5.8%
South Africa	7.2%
Sweden	6.1%
United Kingdom	5.2%
United States	6.2%
World Stock Average	5.4%

SOURCE: *Credit Suisse Global Investment Returns Yearbook 2012.*

Australia from 1900 to 2012, and if the Australian stock market had averaged 5 percent per year, then Australian stocks would have earned a 1 percent annual return after inflation. Fortunately, Aussie stocks tied inflation to a post and beat it mercilessly: by 7.2 percent per year. You can see Australia's after-inflation performance as well as those of 11 other global markets in Table 3.3. Such returns (above inflation) are called *real returns*.

On average, global stocks beat inflation by 5.4 percent per year since 1900. Whether such outperformance will continue is anyone's guess. But over long periods of time, stocks have dominated. For this reason, having stock market exposure is a wise idea.

What Has the Stock Market Done for You Lately?

Some investors, over the past few years, have wondered what the stock market has done for them lately. If your investments have acted more like a deadbeat boyfriend than a moody yet productive home renovator, you have some legitimate factors to blame: high fees, a knucklehead behind

Table 3.4 What $10,000 Invested In U.S. and International Stocks Would Have Grown To

Time Period	Initial Investment	Grew to (U.S. Stock Market)	Grew to (International Stock Markets)
1 Year (2013–2014)	$10,000	$13,334	$11,504
3 Years (2011–2014)	$10,000	$15,650	$11,612
5 Years (2009–2014)	$10,000	$23,580	$17,642
10 Years (2004–2014)	$10,000	$21,577	$20,148

Measured in U.S. dollars.

SOURCE: Morningstar.com: Vanguard's Total Stock Market Index; Vanguard's International Stock Market Index.

the portfolio's decisions, or both. If your money were diversified across a variety of global stock markets over one-, three-, five-, and 10-year periods between 2004 and 2014, you would have earned the returns listed in Table 3.4.

Undressing Stocks with 50 Shades of Gray

You might wonder how money grows in the stock market. Such profits derive from two sources: capital appreciation and dividends. Let me explain with a story.

Imagine you've started a business called Fifty Shades, designing and manufacturing sexy underwear for men and women. After signing seductive advertising deals with Madonna and Miley Cyrus, sales thrust upward across every female age demographic. But as the company's CEO, you recognize a problem. Fruit of the Loom is spanking you silly in sales to aging baby booming males. Only one solution makes sense: Sign Sylvester Stallone to a multiyear television-advertising contract. He could dance around a boxing ring, wearing Fifty Shades skivvies while pounding away at Siberian-sized strawberries and apples.

Such advertising should increase sales, but then you'll need to meet the product demand. New factories will be required; new distribution networks will be needed. They won't be cheap. To make more money, you're going to *need* more money.

So you hire someone to approach the New York Stock Exchange, and before you know it you have investors in your business. They buy parts of your business, also known as shares or stock. You're no longer the sole owner, but, by selling part of your business to new stockholders, you're able to build a larger, more efficient underwear business with the shareholder proceeds.

Your company, though, is now public, meaning the share owners (should they choose) could sell their stakes in Fifty Shades to other willing buyers. When a publicly traded company has shares that trade on a stock market, the trading activity has a negligible effect on the business. So you're able to concentrate on creating the sexiest underwear in the business. The shareholders don't bother you, because generally minority shareholders don't have any influence in a company's day-to-day operations.

Your underwear catches fire globally, which pleases shareholders. But they want more than a certificate from the New York Stock Exchange or their local brokerage firm proving they're partial owners of Fifty Shades. They want to share in the business profits. This makes sense because stockholders in a company are technically owners.

So the board of directors (who were voted into their positions by the shareholders) decides to give the owners an annual percentage of the profits, known as a dividend. This is how it works. Assume that Fifty Shades sells $1,000,000 worth of garments each year. After paying taxes on the earnings, employee wages, and business costs, the company makes an annual profit of $100,000. So the company's board of directors decides to pay its shareholders $50,000 of that annual $100,000 profit and split it among the shareholders. This is known as a dividend.

The remaining $50,000 profit would be reinvested back into the business—so the company can pay for bigger and better facilities, develop new products, increase advertising, and generate even higher profits.

Those reinvested profits make Fifty Shades even more profitable. As a result, the company doubles its profits to $200,000 the following year, and increases its dividend payout to shareholders.

This, of course, causes other potential investors to drool. They want to buy shares in this hot undergarment company. So now there are more people wanting to buy shares than there are people wanting to sell them.

This creates a demand for the shares, causing the share price on the New York Stock Exchange to rise. The price of any asset, whether it's real estate, gold, oil, stock, or a bond, is entirely based on supply and demand. If there are more buyers than sellers, the price rises. If there are more sellers than buyers, the price falls.

Over time, Fifty Shades' share price fluctuates: sometimes climbing, sometimes falling, depending on investor sentiment. If news about the company arouses the public, demand for the shares increases. On other days, investors grow pessimistic, causing the share price to limp.

But your company continues to make more money over the years. And over the long term, when a company increases its profits, the stock price generally rises with it.

Shareholders are able to make money two different ways. They can realize a profit from dividends (cash payments given to shareholders usually four times each year), or they can wait until their stock price increases substantially on the stock market and choose to sell some or all of their shares.

Here's how an investor could hypothetically make 10 percent a year from owning shares in Fifty Shades:

Warren Buffett has his eye on your business, so he decides to invest $10,000 in the company's stock at $10 a share. After one year, if the share price rises to $10.50, this would amount to a 5 percent increase in the share price ($10.50 is 5 percent higher than the $10 that Mr. Buffett paid).

And if Mr. Buffett receives a $500 dividend, he earns an additional 5 percent because a $500 dividend is 5 percent of his initial $10,000 investment.

So if his shares gain 5 percent in value from the share price increase, and he makes an extra 5 percent from the dividend payment, then after one year Mr. Buffett would have earned 10 percent on his shares. Of course, only the 5 percent dividend payout would go into his pocket as a *realized* profit. The 5 percent "profit" from the price appreciation (as the stock rose in value) would be realized only if Mr. Buffett sold his Fifty Shades shares.

Warren Buffett, however, didn't become one of the world's richest men by trading shares that fluctuate in price. Studies have shown that, on average, people who trade stocks (buying and selling them) don't tend to make investment profits that are as high as those of investors who do very little (if any) trading. What's more, to maximize profits, investors should reinvest dividends into new shares.

Doing so increases the number of shares you own. And the more shares you have, the greater the dividend income you'll receive. Joshua Kennon, a financial author at About.com (a division of the New York Times Company), calculated how valuable reinvested dividends are. He assumed an investor purchased $10,000 of Coca-Cola stock in June 1962. If that person didn't reinvest the stock's dividends into additional Coca-Cola shares, the initial $10,000 would have earned $136,270 in cash dividends by 2012 and the shares would be worth $503,103.

If the person had invested the cash dividends, however, the $10,000 would have grown to $1,750,000.[3]

Let's assume Mr. Buffett holds shares in Fifty Shades while reinvesting dividends. Some years the share price rises. Other years it falls. But the company keeps increasing its profits, so the share price increases over time. The annual dividends keep a smile on Buffett's face as he reinvests them in additional shares. His profits from the rising stock price coupled with dividends earn him an average return (let's assume) of 10 percent a year.

The Stock Market Stars as the Great Humiliator

Choosing a company to invest in isn't easy, even if you think you can predict its business earnings. Over the long term, stock price increases correlate directly with business earnings. But over a short period of time (and 10 years is considered a stock market blip), anything can happen. This is why the famous money manager Kenneth Fisher refers to the stock market as the Great Humiliator.[4] Over a handful of years, a company's business profits can grow by 8 percent per year, while the stock price stagnates. Or business earnings could limp along at 4 percent per year, while the stock market pushes the share price along by 13 percent.

Such a disconnection never lasts. Ultimately a company's stock price growth will mirror its business's profit growth. If a stock's price appreciation outpaces business earnings, the stock price will either flatline or fall until it realigns with business earnings.

If business profit growth exceeds the stock's appreciation, at some point the stock will dramatically rise, realigning share price growth with that of business profits.

Connections between stock and business profits correlate strongly over long time periods—15 years or more. But short term, markets are mad because people are crazy.

Those trying to buy individual stocks need to forecast two things: future business earnings and people's reactions to those business earnings. For example, if financial analysts and the general investment public felt that Google's business earnings would grow by 15 percent next year, and the company's earnings grew by 13 percent instead, many shareholders would sell. No, I'm not suggesting such a move would be rational. It wouldn't be. But people aren't rational. Such selling would drop Google's share price, despite the impressive 13 percent business growth rate.

Predicting the general direction of the stock market is just as difficult. Even with a solid eye on the economy, human sentiment moves stock prices in the short term, not government policies or economic data. The existence of more buyers than sellers increases demand, so stock prices rise. Having more sellers than buyers increases supply, so prices fall. That's it: nothing more, nothing less. The stock market isn't its own entity, moving up and down like some kind of mystical scepter. Instead, its movements are a short-term manifestation of what people do. Are they buying or are they selling? We move stock prices: the aggregate activities of you, global institutional investors, and me. Our groupthink is so unpredictable that most economists can't determine the market's direction. To do so accurately, they would have to predict human behavior. And they can't.

But over the long term, there's always a direct correlation between business earnings and stock prices. Warren Buffett's former Columbia University professor, Benjamin Graham, referred to the stock market as a short-term voting machine or popularity contest, but a long-term weighing machine.[5] Business earnings and stock price growth are two separate things. But in the long term, they tend to reflect the same result. For example, if a business grew its profits by 1,000 percent over a 30-year period, the stock price, including dividends, would perform similarly.

It's the same for a stock market in general. If the average company within a stock market grows by 1,000 percent over 30 years (that's 8.32 percent annually), the stock market would reflect such growth. Over the long term, stock markets predictably reflect the fortunes of the businesses within them. But over shorter time periods, the stock market is nuts.

Fast-Growing Economies Can Produce Weak Returns

Adding to the difficulty of predicting stock market growth is the fact that emerging stock markets don't seem to follow the same rules. For example, everybody knows that China's economic growth has run circles around U.S. growth for the past 20 years. But here's a trivia question to ask a friend. Knowing what you know now, if you went back 20 years in a time machine with $10,000 to invest, would you want to spread your money among 100 randomly selected Chinese stocks or 100 randomly selected U.S. stocks?

Most people would choose China. But inflation would have crushed them for it. According to a July 15, 2013, article in Bloomberg.com, since the Chinese market opened up (in 1993), "Foreigners earned less than 1 percent a year investing in Chinese stocks, a sixth of what they would have made owning U.S. Treasury bills."[6] This means an investor in Chinese stocks would have turned $10,000 into less than $12,200 between 1993 and 2013. However, the same investment in U.S. stocks would have grown to $47,655.[7]

Such disparity between economic growth and stock market growth isn't prevalent just in China. Emerging markets (India, Thailand, Indonesia, etc.) have definitely benefited as villagers have migrated to cities, worked at better jobs, and spent higher wages. But shadier legal frameworks and poor corporate governance in such markets can erode profits for shareholders.

As Yale University finance professor David Swensen writes in his book *Pioneering Portfolio Management*, "A particularly prevalent problem in many Asian countries involves family-controlled companies satisfying family desires at the expense of external minority shareholder wishes."[8]

Most global expats are aware of the corruption among many emerging market businesses. Such palm greasing is one of the reasons strong economic growth doesn't always manifest itself in the stock market.

While emerging market economic growth has run circles around U.S. growth, the developed world's stock markets have comfortably beaten aggregate emerging market returns over the past quarter century.

Numbers from the World Bank's International Finance Corporation, for instance, reveal that $100,000 invested in a broad, random selection of emerging market stocks in 1985 (the earliest date from which we have emerging market data) would have been worth $1.08 million by 2006. The same $100,000 invested in U.S. markets would have grown to more than $1.3 million. And if invested in developed world stock markets (excluding the United States), it would have grown to $1.16 million.[9]

Nobody knows which stock markets are going to do well this year or over the next decade. Sometimes emerging markets do well. Sometimes developed markets win.

Many people hire advisors to guess. But speculating is silly, as I'll show in later chapters. Instead of rolling the dice with a soothsayer, trying to predict which market will outperform, it's better to diversify money across every sector at the lowest possible cost.

Unfortunately, many global expatriates fail to do so. And their retirements pay the price.

Bonds Are Protective Nets for Jumpers

Besides investing in stocks, smart investors choose bonds as well. When investing in bonds, individuals loan a government or corporation money in exchange for a fixed rate of interest. Bonds underperform stocks—not every year or every decade, but over the long haul they do. But they aren't as volatile. An investor, for example, with the majority of his or her money in bonds issued by a developed country's government wouldn't suffer a 50 percent investment loss if the stock market dropped by half. In some cases, such an investor may gain money when stocks drop.

Investment portfolios composed of stocks and bonds are less volatile and more diversified than those made up solely of stocks. So they're safer.

In the short term, investments get yanked about based on supply and demand. When demand for stocks is especially high (many more buyers than sellers), stocks rocket. But for stocks to rise so quickly, people would be buying them with abandon. Where do they get such money for their stock market purchases? Many pull proceeds from savings accounts, mattresses (if they're nuts), gold, real estate, and bonds. If enough money is pulled from gold, real estate, and bonds, these asset classes fall in price. Their supply would exceed their demand.

When stocks are roaring, investors selling bonds can force bond prices to drop. Always remember that short-term asset class movements are a result of supply and demand. If more people are selling bonds than buying, supply outweighs demand. So bond prices fall. If more people are buying bonds than selling, bond prices rise.

There are a few different types of bonds, but I'll explain the most common with a story. Assume your eccentric Uncle James wants you to save, so he makes you a deal. If you give him $10,000, he'll invest the money for himself however he sees fit. You arrange for him to keep the money for five years. In the meantime, he gives you cash interest. He promises 5 percent per year. This is called a 5 percent coupon. In this case, the yield is also 5 percent. Uncle James promises to pay you $500 annually. He pays it twice a year, $250 each time.

At the end of the five-year term, Uncle James will return the $10,000. You will have recouped the $10,000, plus earned $500 for every year your uncle held your money.

But what if you had asked him to return the $10,000 before the end of the five-year term? This is where Uncle James's quirkiness shines. He may decide to return just $9,800. Or he may give you a gift, handing over $10,300.

Uncle James guarantees he'll return exactly what you give him only if he's able to hold the money for the duration agreed upon. If you want the money early, the strange duck might return more than you gave him, or less.

Here's where Uncle James gets weirder. Assume that one year after you invested your initial $10,000 with him, your friend Amy wants in on the action. She approaches your uncle, who makes her a deal. "Amy, you can buy into the same scheme, but it expires in 2019. This means you have only four years to earn interest, not five. I'm returning all money in 2019—yours (if you choose to invest) and your friend's." But bank interest rates have risen, so Amy starts wondering why she would invest with your uncle when the interest rate he promises is now lower than what she can earn elsewhere. "I'll tell you what," says Uncle James. "If you invest just $9,500, I'll pay you $500 per year (equivalent to 5 percent of $10,000), but when the term expires in four years, I'll give you $10,000 instead of just the $9,500 you invested."

In such a case, the investment's coupon is 5 percent of $10,000. It was the set interest rate on the initial $10,000 investment deal you made with Uncle James. But the investment yield is higher for Amy because she gets her $500 per year at a discount. She invests $9,500, will earn $500 per year in interest, and will receive $10,000 back at the end of four years. Consequently, her investment yields 5.3 percent per year.

If bank interest rates had dropped instead, Uncle James would have done something different. Realizing what a great deal he was offering compared to the dropping interest rates of the banks, he would have told Amy, "You can invest in this scheme. You will receive a 5 percent coupon on $10,000 but it will cost you $10,500, not $10,000. Therefore, your yield would be 4.8 percent, not 5 percent, because I'll return less than what you invested. It would still be profitable, of course, because you would receive $500 per year. But it would be less so."

If you followed this strange little story, then you'll understand how most bonds work. Newly issued bonds have an expiration term and a fixed rate of interest. Investors purchasing such bonds when they're launched earn the same coupon and yield. If the interest paid amounts to 3 percent per year, this is what investors will make each year if they hold the bonds to maturity. If they sell early, they would receive more or less than what they deposited, depending on current bond prices. If they hold the bonds to maturity, they would receive exactly what they had invested, plus the cash interest they had earned twice a year.

Other investors can jump into a bond after the initial launch date. But if demand for bonds is high, they'll pay a premium for the bond. So their yield will be lower than the coupon rate that was advertised when the bond was launched. If demand for bonds is lower (this occurs when bank interest rates rise), bond prices drop. This increases the yield for new investors jumping into the same bond.

Can You Lose Money with Bonds?

Those buying low-grade corporate bonds from companies with shaky financial foundations can certainly lose money. To entice investors, such companies offer higher than average interest rates. For example, assume a new technology company needs money for research and development. It might issue a bond with a 10 percent coupon, which is well above typical rates. But if the company goes bankrupt, investors might lose some or all of their original capital. It could get flushed down the toilet, along with the company's future.

Likewise, investors loading up on long-term bonds can lose money in real terms. Remember that a real return is the profit made after inflation. If investors bought bonds maturing in 20 years with coupons of 3 percent per year, inflation could devour the profits. Sure, they would still earn 3 percent per year on their investment. But if inflation averaged 4 percent, the investor's real return would be negative. Such interest payments wouldn't keep pace with inflation.

Bonds can drop in price. But even when they do, high-quality bonds never collapse the way stocks can. Plus, as with stocks, I'll show how to diversify across different bonds so you never have to worry about losing money, or losing in the long term to inflation.

In the chart in Figure 3.2, you can see how bonds are less volatile than stocks. The roller-coaster line on top is the S&P 500. You should be able to see the crash of 1987, the crash of 2002–2003, and the crash of 2008–2009. The three lines below it represent total returns of three U.S. bond indexes, with interest reinvested.

While the media, from time to time, may headline upcoming bond crashes or stock plunges, keep bond-crashing forecasts in perspective. Bonds sometimes fall in price. But their drops are nothing compared to how far stocks fall in a bad year.

Patience, diversification, and low investment costs are keys to large profits in the stock and bond markets. To earn such returns, however, investors must sidestep the industry's traps. Let me show you how.

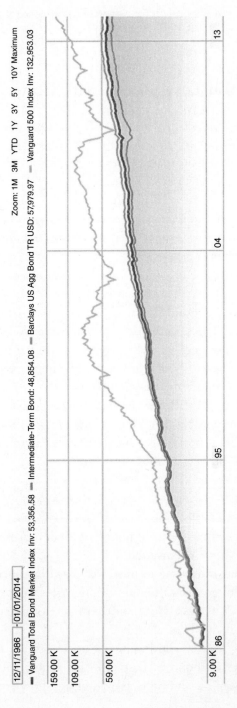

Figure 3.2   Bonds Are More Stable Than Stocks

SOURCE: Morningstar.com.

Notes

1. "S&P 500 Index," Bogleheads. Accessed May 1, 2014. www.bogleheads.org/wiki/S%26P_500_index.

2. Kenneth L. Fisher and Lara Hoffmans, *Markets Never Forget (but People Do): How Your Memory Is Costing You Money—and Why This Time Isn't Different* (Hoboken, NJ: John Wiley & Sons, 2012).

3. Joshua Kennon, "Reinvesting Dividends vs. Not Reinvesting Dividends: A 50-Year Case Study of Coca-Cola Stock." Accessed May 1, 2014. www.joshuakennon.com/reinvesting-dividends-versus-not-reinvesting-dividends-coca-cola/.

4. Kenneth L. Fisher, Jennifer Chou, and Lara Hoffmans, *The Only Three Questions That Count: Investing by Knowing What Others Don't* (Hoboken, NJ: John Wiley & Sons, 2007).

5. "The Voting and Weighing Machines," Morningstar News. Accessed May 1, 2014. http://news.morningstar.com/classroom2/course.asp?docId=142901&page=7.

6. "China Wealth Proves Elusive as Stocks Earn 1% in 20 Years," Bloomberg.com. Accessed May 1, 2014. www.bloomberg.com/news/2013-07-14/china-wealth-eluding-foreigners-as-equities-earn-1-for-20-years.html.

7. "Vanguard 500 Index Inv | VFINX," Morningstar.com. Accessed May 1, 2014. http://quote.morningstar.com/fund/chart.aspx?&t=VFINX®ion=usa&culture=en-US.

8. David F. Swensen, *Pioneering Portfolio Management: An Unconventional Approach to Institutional Investment* (New York: Free Press, 2000).

9. Ibid.

Chapter 4

Don't Start a Fight with an Escalator

A dmit it. When you were a kid, you were tempted at least once to run up an escalator that was heading down. Sure, it was tougher than taking the stairs, but mastering the mechanical monster was part of the fun.

Unfortunately, most global expatriates trudge against an escalator full-time with their investments.

I could use any of the world's stock markets to explain this. But in honor of roast beef, Yorkshire pudding, and mushy peas, let's give a nod to the British.

During the decade ending 2013, the typical UK stock earned 132 percent.[1]

This means £10,000 invested in the average British stock grew to £23,200. Did most British investors make such profits? Not even close. Instead, most financed the lavish lifestyles of those working in the financial services industry.

If every stock on the British market were sold, most of the direct recipients would be pension funds, unit trusts (mutual funds), college endowment funds, and hedge funds. The money would then be paid to investors with stakes in such products. Because the vast majority of the money in the markets is professionally managed, when the UK market earns 132 percent over a given decade, it means the average professional fund earned roughly 132 percent—before fees.

The same premise applies to other countries' stock markets. As a group, because institutional and unit trust money represents the vast majority of assets invested in a given market, the average institutional investor and unit trust will earn (on average, before fees) the market's return. William F. Sharpe explained this in the *Financial Analysts Journal* in 1991, one year after he won the Nobel Prize in economic sciences.[2]

It's easy to visualize with a story. Imagine 100 students in a school called Unit Trust. Assume all 100 take an exam, and the school invites four or five kids from outside the district to join them. If the average exam score is 80 percent, the average Unit Trust student would have earned close to 80 percent. The four or five students from outside the district would barely affect the average.

In the same vein, because institutional and unit trust money comprises nearly all of the assets in the British market, the return of the stock index will be close to the average British professional's stock market performance. People like your Uncle Toby and Richard Branson, who might buy their own stocks, have a minor influence on the market because they invest so little money compared to institutional traders. They're like the four or five kids outside the Unit Trust school district whose test scores barely budge the average of the other 100 test-taking students.

Yes, the Financial District Loves You!

You don't need to be Stephen Hawking to know that those in the British financial district don't work for free. Instead, they're among the highest-paid people in Britain. Who pays them? British investors, of course. If you invest in a pension or a unit trust, you're paying their salaries.

Most retail investors buy actively managed unit trusts. In North America, they're called actively managed mutual funds. In most cases, they're purchased through an intermediary advisor or broker. The broker then puts the money into a mutual fund. Once there, the cash gets pooled with money from other investors, like your Aunt Lucy, your friend Bob, and the strange homebound bloke with the telescope.

A fund manager then trades stocks within the unit trust. A large brokerage house charges commissions for each trade. But neither the fund manager nor his or her firm is generous enough to pay those commissions. Instead, the costs are skimmed from the mutual fund's proceeds. Can you see where this is headed?

The brokerage firm incurs other costs as well: salaries for employees, research expenses, electricity expenses, advertising expenses, lease expenses, and often a commission for the broker selling the products. Owners of the firm, as well, demand their share of profits. Where does this money come from? It all gets siphoned from the investment assets. Can you hear that escalator whirling?

Recall that the typical British stock earned 132 percent for the decade ending 2013. This means the typical professional investor (in British stocks) earned about the same. But that's before fees.

Add the plethora of costs, and the escalator starts smoking. It's a mathematical certainty that the average retail investor earns nothing close to the return delivered by the average stock, also known as the market average. Whether investors are Canadian, American, European, or Australian, they pay insidious fees to the financial services industry. Such costs jeopardize their futures.

Most of these fees, of course, are hidden from your investment statement. But they're real. And they're punishing. They also draw the ire of many.

Global Investors Getting Fleeced

Warren Buffett says, "Full-time professionals in other fields, let's say dentists, bring a lot to the layman. But in aggregate, people get nothing for their money from professional money managers."[3] David Swensen, Yale University's endowment fund manager, suggests that the government needs to stop the mutual fund industry's exploitation of individual investors.[4]

"Talk about irony!"

Illustration by Chad Crowe: Printed with permission.

Jack Meyer, the leader of Harvard University's endowment fund, says, "The investment business is a giant scam. It deletes billions of dollars every year in transaction costs and fees."[5]

Perhaps you're shaking your head right now. "These blokes are Americans," you're thinking. "We all know Wall Street gouges the typical Yank."

Do investors in other countries pay such fees? The answer is no. Most non-Americans pay *much more*.

In a study published in 2008 by Oxford University Press, researchers Ajay Khorana, Henri Servaes, and Peter Tufano compared international fund costs, including estimates for sales fees. British investors pay 51 percent more in fees than Americans pay. Canadians pay nearly 100 percent more.[6]

Understanding the impact of fees is important. If you're paying 2 percent in annual fees each year to have your money managed, you may see this as a paltry sum. But it isn't. If the markets make 6 percent in

Table 4.1 Single-Year Profits Siphoned by Financial Industry When Markets Earn 6 Percent

Country	Total Estimated Expenses, Including Sales Costs	Percentage of Annual Profits Lost by the Investor
Netherlands	0.82%	13.6%
Australia	1.41%	23.5%
Sweden	1.51%	25.1%
United States	1.53%	25.5%
Belgium	1.76%	29.3%
Denmark	1.85%	30.8%
France	1.88%	31.3%
Finland	1.91%	31.8%
Germany	1.97%	32.8%
Austria	2.26%	37.6%
United Kingdom	2.28%	38.0%
Ireland	2.40%	40.0%
Norway	2.43%	40.5%
Italy	2.44%	40.6%
Luxembourg	2.63%	43.8%
Spain	2.70%	45.0%
Canada	3.0%	50.0%

SOURCE: Ajay Khorana, Henri Servaes, and Peter Tufano, "Mutual Fund Fees around the World," *Review of Financial Studies* 22, no. 3 (2009): 1279–1310. http://faculty.london.edu/hservaes/rfs2009.pdf.

a given year, and you're paying 2 percent in fees, then you're giving away 33 percent of your profits to the financial services industry.

Table 4.1 shows the percentages of annual fees paid by international investors. More important, note the annual profits that investors would lose if their respective stock markets earned 6 percent next year.

During years when stock markets don't perform well, the industry takes an even bigger chunk of your profits. Assume the German stock market earns 3 percent in a given year. The typical German fund investor pays a 1.97 percent annual fee. In this case, the average mutual fund (unit trust) investor relinquishes 65.6 percent of his or her annual profit.

High fees create a maddening process of two steps forward and one step back. Fortunately, there's an alternative. And by choosing it, global expats give less to the financial services industry and much more to themselves.

In the chapters ahead, I'll show how to bypass a fight with a downward-heading escalator.

Notes

1. "MSCI UK Index," iShares UK. www.ishares.com/uk/individual/en/products/253739/ishares-msci-uk-ucits-etf.
2. William F. Sharpe, "The Arithmetic of Active Management," *Financial Analysts Journal*, 1991. Accessed May 4, 2014. www.stanford.edu/~wfsharpe/art/active/active.htm.
3. Warren Buffett and Janet Lowe, *Warren Buffett Speaks: Wit and Wisdom from the World's Greatest Investor* (New York: John Wiley & Sons, 1997).
4. David F. Swensen, *Unconventional Success: A Fundamental Approach to Personal Investment* (New York: Free Press, 2005).
5. "Online Extra: Husbanding That $27 Billion (Extended)," *Bloomberg Businessweek*, December 26, 2004. Accessed May 4, 2014. www.businessweek.com/stories/2004-12-26/online-extra-husbanding-that-27-billion-extended.
6. Ajay Khorana, Henri Servaes, and Peter Tufano, "Mutual Fund Fees around the World," *Review of Financial Studies* 22, no. 3 (2009): 1279–1310. Accessed May 4, 2014. http://faculty.london.edu/hservaes/rfs2009.pdf.

Chapter 5

Where Are the Customers' Yachts?

An out-of-town visitor was being shown the wonders of the New York financial district. When the party arrived at the Battery, one of his guides indicated some handsome ships riding at anchor. He said,
    "Look, those are the bankers' and brokers' yachts."
    "Where are the customers' yachts?" asked the naïve visitor.
    —Fred Schwed, *Where Are the Customers' Yachts?*[1]

I f you've never read an investment book before, chances are you've never heard of index funds. No, your financial advisor won't likely discuss them. Index funds are flies in caviar dishes for most financial

51

advisors. From their perspective, selling them to clients makes little sense. If they sell index funds, they make less money for themselves. If they sell actively managed mutual funds, advisors make more. It really is that simple.

Most expats, however, should be interested in funding their own retirement, not somebody else's.

The term *index* refers to a collection of something. Think of a collection of key words at the back of a book, representing the book's content. An index fund is much the same: a collection of stocks representing the content in a given market.

For example, a total Australian stock market index is a collection of stocks compiled to represent the entire Australian market. If a single index fund consisted of every Australian stock, for example, and nobody traded those index fund shares back and forth (thus avoiding transaction costs), then the profits for investors in the index fund would perfectly match the return of the Australian stock market before fees. Stated another way, investors in a total Australian stock market index would earn roughly the same return as the average Australian stock.

Global Investors Bleed by the Same Sword

Now toss a professional fund manager into the mix—somebody trained to choose the very best stocks for the given fund. Unfortunately, the fund's performance will likely lag the stock market index. Most active funds do. Regardless of the country you choose, actively managed mutual funds sing the same sad song.

Recall why from the previous chapter. Professionally managed money represents nearly all of the money invested in a given market. Consequently, the average money manager's return will equal the return of the market—before fees. Add costs, and we're trying to run up that downward-heading escalator.

Consider the UK market. According to a study published by the Oxford University Press, "Mutual Fund Fees around the World," the average actively managed fund in Great Britain costs 2.28 percent each year, including sales costs.[2] Regardless of the market, the average professionally managed fund will underperform the market's index in equal proportion to the fees charged.

Ron Sandler, former chief executive for Lloyds of London, reported a study for *The Economist*, suggesting that the average actively managed unit trust in Great Britain underperformed the British market index by 2.5 percent each year. It's no coincidence that the average UK unit trust (mutual fund) cost British investors nearly 2.5 percent per year.[3]

In Canada, Standard & Poor's reported that 97.5 percent of actively managed Canadian stock market funds underperformed the Canadian stock market index from 2005 to 2010, thanks largely to the funds' high management expenses.[4]

In South Africa, nearly 90 percent of actively managed unit trusts underperformed the South African stock index, as measured by the Satrix 40 exchange-traded fund (ETF) during the five years ending 2010.[5]

In Australia, according to the Standard & Poor's Indices versus Active (SPIVA) funds scorecard, 72 percent of actively managed funds underperformed their indexed benchmarks over the three-year period ending 2012.[6]

As for American expatriates, beating a portfolio of index funds with actively managed funds (especially after taxes) is about as likely as growing a third eye.

American Expatriates Run Naked

Unlike most global expats, Americans can't legally shelter their money in a country that doesn't charge capital gains taxes. And actively managed mutual funds attract high levels of tax. There are two forms of American capital gains taxes. One is called *short-term*; the other, *long-term*. Short-term capital gains are taxed at the investor's ordinary income tax rate. Such taxes are triggered when a profitable investment in a non-tax-deferred account is sold within one year.

I can hear what you're thinking: "I don't sell my mutual funds on an annual basis, so I wouldn't incur such costs when my funds make money." Unfortunately, if you're an American expat invested in actively managed mutual funds, you sell without realizing it. Fund managers do it for you by constantly trading stocks within their respective funds. In a non-tax-sheltered account, it's a heavy tax to pay.

Stanford University economists Joel Dickson and John Shoven examined a sample of 62 actively managed mutual funds with long-term track records. Before taxes, $1,000 invested in those funds between 1962 and 1992 would have grown to $21,890. After capital gains and dividend taxes, however, that same $1,000 would have grown to just $9,870 in a high-income earner's taxable account.[7] American expats, as I'll explain in a later chapter, must invest the majority of their money in taxable accounts.

Because index fund holdings don't get actively traded, they trigger minimal capital gains taxes until investors are ready to sell. And even then, they're taxed at the far more lenient long-term capital gains tax rate.

In a 2009 *New York Times* article, "The Index Funds Win Again," Mark Hulbert reported that Mark Kritzman, president and chief executive of Windham Capital Management of Boston, had conducted a 20-year study on after-tax performances of index funds and actively managed funds. He found that, before fees and taxes, an actively managed fund would have to beat an index fund by 4.3 percent a year just to match the performance of the index fund.[8]

Flying parrots will serve you breakfast before a portfolio of actively managed funds beats a portfolio of index funds (before fees) by 4.3 percent over an investment lifetime. Researchers Richard A. Ferri and Alex C. Benke reported in their 2013 research paper, "A Case for Index Fund Portfolios," that the slim number of portfolios that beat index funds before taxes between 2003 and 2012 did so with an annual advantage ranging between only 0.29 percent and 0.54 percent per year.[9] And that's before taxes.

Why Brokers Want to Muzzle Warren Buffett

Most financial advisors wish to muzzle the brightest minds in finance: professors at leading business universities, Nobel Prize laureates in economics, the (rare) advisors with integrity, and billionaire businessmen like Warren Buffett. Brokers make more when experts are mute.

Warren Buffett, chairman of Berkshire Hathaway, is well known as history's greatest investor. And he criticizes the mutual fund industry, suggesting, "The best way to own common stocks is through an index fund."[10]

Buffett wrote a parable of the money management industry in Berkshire Hathaway's 2006 annual report. It stars a family called the Gotrocks.[11]

The family owns every stock in the United States; nobody else owns a single share.

Consequently, the family shares all of the revenue generated by those businesses. But instead of harmoniously splitting that money forever, they live up to their name ("got rocks" in the head) by hiring helpers to redistribute those earnings to the family, with the helpers charging the family fees to do so. Those helpers, of course, are brokers, mutual fund salespeople, and financial services companies. Their fees detract from the wealth the Gotrocks are entitled to.

The parable synchronizes with William F. Sharpe's thesis in "The Arithmetic of Active Management."[12] In it, the economic sciences Nobel Prize laureate proves that, before fees, investors in the stock market earn the return of the market, on average. After fees, as a group, they get scalped. Referencing a parasitic industry, Warren Buffett laments, "People get nothing for their money from professional money managers."[13]

Nobel laureate Sharpe explains it's delusional for most people (and most advisors) to anticipate beating market indexes over the long term. In a 2007 interview with Jason Zweig for *Money* magazine, he stated his view:

Sharpe: The only way to be assured of higher expected return is to own the entire market portfolio.

Zweig: You can easily do that through a simple, cheap index mutual fund. Why doesn't everyone invest that way?

Sharpe: Hope springs eternal. We all tend to think either that we're above average or that we can pick other people [to manage our money] who are above average . . . and those of us who put our money in index funds say, "Thank you very much."[14]

Daniel Kahneman, another famed Nobel Prize–winning economist, echoed the sentiment during a 2012 interview with the magazine *Der Spiegel*:

In the stock market . . . the predictions of experts are practically worthless. Anyone who wants to invest money is better off choosing index funds, which simply follow a certain stock index without any intervention of gifted stock pickers . . . we want to invest our money with somebody who appears to understand, even though the statistical evidence is plain that they are very unlikely to do so.[15]

Merton Miller, a 1990 Nobel Prize winner in economics, says even professionals managing money for governments or corporations shouldn't delude themselves about beating a portfolio of index funds:

Any pension fund manager who doesn't have the vast majority— and I mean 70 percent or 80 percent of his or her portfolio— in passive investments [index funds] is guilty of malfeasance, nonfeasance, or some other kind of bad feasance! There's just no sense for most of them to have anything but a passive [indexed] investment policy.[16]

In the documentary program *Passive Investing: The Evidence the Fund Management Industry Would Prefer You Not See*, many of the world's top economists and financial academics voice the futility of buying actively managed funds. But as the title suggests, it's the program most financial advisors will never want you watching.[17]

Financial Advisors Touting "The World Is Flat!"

Your financial education is the biggest threat to most globe-trotting financial advisors seeking expatriate spoils. Consequently, many are motivated to derail would-be index investors from gaining financial knowledge.

Self-Serving Argument Stomped by Evidence

Here is one of the most common arguments you'll hear from desperate advisors hoping to keep their gravy trains running:

Index funds are dangerous when stock markets fall. In an active fund, we can protect your money in case the markets crash.

This is where a salesperson tries scaring you—suggesting active managers have the ability to quickly sell stock market assets before the markets drop, saving your mutual fund assets from falling too far during a crash. And then, when the markets are looking safer (or so the pitch goes), a mutual fund manager will then buy stocks again, allowing you to ride the wave of profits back as the stock market recovers.

There are problems with this smoke screen. First, nobody should have all of his or her investments in a single stock market index fund. Investors require a combination: a domestic stock index fund to represent their home country stock market, an international stock market index fund to provide global exposure, and a bond market index fund for added stability. (Bonds act like portfolio parachutes. They're loans investors make to governments or corporations in exchange for a guaranteed rate of interest.) If the global stock markets dropped by 30 percent in a given year, a diversified portfolio of stock and bond market indexes wouldn't do the same.

Have some fun with self-proclaimed financial soothsayers. Ask which calendar year in recent memory saw the biggest stock market decline. They should say 2008. Ask them if most actively managed funds beat the total stock market index during 2008. If they say, "Yes," you've exposed your Pinocchios. A Standard & Poor's study cited in the *Wall Street Journal* in 2009 detailed that the vast majority of actively managed funds still lost to their counterpart stock market index funds during 2008— the worst market drop in recent memory. Clearly, active fund managers weren't able to dive out of the markets in time.[18]

Warren Buffett wagered a $1 million bet in 2008, unveiling more damning evidence against expensive money management. A few years previously, the great investor claimed nobody could handpick a group of hedge funds that would outperform the U.S. stock market index over the following 10 years.

Hedge funds are like actively managed mutual funds for the Gucci, Prada, Rolex crowd. To invest in a hedge fund, you must be an accredited investor—somebody with a huge salary or net worth. Hedge fund managers market themselves as the best professional investors in the industry. They certainly have plenty of flexibility. Hedge funds (according to marketing lore) make money during both rising and falling markets. Managers can invest in any asset class they wish; they can even bet against the stock market. Doing so is called "shorting the market" where fund managers bet that the markets will fall, and then collect on those bets if they're right.

Buffett, however, doesn't believe people can predict such stock market movements, charge high fees to do so, and make investors money.

Hedge Fund Money Spanked for Its Con

Grabbing Warren Buffett's gauntlet in 2008, New York asset management firm Protégé Partners bet history's greatest investor that five handpicked hedge funds would beat the S&P 500 index, a large U.S. stock index, over the following 10 years. Protégé Partners selected five hedge funds with solid management and great track records. But historical results are rarely repeated in the future. From 2008 to 2013, Protégé's pet funds rose 12.5 percent. But they were spanked by the index, which gained 43.8 percent.

If these hedge fund managers could have foreseen the stock market crash of 2008, they would have made a fortune by shorting (betting against) the market. But that wasn't the case. Six years into Buffett's bet, the stock market index was thumping Protégé's handpicked hedge funds by 31.3 percent.[19]

As of this writing, a few years remain on the bet. But if you've read Simon Lack's book, *The Hedge Fund Mirage*, you would place your money on the index. Lack reveals that a portfolio balanced between a U.S. stock index and a U.S. bond index would have beaten the typical hedge fund in 2003, 2004, 2005, 2006, 2007, 2008, 2009, 2010, and 2011.[20] Hedge funds continued to underperform the balanced stock and bond index in 2012 and 2013, falling 75 percent behind within the span of a decade (see Figure 5.1).[21] Such a shortfall for the masters of the universe is so great, in fact, that even if they had worked for free (not charging their usual 2 percent per year plus 20 percent of any profits) they still would have underperformed!

Consider the hedge fund industry's failure to beat portfolios of market indexes. If they can't do it, what chance does your financial advisor have? If your advisor has Olympian persistence, you might hear this:

You can't beat the market with an index fund. An index fund will give you just an average return. Why saddle yourself with mediocrity when we have teams of people to select the best funds for you?

If the average mutual fund had no costs associated with it, then the salesperson would be right. A total stock market index fund's return

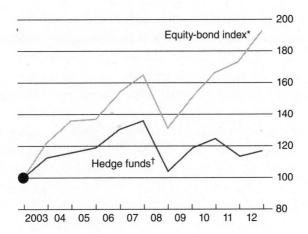

Figure 5.1   Hedge Fund Returns versus 60 Percent Stock Index/40 Percent Bond Index

*Weighted index: S&P 500 (60%) and world government bonds (40%).

†HFRX global index.

SOURCES: Hedge Fund Research; Thomson Reuters; *The Economist*; Matthew O'Brien, "Don't Invest in Hedge Funds," *The Atlantic*, July 10, 2013. Accessed May 5, 2014. www.theatlantic.com/business/archive/2013/07/dont-invest-in-hedge-funds/277697/.

would be pretty close to average. In the long term, roughly half of the world's actively managed funds would beat the world stock market index, and roughly half of the world's funds would be beaten by it. But for that to happen, you would have to live in a fantasy world where the world's bankers, money managers, and financial planners all worked for nothing—and their firms would have to be charitable foundations.

If your advisor's skin is thicker than that of a holiday time-share salesperson's, you might hear this next:

I can show you plenty of mutual funds that have beaten the indexes. We'd buy you only the very best funds.

Studies prove that selecting mutual funds based on high-performance track records is naive. Morningstar is a firm that rates mutual fund performances, giving five stars for funds that have beaten their peers and the comparative index, down to one star for funds with disappointing track records.

According to Morningstar, 72 percent of investors purchased funds rated four or five stars between 1999 and 2009. And why wouldn't they? Whether you're selecting mutual funds on your own or hiring an advisor to do so, going with a proven winner makes sense. But ironically, it's as smart as sipping seawater.

Star ratings change all the time, and funds earning five stars during one time period are rarely the top-rated funds during subsequent years.

Tim Courtney is the chief investment officer of U.S.-based Burns Advisory. He grew frustrated that so many of his clients insisted he choose actively managed mutual funds with five-star ratings. After back-testing the performances of the funds most highly rated by Morningstar during the decade ending in 2009, he found that they usually performed poorly after earning five-star designations. Not only did most of the funds go on to underperform their benchmark indexes, but they also underperformed the average actively managed mutual fund.[22]

What if, however, your advisor kept an eye on the star ratings, moving your money from funds that slip in the rankings to newly crowned five-star funds? Such attention to detail isn't likely, which is good, because it's a terrible strategy.

Hulbert's Financial Digest is an investment newsletter that rates the performance predictions of other newsletters. Studying Morningstar's five-star U.S. funds from 1994 to 2004, *Hulbert's* found that if investors continually adjusted their mutual fund holdings to hold only the highest-rated funds, they would have underperformed a total stock market index by 45.8 percent over the decade. In an American expatriate's taxable account, the deficit would be even greater. After taxes, Morningstar's top-rated funds underperformed the U.S. stock market index by 64.2 percent.[23]

Historical track records mean little. Even Morningstar's director of research, John Rekenthaler, recognizes the incongruity. In the fall 2000 edition of *In the Vanguard*, he said, "To be fair, I don't think that you'd want to pay much attention to Morningstar's ratings either."[24]

So if Morningstar can't pick the future's top funds, what odds does your financial planner have—especially when trying to dazzle you with a fund's historical track record?

What's maddening about such forecasting attempts is that only 7 percent of funds performing among the top 100 in a given year are able to land there again the following year. The chart in Figure 5.2, courtesy of Index Fund Advisors (IFA), shows the shocking reality.

If the salesperson's tenacity is tougher than a foot wart, you'll get this as the next response:

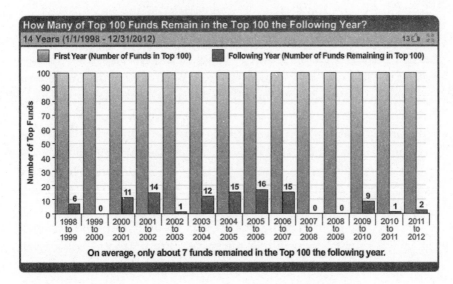

How Many of Top 100 Funds Remain in the Top 100 the Following Year?
14 Years (1/1/1998 - 12/31/2012)   13€▸

On average, only about 7 funds remained in the Top 100 the following year.

Figure 5.2 How Many Top 100 Funds Remain in the Top 100 the Following Year?
SOURCES: © 2013 Index Fund Advisors, Inc. (IFA); © Morningstar, Inc. Printed with permission.

I'm a professional. I can bounce your money around from fund to fund, taking advantage of global economic swings and hot fund manager streaks, and easily beat a portfolio of diversified indexes.

Sadly, many investors fall victim to their advisor's overconfidence. Instead of building diversified accounts of index funds, they build actively managed portfolios with yesterday's winners. Sometimes it's a collection of mutual funds with strong historical track records, or a focus on funds from a recently profitable geographic region. The results are often disastrous.

Adam Zargar, a British expatriate in Dubai, had such an experience with an investment representative from Royal Skandia. On October 29, 2010, the advisor built a portfolio of funds heavily tilted toward emerging markets, such as India, Thailand, and China. By doing so, Adam's advisor violated investing's golden rule: diversification. Spreading assets among a variety of markets and asset classes increases safety. We shouldn't try to gamble that a recently scorching fund from a specific geographic region or asset class (gold, oil, commodities, etc.) will continue to blaze, just because it did so recently.

But that's how most people invest. Adam's advisor was no exception. During the 12 months *before* Adam's advisor selected his funds, the emerging markets had increased by roughly 25 percent. His World Materials fund had gained 40 percent—before Adam bought it. The advisor chose funds by looking through the rearview mirror, and he failed to diversify. Three years later, Adam's portfolio was in the ditch.[25]

Nobody makes money every year, of course. But in the three years following the inception of Adam's portfolio in 2010, the British stock market soared 43 percent. Vanguard's Global Stock Market Index (an average of the world's stock markets) rose 32 percent. The U.S. stock market jumped 61 percent.

Despite the globally rising tide, Adam's portfolio lost money. Often, yesterday's hottest geographic sector becomes tomorrow's biggest loser. Futile performance chasing is common. Failing to diversify is common. And *most* people fall victim.

Why Most Investors Underperform Their Funds

Chicago-based Dalbar Inc. compares the results of the U.S. stock and bond market indexes with the profits earned by the average investor. The firm calls this the Quantitative Analysis of Investor Behavior.

Between 1990 and 2010, the average investor in U.S. stocks averaged 3.83 percent a year (see Figure 5.3). The U.S. stock market index, in comparison, gained 9.14 percent annually.

A similar performance gap exists with bonds. During the same 20-year period, the average investor in U.S. bonds earned just 1.81 percent per year, compared to 6.89 percent for the U.S. bond index.

Like Adam Zargar's advisor, most people feel good about investing in a market that has recently risen in price, extrapolating that pattern into the future. But stock markets are as unpredictable as the next earthquake. When markets are diving, many investors sell or at least cease to continue buying. By loading up on what's expensive and shunning what's cheap, they buy high and sell low.

Smart investors aren't so silly. Realizing that the markets are random, they buy low-cost investment products representing the entire global market. They invest regularly regardless of what the markets are doing,

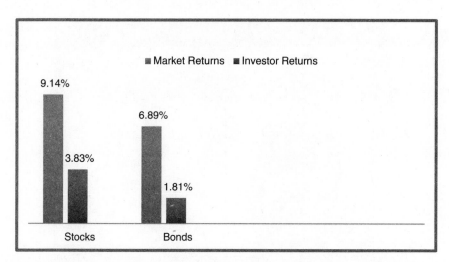

Figure 5.3　U.S. Stock and Bond Market Returns versus Investor Returns, 1990–2010
SOURCE: Dalbar Group.

and they diversify their assets broadly without speculating. Owning a global representation of investments is much easier than trying to predict the future (see Figure 5.4).

The next time an advisor tries to excite you with a hot fund or economic sector, let him burn his own money—not yours.

If you're countering your advisor's market-beating claims with proof, he or she might start to panic. When the advisor's desperation peaks, you might here this:

We use professional guidance to determine which economic sectors look most promising. With help from our professionals, we can beat a portfolio of index funds.

Many of the world's smartest money minds run state and corporate pension funds. I'm not talking about the expensive, dodgy offshore pensions hawked to unwary expats. State and corporate pensions are run at extraordinarily low costs—a fraction of what you would pay for services from a financial advisory firm. Yet they're still humbled by a portfolio of index funds.

Most pension funds have their money in a 60/40 split: 60 percent stocks and 40 percent bonds. The consulting firm FutureMetrics

One of these two dresses in an elaborate costume to make you think he can predict the future. The other wears a turban.

Figure 5.4   Financial Advisors Can't Predict the Future
Illustration by Chad Crowe: Printed with permission.

studied the performance of 192 U.S. major corporate pension plans between 1988 and 2005. Fewer than 30 percent of the pension funds outperformed a portfolio of 60 percent S&P 500 index and 40 percent intermediate corporate bond index.[26] You could have beaten more than 70 percent of pension fund managers with a diversified portfolio of index funds, while allocating less than an hour a year to your investments.

Armed with such knowledge, you should be able to fend off advisors selling inefficient investment products. As an expat, your future may depend on it.

But what if your employer demonstrates ignorance? This is the problem many expats face. Their employers, without understanding the importance of sidestepping unfair financial services options, invite self-serving sales reps into their establishments. Offshore pension platforms are often offered. They're expensive, charging up to 10 times more than what people could be paying; they're inflexible, penalizing people heavily for withdrawing funds earlier than a predetermined date; and (no surprise here) they pay high-enough commissions to satisfy a sultan.

How do smart, innovative companies prevent their employees from getting leeched? Google serves as a great example.

In a 2008 article for *San Francisco* magazine, Mark Dowie reported that Google's progressiveness extends far beyond the World Wide Web:

In August 2004, shares of the company were about to go public on the stock exchange. Hundreds of young Google employees were going to automatically become multimillionaires. But senior vice president Jonathan Rosenberg wanted to protect them from Wall Street's brokers and financial advisors. Company founders Sergey Brin and Larry Page and CEO Eric Schmidt agreed.

They invited experts to speak, including an economic sciences Nobel Prize winner (Bill Sharpe), a legendary Princeton economics professor (Burton Malkiel), and a man named by *Fortune* magazine as one of the four investment giants of the twentieth century (John Bogle).

All of the experts said the same thing. The financial service reps that were circling Google at the time were after one thing: fees and commissions for themselves and their firms. Each expert told Google's staff to build low-cost portfolios of index funds instead.[27]

Unfortunately, few global firms educate employees on suitable investment products. Many employers, without realizing it, push employees into bed with investment providers they should avoid. Sleeping with silver-tongued players has devastating consequences.

Notes

1. Fred Schwed, *Where Are the Customers' Yachts? Or, A Good Hard Look at Wall Street* (New York: John Wiley & Sons, 1995), 1.
2. Ajay Khorana, Henri Servaes, and Peter Tufano, "Mutual Fund Fees around the World," *Review of Financial Studies* 22, no. 3 (Oxford University Press, 2008). Accessed May 4, 2014. http://faculty.london.edu/hservaes/rfs2009.pdf.
3. "Actively Cheated," *The Economist*, July 13, 2002. Accessed May 5, 2014. www.economist.com/node/1224513.

4. "S&P Indices Research and Design Year End 2010," Standard & Poor's Indices versus Active Funds Scorecard (SPIVA Canada). Accessed May 5, 2014. www .spindices.com/documents/spiva/spiva-canada-year-end-2010.pdf.

5. Maya Fisher-French, "The ETF vs Unit Trust Debate," M&G Online. Accessed May 5, 2014. http://mg.co.za/article/2010-06-03-the-etf-vs-unit-trust-debate.

6. S&P Indices versus Active Funds Scorecard (SPIVA Australia). Accessed May 5, 2014. www.spindices.com/documents/spiva/spiva-australia-mid-year-2012.pdf.

7. Burton G. Malkiel, *A Random Walk Down Wall Street: The Time-Tested Strategy for Successful Investing*, 11th ed. (New York: W.W. Norton, 2012), 399.

8. Mark Hulbert, "The Index Funds Win Again," *New York Times*, February 21, 2009. Accessed May 5, 2014. www.nytimes.com/2009/02/22/your-money/stocks-and-bonds/22stra.html.

9. Richard A. Ferri and Alex C. Benke, "A Case for Index Fund Portfolios." Accessed May 5, 2014. www.rickferri.com/WhitePaper.pdf.

10. Warren E. Buffett, "Chairman's Letter—1996." Accessed May 5, 2014. www .berkshirehathaway.com/letters/1996.html.

11. "Berkshire Hathaway Inc., 2006 Annual Report," Berkshirehathaway.com. Accessed May 5, 2014. www.berkshirehathaway.com/2006ar/2006ar.pdf.

12. William F. Sharpe, "The Arithmetic of Active Management," *Financial Analysts Journal* 47, no. 1 (January/February 1991): 7–9. Accessed May 4, 2014. www .stanford.edu/~wfsharpe/art/active/active.htm.

13. Warren Buffett and Janet Lowe, *Warren Buffett Speaks: Wit and Wisdom from the World's Greatest Investor* (Hoboken, NJ: John Wiley & Sons, 2007), 151.

14. Jason Zweig, "The Man Who Explained It All," CNNMoney, July 6, 2007. Accessed May 5, 2014. http://money.cnn.com/2007/05/21/pf/sharpe .moneymag/index.htm?postversion=2007070616.

15. "Spiegel Interview with Daniel Kahneman: Debunking the Myth of Intuition," Spiegel Online. Accessed May 5, 2014. www.spiegel.de/international/zeitgeist/interview-with-daniel-kahneman-on-the-pitfalls-of-intuition-and-memory-a-834407-2.html.

16. Peter Tanous, "An Interview with Merton Miller," Index Fund Advisors, February 1, 1997. Accessed May 5, 2014. www.ifa.com/Articles/An_Interview_ with_Merton_Miller.aspx.

17. *Passive Investing: The Evidence the Fund Management Industry Would Prefer You Not See* (documentary), Sensible Investing. Accessed May 5, 2014. www .sensibleinvesting.tv/ViewAll.aspx?id=8B9BC346-E853-475D-9050-889 E41CE0289.

18. Andrew Hallam, *Millionaire Teacher: The Nine Rules of Wealth You Should Have Learned in School* (Singapore: John Wiley & Sons (Asia), 2011), 126.

19. Alex Crippen, "Buffett Has Big Lead in Bet against Hedge Funds," CNBC .com, February 6, 2014. Accessed May 5, 2014. www.cnbc.com/id/101394085.

20. Simon Lack, *The Hedge Fund Mirage: The Illusion of Big Money and Why It's Too Good to Be True* (Hoboken, NJ: John Wiley & Sons, 2012), 175.

21. "HFRX Indices," HFRX Hedge Fund Indices, HFRX Global Hedge Fund Index. Accessed May 5, 2014. https://www.hedgefundresearch.com/hfrx_reg/index.php?fuse=login&hi.

22. Sam Mamudi, "Five-Star Mutual Funds Don't Live Up to Their Past," Market-Watch, May 28, 2010. Accessed May 5, 2014. www.marketwatch.com/story/five-star-mutual-funds-dont-live-up-to-their-past-2010-05-28.

23. John C. Bogle, *Don't Count on It!: Reflections on Investment Illusions, Capitalism, "Mutual" Funds, Indexing, Entrepreneurship, Idealism, and Heroes* (Hoboken, NJ: John Wiley & Sons, 2011), 382.

24. "An Interview with Morningstar Research Director John Rekenthaler," *In the Vanguard*, Fall 2000. Accessed May 5, 2014. www.vanguard.com/pdf/itvautumn2000.pdf.

25. Interview with Adam Zargar. E-mail interview by author, June 14, 2013.

26. Larry E. Swedroe, *The Quest for Alpha: The Holy Grail of Investing* (Hoboken, NJ: John Wiley & Sons, 2011), 134.

27. Mark Dowie, "The Best Investment Advice You'll Never Get," *Modern Luxury/San Francisco*, January 18, 2008. Accessed May 5, 2014. www.modernluxury.com/san-francisco/story/the-best-investment-advice-youll-never-get.

Chapter 6

Don't Climb into Bed with a Silver-Tongued Player

I nvesting with actively managed funds is like walking up a downward-heading escalator. Those doing so fight more than gravity. But many expats face the same daunting task with 80-pound rucksacks. They're sold debilitating offshore pensions, otherwise known as investment-linked assurance schemes (ILASs). If you're an expatriate, chances are either you or someone you know has fallen into one of these schemes.

Advisors selling such products promise high, tax-free returns. Americans aren't usually targeted, as they must declare their worldwide income to the U.S. Internal Revenue Service (IRS). For them, the "tax-free" sales pitch smacks of Al Capone: The infamous gangster wasn't tossed into Alcatraz for bootlegging or murder—but for tax evasion.

Europeans, Canadians, Australians, New Zealanders, Asians, South Americans, and Africans, however, are ripe pickings for silver-tongued sharks. If they're living in a country where they don't have to pay tax on foreign investment income (check with a tax accountant), many expats can legally invest offshore where capital gains aren't taxed. Many don't realize, however, that they can do so without buying an expensive, inflexible offshore pension.

Advisors selling such products earn commissions high enough to make a cadaver blush. Investors buying them get stiffed.

The investments are usually portfolios of actively managed mutual funds coupled with an insurance component. Neither the investment nor the insurance is typically worth the money.

To be fair, not all advisors selling offshore pensions understand their total costs. Question them about fees and they might dig into the fund prospectus, citing costs of 1.5 percent or less. Or they'll glibly state that the fees are low—without understanding the ravages beneath the surface. Offshore pensions commonly cost 4 percent or more each year.

As American writer Upton Sinclair once said, "It is difficult to get a man to understand something, when his salary depends upon his not understanding it." Many sales representatives flog offshore pensions from companies like Zurich International, Friends Provident, Generali, Aviva, and Royal Skandia without realizing their clients are usually charged on three levels: annual management costs, establishment costs, and hidden mutual fund management fees.

Peggy Creveling, a Chartered Financial Analyst (CFA) and Certified Financial Planner (CFP) based in Bangkok, says such products are long on promises and short on profits.

"What the sales literature does not expressly tell you may become clear—once you agree to purchase the scheme. Your investment is subjected to a layered fee structure that can lower your earnings significantly, perhaps by 30 to 40 percent per year."[1]

Creveling is right. But the reality can be even worse. If global stock markets disappoint investors, earning just 4 percent per year over the next decade, many offshore pension investors would make nothing after paying 4 percent in fees.

This is based on the premise in the Stanford University published paper, "The Arithmetic of Active Management." Written by economic

Table 6.1   Results of $10,000 Invested Annually If Global Stock and Bond Markets Averaged 9 Percent

Investment Duration	Indexed Portfolio Averaging 8.8% after Costs	Offshore Pension Averaging 5% after Costs	Paying 3.3% Less Each Year Would Earn
15 years	$314,470	$226,574	39% more
20 years	$544,283	$347,192	57% more
25 years	$894,646	$501,134	79% more
30 years	$1,428,797	$697,607	105% more
35 years	$2,243,141	$948,363	137% more

sciences Nobel Prize winner William Sharpe, it asserts that the typical actively managed dollar will underperform the market in direct proportion to the fees charged.[2]

Investors don't need to pay 4 percent in annual fees. Most expatriate investors could pay as little as 0.2 percent by building a portfolio of index funds. There's a 3.8 percent annual differential between paying 4 percent and paying 0.2 percent. But are the savings such a big deal? That depends on whether you want to retire on caviar or cat food.

After 15 years, a 3.8 percent annual difference between an indexed portfolio and an offshore pension (ILAS) would likely put 39 percent more in the index investor's pocket, 57 percent more after 20 years, 79 percent more after 25 years, 105 percent more after 30 years, and 137 percent more after 35 years. (See Table 6.1.) Over an expat's career, the difference could exceed one million dollars, one million pounds, or one million euros. We're not talking chump change.

Featuring the Rip-Offers

Certified Financial Planner Tony Noto was once hired by a firm to sell offshore pensions to expatriates. But the more he learned about them, the sketchier they appeared. After two weeks of dissecting these products, he quit and established his own firm to build indexed portfolios for clients.

"These offshore pensions are popularly sold," he says, "because they offer lucrative up-front commissions, often equivalent to the total sum of an investor's deposit during their first year of the scheme. Those convincing you to invest $15,000 per year for 25 years, for example, often reap an up-front commission of roughly $15,000 from the insurance company, shortly after the contractual ink dries. There is no question of who ultimately pays that bill—the investor."[3]

Benjamin Robertson revealed the commissions paid to brokers in his September 2013 article in the *South China Morning Post*, "Investment-Linked Insurance Schemes a Trap for Unwary Investors." On a 20-year policy, a broker convincing a client to add $1,000 per month ($12,000 per year) would receive an up-front commission of $10,800, split between the broker and his or her employer.

On a 25-year policy, the commission would be higher. It's based on a formula multiplying the number of years of the policy × 12 (months in the year) × monthly dollar contribution × 4.2 percent. A 25-year policy in which the investor adds $1,000 per month would earn a brokerage commission of $12,600.[4]

Recognizing a winning lottery ticket when they see it, many expatriate advisors flog the products exclusively. To a hammer, everything looks like a nail. Consequently, these expensive, inflexible platforms have spread like pandemics among global expats.

The Ten Habits of Successful Financial Advisors . . . Really?

Former expatriate financial advisor Frank Furness created a series of training videos for advisors. One of them is titled "The 10 Habits of Successful Financial Advisors." Not one of the habits deals with investors' welfare. Instead, the video outlines strategies expatriate advisors use to make millions of dollars a year in commissions. As Furness says, "For me, it's the best job in the world. Where else can I go out and meet somebody, drink their coffee, eat their cake, and walk out with $5,000 in my pocket? No other business."[5]

Much like car salesmen, many measure success by how many deals they can close. In the video, Furness interviews Steve Young, a representative working for International Financial Services (Singapore), described as one of the region's top advisors—one of "the true tigers in the industry." The advisor explains that his team puts prospective clients in front of him "to let me do what I'm good at, which is closing the deals out."

Young adds, "If I can delegate the paperwork, all I want to do is see the checks from the clients." The advisor is so good at selling, in fact, that he once established 198 new clients in a single calendar month, claiming to set a world record in the process. Furness closes the video by saying to the camera, "If you live anywhere in Asia, especially in the Singapore area, and you want to deal with the best . . . why not contact Steve?"[6] Unfortunately, "the best" advisor in sales lore isn't necessarily the best advisor for clients.

When Your Advisor Is a Sales Commando

In April 2014, online publication International Adviser highlighted quotes from Doug Tucker's new book, *Sales Commando: Unleash Your Potential* (PG Press). Tucker, a former offshore pension seller, says that to generate clients "you have to go into full-frontal attack mode. This means huge, massive action. To do this you need a strategy, a plan of attack, and the absolute certainty you are going to win."

Before a prospective client can object to a product, Tucker suggests to advisors: "Create a mental picture of each objection as a small monster being born and figuratively popping out of the client's mouth. The minute you pay attention to the fledgling monster you will be feeding it with energy, because this little monster thrives on encouragement. The more you acknowledge its presence, the more it will grow and grow."[7]

Lucrative up-front commissions encourage such aggressive winner-take-all strategies. In some cases, advisors convince their clients to invest far more than they can afford. Such was the case with Sit-Wai Long, a former HSBC Bank representative. He convinced a client with a comparatively low income to invest a ridiculously high monthly sum. Fortunately, he was caught. Hong Kong regulatory authorities slapped him with a three-year suspension from selling financial products.[8]

While the city's customer complaints about offshore pensions doubled in 2013 compared to 2012, much of the abuse still gets unreported.

Welcoming Sharks into the Seal Pool

Few expatriate employers understand how offshore pensions work. Yet many invite sharks into the company seal pools. Chip Kimball, superintendent at Singapore American School, says, "Many international schools don't have any form of regulation, and little to no vetting or oversight regarding the financial products that salespeople try selling on campuses." Some schools embrace expensive, inflexible official providers, while encouraging staff to use them. "This is dangerous," adds Kimball. "High fees and commissions for poor financial products cost teachers dearly."[9] International teachers aren't the only expats at risk.

Here's how the process often begins. A representative from a brokerage firm slides into a workplace. Nearly all of them claim their costs are low and transparent. Some of the more common brokerages selling offshore pensions include the deVere Group, Montpelier Financial Consultants, Austen Morris Associates, Globaleye Financial Planning, the Henley Group, Gilt Edge International, Warrick Mann International, the Alexander Beard Group, SCI Group Ltd., and the Sovereign Group.

The broker convinces management to endorse the broker's firm, resulting in a ready-made customer base. Such brokers are intermediaries for offshore pension providers, many of which are based in the British Channel Islands, Luxembourg, or the Isle of Man.

Some common pension providers include Zurich International, Friends Provident, Generali International, Aviva, and Royal Skandia. When an advisor for the deVere Group, for example, sells a Friends Provident pension, the deVere advisor receives an up-front commission from Friends Provident.

To recoup that commission, Friends Provident must keep the investor's money with the firm as long as possible. Doing so allows the company to reap more client fees over time. As an investor adds more money, fees mount. But investors awakening to the tyranny of costs find their private parts stuck in a zipper. Early redemption penalties might cost 80 percent (or more) of the investor's total proceeds.

Jon Williams, formerly a British information technology (IT) worker in Dubai, explains how these offshore pensions can gain traction away from the workplace. "A friend of mine gave my contact information to an advisor working for PIC [Professional Investment Consultants]. It's an affiliate of the deVere Group." Jon met the representative in his apartment. "I wanted a breakdown of costs," says Jon, "so the advisor promised to send it the following day."

In return, the advisor wanted the names and contact details for 10 of Jon's friends or colleagues. "I felt Jedi mind-tricked by the guy and did what he asked." The following day, Jon received the breakdown of fees, entered the particulars into an Excel spreadsheet, and was horrified by the costs. "I didn't sign up, even though the rep told me he was offering a special one-time offer—one that needed an immediate decision." Promises of urgent, one-time offers should always raise red flags, whether you're buying financial products or a holiday time-share. Jon also asked the advisor not to contact his friends. "I made a lucky escape. But many of my friends weren't as fortunate."[10]

Misled Investors Pay the Price

High-commission-paying products often distract advisors from telling the entire truth. Those selling offshore pensions should always discuss withdrawal penalties. Not doing so, unfortunately, is common.

Indian national Alla Rao was working in Abu Dhabi when he met an agent selling a Zurich International Vista offshore pension. As he explains, "After constant pestering by the advisor and after him showing me charts representing great investment returns, I ended up signing. Never a word was mentioned about early surrender penalties. I was told I could sell the Zurich policy anytime, with a maximum surrender cost of 1 or 2 percent. But despite rising global stock markets during my 4.5 years of owning the plan [global stocks rose 40 percent], my investments had dropped 10 percent. I've since learned that to sell will cost me 33 percent of everything I've invested, from early redemption penalties. The advisor certainly never told me that when he sold me the plan."[11]

A Canadian Investor Gets Bled

Alla Rao wasn't alone. Steve Batchelor knew nothing about offshore pensions when he moved overseas in 2007. The 39-year-old Canadian realized he couldn't contribute to a Canadian socialized pension plan while working in Beijing, so he welcomed the idea of investing in a private pension.

His employer encouraged it. Instead of providing educational sessions for staff about appropriate investments and fees, the employer invited some hungry offshore pension peddlers. "We were told," says Steve, "that our employer would match some of our savings if we invested with one of the pension firms."

Steve warmed to a representative selling a Friends Provident scheme. Describing the perks, the representative told Steve he could earn loyalty bonuses after the 10th year. He also said Steve could switch his money between funds at no extra cost, and that the money would grow tax free, offshore.

Steve felt confused by the advisor's explanation of the pension's inner workings: a percentage in fees taken here, a percentage taken there, reduced costs here, bonuses gained there. It looked messy. But Steve trusted the advisor. "I was really proud of myself for setting this up at first," he said. "But I wish I knew then what I know now."[12]

Steve's money was invested in actively managed mutual funds, costing an average of 1.97 percent a year. Not only was he paying high costs for the funds, but his first 18 months of savings will bleed for 25 years.

Steve invested $9,266 during the first year and a half. His Friends Provident Premier Advance plan charges 7.2 percent annually in fees for the first 18 months. External mutual fund costs deducted an additional 1.97 percent per year. Consequently, during his first year and a half, he paid gob-smacking costs of 9.17 percent annually.[13] Even if Steve's investments had made 9 percent a year (before fees) during this 18-month period, Steve would have lost money.

As stated in the contract, Friends Provident would reduce Steve's annual charges by 6 percent on all deposits made after 18 months. But he's stuck paying costs of 9.17 percent per year for 25 years on the first $9,266 he deposited. If the money Steve invested during the first 18 months earns (before fees) 9.17 percent per year for 25 years, it will match Steve's investment costs. His initial $9,266 becomes a corporate Dracula's drinking fountain.

Some people donate to charity; others give to family. Few place financial firms on their philanthropic lists.

Would You Like a Band-Aid for That Bleeding Gash?

After the tenth year, Friends Provident pays loyalty bonuses of 0.5 per-cent annually on Steve's investments. But it's a small Band-Aid for a bleeding gash. Steve's total annual charges on deposits made after the 18th month are six times greater than the bonus offered. Charges on the deposits made during the first 18 months continue to exceed 9 percent per year: more than 18 times higher than the 0.5 percent bonus offered by Friends Provident after the tenth year.

Investors building a low-cost portfolio of index funds costing just 0.2 percent per year (and I'll show you how to do this) would likely have much more money than Steve would at the end of the 25-year term. Unlike Steve, they would also have the flexibility to sell their invest-ments without penalty at any time. And as long as their home or resident country doesn't tax them on worldwide income, they wouldn't have to pay capital gains taxes. I'll explain how in subsequent chapters.

Masters of the Insured Death Benefit Illusion

Those flogging offshore pensions, however, may point to the insured death benefit. It's often craftily worded. This was Steve's:

> In the event of the death of the Life Assured (or the last surviv-ing Life Assured if the policy is written on more than one life) while the policy is in force, 101 percent of the cash-in value of your plan will be payable.

The literature accompanying the policy offered no other reference or explanation of what this meant. So I wondered: Did it mean the de-ceased earned a 101 percent bonus on top of the investment portfolio's actual value?

I had to call four separate advisors flogging Friends Provident pen-sions before one of them even attempted to explain the insurance policy. He said that if the policy holder (the investor) dies, then his or her heirs would receive the account's proceeds, or if the account were valued less than what was deposited into it, the surviving members (spouse, brother, sister, whoever was on the policy) would earn an amount equal to 101 percent of what the deceased had invested.

Manipulation with numbers is an art. The contract claims the descendant receives "101 percent of the cash-in value." But consider this. If I loaned you $5 and you gave the $5 back, you would have returned 100 percent of what I had loaned you. By offering 101 percent of the "cash-in value," Friends Provident offers to pay back 1 percent more than what was invested: not 1 percent per year, but 1 percent overall. There's no upward adjustment to cover inflation. If inflation averaged 3.5 percent per year, the insurance guarantee equals a real (inflation-adjusted) loss exceeding 40 percent for the decade, if the investor died while the portfolio was worth less than what he or she had deposited.

Free Fund Switching Isn't a Perk

Sales reps also promote the idea that clients dissatisfied with their fund performances can switch into other funds for free. Costs to switch into different funds are called sales loads. In a 2012 Bloomberg.com article titled "The Worst Deal in Mutual Funds Faces a Reckoning," Ben Steverman writes, "those paying loads are the poorest and least sophisticated of investors."[14] Only the naive would believe that free fund switching is a perk. Load fees are as easy to avoid as a 10-foot-wide drainage ditch.

Such costs are even banned in Australia and the United Kingdom.[15]

Expatriate workplaces, however, aren't the only feeding grounds for commission-hungry sales reps; some do almost anything to build a client base. Random cold calls aren't beneath them. A sales representative from Austen Morris Associates cold-called Icelander Lawrence Graham just three to four months after he became an expatriate.

"I have no idea how he found my number," Graham says. "The rep explained the expected returns over the next few decades and made it all sound fairly good: low expected returns for the first few years with exponential growth in the later years of the plan due to the larger amount of money that would have been invested by that point. But there's a lot they didn't tell me. I had no idea how much the fees would eat into my profits. The money I gave them during the first 18 months has to stay with the firm for 30 years. I can't take it out earlier without paying a hefty penalty. They didn't tell me that when I signed up."[16]

Making Millions off the General Public

With such massive commissions paid to brokers, sales of these products won't likely abate any time soon. When BBC Panorama investigated one of the largest offshore pension sellers, deVere Group, the investigators revealed that the company's top sales brokers earned on average more than £220,000 in the first three months of 2010. The top broker was on track to exceed £1 million for the year.

Penny Haslam reported such findings in the BBC Panorama documentary, *Who Took My Pension?* After asking pension providers to supply data on charges, she revealed the most expensive pensions in Great Britain.

Here's how they stacked up if investors had contributed £120,000 over 40 years. Legal and General's Co-Funds Portfolio Pension would have taken £61,000 in fees, the Co-operative Bank's Personal Pension would have absconded with £95,900 in fees, and HSBC's World Selection Personal Pension would have lifted £99,900 in total fees.[17]

The documentary included costs of management fees in these calculations, but didn't include costs of actively managed funds within the pensions themselves. Doing so would have doubled total fees, aligning them closely with offshore pension costs.

Fooling the Masses with Numbers

While the offshore pension providers have subtle differences, most seduce investors with the promise of loyalty bonuses. But it's a smoke and mirrors show.

To dramatize an example, I'll introduce you to a hypothetical bonus platform that's far more generous than anything offered by an offshore pension. It's going to look amazing. But don't be fooled.

Hallam's offshore pension guarantees a 50 percent bonus on unlimited cash deposits. If you invest $10,000 each year, we'll chip in an extra 50 percent, ramping your invested proceeds to $15,000 per year.

Table 6.2   Bonuses Don't Offset Costs

Investor Has $10,000 per Year to Invest

	Fantasy Offshore 50% Bonus Pension	Low-Cost Indexed Portfolio
Amount annually invested by client	$10,000	$10,000
Annual bonus paid on deposits	50%	0%
Total annual amount invested after bonus	$15,000	$10,000
Assumed global markets' average return	10%	10%
Annual fees paid on total portfolio value	3.5%	0.2%
Annual returns after fees	6.5%	9.8%
Total portfolio value after 30 years	$1,379,838	$1,739,129

Annual management charges are just 1.5 percent per year. How can you lose when receiving a 50 percent annual bonus?

In this fantasy broker scenario, I haven't included costs of the actively managed funds. If the fund expenses added another 2 percent per year, total costs for the account would run 3.5 percent per year (1.5 percent for the management fee plus 2 percent for the mutual funds).

Still, that 50 percent bonus *appears* to trump the comparatively small 3.5 percent annual account charge. Or does it?

Keep in mind that no offshore pension firm offers a 50 percent bonus every year on annual deposits. But even if one did, investors could still get fleeced. Deception with numbers is an art. Not receiving a bonus but paying just 0.2 percent in annual fees would reap far greater rewards.

Table 6.2 lists the fantasy bonus pension alongside an indexed portfolio.

No offshore pension provider offers a 50 percent annual bonus on unlimited deposits every year. But even if one did, the investor could still end up hundreds of thousands of dollars poorer.

Regulators Making an Effort

Attractive distractions sold as "bonuses" or "fee reductions" have caught the attention of Hong Kong's Monetary Authority. In March 2011, Meena Datwani, Chief Executor for Banking Conduct, distributed a memo to the city's ILAS product sellers. Complaints about offshore pensions had caused regulators to set certain requirements for the products.

But despite the effort, interpretations of fees, bonuses, and promises vary. Consequently, they're difficult to enforce.[18]

Hong Kong's Monetary Authority worded its restrictions the following way:

> **Use of Gifts or Promises of Reduced Fees over Time**
> To avoid distracting customers' attention from the nature and risks associated with ILAS [offshore pension] products, AIs [authorized institutions] should not offer financial or other incentives (e.g., gifts) for promoting ILAS products. Discount of fees and charges, and the offering of any gifts for brand promotion, relationship building, or other purposes . . .

Bonuses and reduced fee offerings can distract customers from the unflattering reality of fees incurred. But what the sales representative doesn't state might be more harmful than what is stated.

Lock-In Periods

> AIs [authorized institutions] should disclose and explain that ILAS [offshore pension] products are designed to be held for a medium/long-term period and that early surrender of the product may be subject to a heavy financial penalty, and disclose the level of penalty.

When I dissected the inner workings of offshore pensions on my blog (www.andrewhallam.com), hundreds of investors holding such products left messages claiming that nobody had explained the penalties incurred if they sold their investments before the termination date of their policy. Not disclosing this information may have helped sales reps close their deals. But it hurt the many investors who required earlier access to their money.

Fees and Charges

> Fees and charges—AIs [authorized institutions] should disclose and explain the fees and charges at both the scheme level and the underlying investment asset level, and that due to the fees and charges, the return on the ILAS [offshore pension] product as a whole may be lower than the return of the underlying investment assets.

Many sales reps fail to mention total charges: the management fees for the portfolio plus the hidden expense ratio costs of the funds themselves. As such, many cite costs of 1.5 percent to clients, when actual costs usually exceed 3.5 percent per year. Would any dare show what a 3.5 percent annual drag on investment returns would do over time?

Even though Hong Kong regulatory authorities distributed the preceding restrictions, they don't appear to be enforced.

You might wonder how prolifically offshore pensions are sold. Reporter Nicky Burridge of the *South China Morning Post* wanted to find out. She generously detailed her findings here.

The Murky World of Offshore Pensions
By Nicky Burridge

As a Hong Kong newspaper reporter, I decided to carry out a mystery shopping exercise to see how ubiquitous the offshore pension (ILAS) products really are and how well they are explained to customers.

Posing as an inexperienced investor who wanted to save HK$10,000 to HK$15,000 a month for around 10 years for no particular purpose, I visited three high street banks, HSBC Bank, DBS Bank, and Bank of China, in 2011, to see what they would recommend.

Unsurprisingly, staff at all three banks were quick to suggest I should put my money into an offshore pension.

The sales pitch for ILAS products revolved around the wide choice of funds I could invest in and unlimited free switching between funds.

The downside of the plans was their eye-watering complexity and the opacity of their charges.

I was told by the Bank of China advisor that the product had both an "A" account and a "B" account, with different charges levied on each one. I can remember feeling a surge of frustration as I tried to establish exactly what the purpose of the two accounts was and whether I would ever receive money back from the "A" account, into which the first 24 months' worth of premiums [monthly investment deposits] would be paid.

The charges were even harder to understand. Although the HSBC advisor told me they were around 5 percent a year, pinning down the exact cost was nearly impossible, even with the product brochure. There were fees for administration and asset maintenance and life insurance charges, all paid to the offshore pension provider, as well as management, custody, trustee, and performance charges levied by the individual funds into which my money would be invested.

Charges levied on the products offered by the other banks were just as difficult to understand. But why were they pushed so exclusively? I was shocked to learn, during a conversation with an independent financial advisor, that it was common for all of the money a new client invests during the first year of an offshore pension to be handed over as an up-front commission to the salesperson. It struck me that this offered little incentive for brokers and advisors to offer any other product.

I was even more shocked when another independent financial advisor told me he estimated that 75 percent of investment products sold to individuals in Hong Kong were sold under the ILAS (offshore pension) umbrella.

They are shockingly bad products: expensive, inflexible, and incredibly difficult to understand.

Can Squeaky Wheels Gain Redemption?

While inappropriate selling of these high-commission products is likely to continue, squeaky wheels occasionally gain attention.

On October 24, 2010, 24-year-old Tsang Sau Ming (known by friends as DeAnn) invested with a firm called Convoy Investment Services in Hong Kong.

The Convoy rep sold her an offshore pension through Zurich Vista, coupling an insurance policy with a high-cost investment platform. The advisor dismissed her insistence that she didn't need an insurance policy and he recommended that she invest 28.6 percent of her HK$126,000 annual salary.

During the first 18 months, she invested HK$54,000, increasing her invested total to HK$93,000 midway through 2013. During that time period, the U.S. stock market gained 50 percent; global stock markets averaged a 25 percent gain. But anchored by heavy administrative fees, high fund costs, and poor fund selection, DeAnn earned less than 1 percent.

Upset with her account's performance and the realization of the costs paid, she inquired about selling her investment policy. But while her statements claimed she had $93,500, Zurich was prepared to give her only $43,000. The remaining $50,500 would be absorbed as a penalty for redeeming her funds early.

Distraught, she contacted Leung Chung-yan, who battled her own offshore pension by going to the media.[19]

Although Leung Chung-yan didn't receive an apology from the firm for wrongdoing, she was offered a full refund.

The offered refund gives hope to many, including DeAnn.

Another precedent-setting investor was a 59-year-old British expatriate living near Alicante, Spain. He saw his savings plummet from £89,000 to just £20,000 after purchasing an offshore pension offered by the deVere Group in June 2010. He wanted to withdraw his remaining money but was told by deVere that he would receive only £11,000 after charges. Rightfully upset, he took his story to the UK financial blog site, This Is Money. Media pressure caused deVere to cave. They reimbursed his entire £89,000.[20]

If Investors Can't Reclaim Their Losses

It's a question many investors in similar predicaments have asked themselves. Should they redeem their investments (taking a kick to the groin), or continue contributing to the plan while getting fleeced by high fees?

Many investors have taken a voluntary kick to the privates by selling their funds before the policy surrender date. They argue that, by doing so, they could invest the leftover proceeds in a low-cost platform and still come out ahead.

Here's an example using DeAnn's scenario. Her policy's fee structure is characteristically murky, but total annual costs (including fund fees) run roughly 3.8 percent per year.

If global markets generate a 9 percent return, she would likely reap about 5.2 percent, as long as her advisor allocated the funds intelligently. Consequently, her HK$93,500, coupled with her annual deposits of HK$35,280 for the next 22 years, could grow to HK$1,748,608.

But taking a financial hit and selling her policy might be the better option. If she took a HK$50,500 penalty for canceling the policy, she would have HK$43,000 remaining. If she paid annual investment fees of 0.2 percent, she could earn 8.8 percent annually on that HK$43,000 if global markets grew by 9 percent. Over 22 years, while adding HK$35,280 annually, she could grow her money to HK$2,622,854 (see Table 6.3).

Despite taking a $50,500 penalty for canceling her policy, she could invest the reduced sum but still retire nearly a million dollars richer by paying lower investment costs.

If you're pondering your own offshore pension predicament, do the math with a compound interest calculator, such as the one at www.moneychimp.com. Understand all of the fees first, along with any bonus units you might be entitled to. Some money could be eligible for a free withdrawal, so contact your advisor about softening redemption costs. After doing so, you could determine whether it's worth hanging on to your policy, taking the hit and canceling, or limiting the damage by simply reducing (or eliminating) new deposits if the policy allows it.

Table 6.3   Would DeAnn Be Wise to Take the Financial Hit?

	DeAnn Pays Redemption Fee and Invests the Remainder	DeAnn Remains with the High-Cost Investment
Investment value	HK$43,000 (amount remaining after redemption penalties)	HK$93,500
Annual addition	HK$35,280	HK$35,280
Estimated growth rate after fees	8.8%	5.2%
Value of portfolio after 22 years	HK$2,628,190	HK$1,748,608

When High Fees Meet Gunslingers

Unfortunately, high costs aren't the only problem with offshore pensions. Many advisors selling them fail to build diversified portfolios. Diversification increases safety. Stuffing too many eggs into the same basket increases risk. And when the basket tips (all baskets tip at some point), the investment portfolio cracks.

Most offshore pension sellers aren't Certified Financial Planners. The CFP designation ensures that advisors have been trained to diversify their clients' money, spreading it across multiple asset classes and geographic regions. Instead, many offshore pension sellers obtain impressive-sounding three-letter credentials that require fewer than three weeks to obtain.

Former broker Shawn Wong says,

> People wanting to sell ILAS products [offshore pensions] don't require strict financial training. The firm I worked at often sold Friends Provident, Zurich, and Standard Life products because they offered high commissions and low-level entry points. Someone directly out of high school could pass the required licensing tests in a couple of weeks. The tests are easy, with minimal focus on multi-asset-class portfolio allocation and rebalancing. Not surprisingly, many client portfolios get built without adequate diversification. The focus on sales and commissions outweighs the need for a responsible portfolio.[21]

Odds are that those investing with a Certified Financial Planner (CFP) won't suffer from a lack of diversification. But CFPs aren't all saints. Such an advisor looking for fat commissions *could* still push your money into an offshore pension. However, CFPs are more likely to diversify their clients' accounts across global stock and bond markets—instead of gambling everything on a few pet sectors.

A Son's Inheritance Gets Plundered

Spaniard Miguel Delgado (not his real name) unfortunately employed an egg basket stuffer. A teacher at an international school in Vietnam, he invested 250,000 euros with an advisor from the SCI Group.

Miguel wanted to invest the money conservatively. His mother had recently died, and the money had come from his inheritance. Having already lost his mother, he couldn't bear the thought of losing her hard-earned money as well. Unfortunately, the advisor convinced him to invest his entire inheritance, plus a further 50,000 euros his wife had saved, into PDL International's Protected Asset TEP Fund (PATF). Failing to diversify is like doing the high jump with a pair of scissors. Daniel R. Solin, the author of *Does Your Broker Owe You Money?*, says when a broker fails to adequately diversify a client's portfolio, it's cause for a lawsuit.[22]

Miguel's advisor described the investment as a fund endowment policy promising broad diversification, low volatility, and consistent returns. The trouble was, Miguel didn't know what endowment policies were. But the advisor had a silver tongue. Miguel, hooked by the salesman's suavity, unknowingly compounded the tragedy. "I convinced my brother to invest his inheritance in the fund as well."

The investment was supposed to be far safer than a regular stock market fund—or so the sales pitch went. It wasn't supposed to drop, even if the stock markets fell. This greatly appealed to Miguel. The money his mother bequeathed was sacred. He didn't want to lose it.

But in 2008, the investment collapsed, dropping 35 percent in 12 months. The United States was the catalyst for the financial crisis, but not even its stock market dropped as far. In euro terms, U.S. stocks fell roughly 30 percent. They soon recovered, and by 2014, U.S. stocks were 50 percent higher than they were before the financial crisis hit.[23]

Unfortunately, the same can't be said for PDL International's PATF fund. By January 2014, it had not fully recovered from its 2008 plunge.[24]

Miguel explains, "When the fund started to rise again, we sold, losing 80,000 euros in a fund that was supposed to be conservative." He claims, however, to have learned his lesson. "Promises of strong returns without risk don't exist, despite what a smooth-talking salesperson might tell you. It's important to fully understand what you're invested in."

Steve Batchelor—the Beijing-based Canadian expat I introduced earlier—also suffered from a lack of diversification. He bought a Friends Provident offshore pension through a firm called Gilt Edge International.

Steve started his offshore pension in late 2007. It didn't have any exposure to U.S. stocks (the world's largest market) or European stocks.

Steve Batchelor's Portfolio Screenshots: 2009-2012

Date: 28th August 2009

Please invest my FUTURE CONTRIBUTIONS as follows;

Code	Fund Name	% IN
M082	BLACKROCK GF WORLD GOLD	20.00
P047	INVESTEC GS GLOBAL ENERGY	20.00
P058	TEMPLETON BRIC	20.00
R051	FIRST STATE CHINA GROWTH	20.00
N/AR072	CASTLESTONE ALIQUOT PRECIOUS METAL	20.00

Date: 22nd July 2010

Please invest my FUTURE CONTRIBUTIONS as follows;

Code	Fund Name	% IN
J052	CIPTADANA INDONESIAN GROWTH	20.00
M082	BLACKROCK GF WORLD GOLD	20.00
P047	INVESTEC GS GLOBAL ENERGY	15.00
P058	TEMPLETON BRIC	15.00
R051	FIRST STATE CHINA GROWTH	15.00
N/AR072	CASTLESTONE ALIQUOT PRECIOUS METAL	15.00

Date: 7th December 2011

Please invest my FUTURE CONTRIBUTIONS as follows;

Code	Fund Name	% IN
J052	CIPTADANA INDONESIAN GROWTH	25.00
M082	BLACKROCK GF WORLD GOLD	25.00
P047	INVESTEC GS GLOBAL ENERGY	25.00
R069	DWS NOOR PRECIOUS METALS SECURITIES	25.00

Date: 13th April 2012

Please invest my FUTURE CONTRIBUTIONS as follows;

Code	Fund Name	% IN
J052	CIPTADANA INDONESIAN GROWTH	25.00
M082	BLACKROCK GF WORLD GOLD	25.00
P047	INVESTEC GS GLOBAL ENERGY	25.00
L029	PICTET (CH) PRECIOUS METALS-PHYSICAL GOLD	25.00

Figure 6.1   Irresponsible Investment Allocations

Nor did it have exposure to bonds. Portfolios such as Steve's are like rock climbers without ropes: exciting perhaps, but irresponsible.

The portfolio was heavily concentrated in gold, other precious metals, and emerging stock markets, such as Brazil, China, India, and Indonesia. At no point, since Steve opened the account in 2007, was it globally diversified across a variety of international stock markets and bonds. Note the screen shots of his portfolio in Figure 6.1, taken in 2009, 2010, 2011, and 2012.

Steve's account was layered with unnecessary fees. What's more, without bonds and with no exposure to the world's biggest markets (U.S. and European stocks), it was lopsided and risky.

Adding alcohol to a climber's water, his advisor significantly increased Steve's gold holdings in late 2011, just in time for gold's 28 percent price plunge. By April 2012, Steve had 50 percent of his portfolio in gold and precious metals. By October 2013, the advisor increased this percentage to 79 percent (not shown).

According to his account statement, Steve's investment value plummeted 20.68 percent between his 2007 account opening date and October 2013. What if, instead of concentrating too much on a specific asset class, Steve's portfolio were properly diversified? If that were the case, he wouldn't be plucking dirt from his wounds. With a blended portfolio, including a U.S. stock index, an international stock index, and a bond index, Steve's money would have grown 35 percent instead of dropping 20.68 percent (see Table 6.4).

How much would Steve's portfolio have to gain to break even after a 20.68 percent loss? An instinctive answer would be 20.68 percent. But the reality is heftier. It can take years for a portfolio to recover large losses (see Table 6.5).

Table 6.4   Undiversified Portfolio Gets Dragged through the Dirt

September 31, 2007, to October 5, 2013

Steve's Undiversified Portfolio	Vanguard Target Retirement 2025 Fund (30% U.S. and International Bonds, 70% U.S. and International Stocks)
−20.68%	+35%

SOURCES: Steve Batchelor's account statement; Morningstar.com.

Table 6.5   Gains Required to Offset Losses

Portfolio Loss	Gain Required to Get Back to Even
−10%	+11.1%
−20%	+25.0%
−30%	+42.9%
−40%	+66.7%
−50%	+100.0%
−60%	+150.0%
−70%	+233.3%

Steve's 20.68 percent drop would require a gain of 26.07 percent to break even. He underperformed a diversified portfolio of stock and bond indexes by more than 55 percent in just six years. The advisor, an offshore pension cowboy, cost the Canadian dearly.

British Teacher Learns a Costly Lesson

While many people hope their advisors will build responsible, diversified portfolios, that isn't always the case. Susan Proctor paid a similar price for her advisor's overconfidence.

A British schoolteacher in Muskat, Oman, Susan told her offshore pension advisor, "I definitely don't want high-risk investments." But instead of spreading her assets among global stocks and bonds, he ignored her request and gambled. "I eventually researched every one of the funds he bought for me, and all of them were classified either high risk or medium risk. I didn't own a single bond fund, either."[25]

Bonds are like parachutes when stocks fall; they cushion portfolios when stock markets drop. They're important components of any responsible portfolio. But Susan, like Steve Batchelor, didn't own any.

Playing Soccer Like Wasps around Honey

Susan's portfolio was built mostly around emerging market funds focused on Thai, Indonesian, Brazilian, Indian, Chinese, and Latin American stocks. She had no exposure to her home British stock market, no exposure to European markets, and limited exposure to the U.S. market. The emerging markets had achieved spectacular returns between 2003 and 2007. But Susan didn't start investing until 2008.

Like a five-year-old soccer player, her advisor ran where the ball had been. More sophisticated players (and investors) space themselves around the pitch instead of chasing the ball like wasps around honey.

Without a single player on left wing, right wing, or defending midfield, Susan missed some wide-open shots. Her home British stock market gained 43 percent over five years. But with no British stock market exposure, not a single portfolio player could pick up the ball and shoot.

Over five years, Susan's portfolio underperformed the average global stock by nearly 40 percent (see Table 6.6). It underperformed her home British stock market by more than 25 percent; and it underperformed a conservative blend of global stocks and global bonds by nearly 22 percent.

"I would like to be able to complain to my advisor," she says, "but a few years after selling me the pension, he created some kind of Ponzi scheme, got caught, and has since fled the country." As of this writing, Bernie Madoff Jr. was still at large.

High fees are troublesome enough. But when investors or advisors speculate, problems compound. Poorly trained (and undisciplined) advisors often build portfolios concentrated on geographic sectors that have recently performed well, instead of properly diversifying. When investors and advisors build today's portfolios based on yesterday's winners, sound retirements are jeopardized.

Table 6.6   Susan Proctor's Five-Year Comparative Portfolio Performance

Susan's Portfolio Growth (not including offshore pension costs)	Vanguard Total World Stock Market Index	UK Stock Market Index (iShares ETF)	Balanced Portfolio: 50% Global Stock Index/50% International Bond Index
+26.66%	+55.7%	+43%	+38%

Measured in U.S. dollars.

SOURCES: Susan Proctor's account; Vanguard US; iShares US.

Most Investors Are Crazy

I've shown this before, but it's worth emphasizing. U.S. stocks averaged 9.14 percent a year between 1990 and 2010 (see Figure 6.2). But the average investor in U.S. stocks made just 3.83 percent annually.[26] Clearly, a 5.31 percent shortfall can't be blamed entirely on fees. The average U.S. stock market fund charges 1.5 percent a year, but the average American investor underperformed the market by 5.31 percent per year.

When U.S. stocks were rising, investors (and their advisors) were piling onto the bandwagon. But when those same stocks stagnated or fell, investors didn't add as much money. Many sold their investments. Others looked for what they hoped would be a far more promising market. Such behavior is crazy. And its results are regularly documented by the Chicago-based Dalbar Group.

Considering how badly the average American investor performed (after paying mutual fund fees of 1.5 percent per year), how do you think the average offshore pension investor performed? Such platforms, after all, charge more than twice as much.

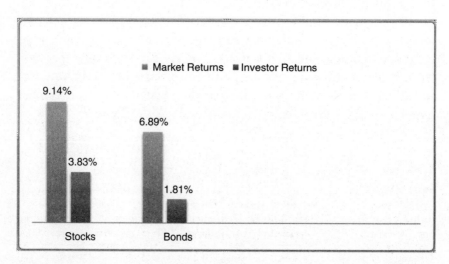

Figure 6.2   U.S. Stock and Bond Market Returns versus the Average American Investor, 1990–2010
SOURCE: Dalbar Group.

Expatriates and their employers need to take responsibility. Some investment products are bona fide rip-offs. Others are solid. But when investors and employers don't know the difference, people suffer.

Notes

1. Peggy Creveling, "Five Things to Consider Before Buying Offshore Pension Schemes," *Creveling & Creveling Private Wealth Advisory* (blog), January 31, 2011. Accessed May 6, 2014. http://crevelingandcreveling.com/blog-list/48-five-things-to-consider-before-buying-offshore-investment-schemes.html.
2. William F. Sharpe, "The Arithmetic of Active Management," *Financial Analysts Journal* 47, no. 1 (January/February 1991): 7–9. Accessed May 6, 2014. www.stanford.edu/~wfsharpe/art/active/active.htm.
3. Interview with Tony Noto. Telephone interview by author, December 22, 2013.
4. Benjamin Robertson, "Investment-Linked Insurance Schemes a Trap for Unwary Investors," *South China Morning Post*, September 30, 2013. Accessed May 6, 2014. www.scmp.com/news/article/1320840/investment-linked-insurance-schemes-trap-unwary-investors?login=1.
5. Frank Furness, "The 10 Habits of Successful Financial Advisors," You-Tube, December 19, 2013. Accessed May 6, 2014. www.youtube.com/watch?v=jOgIMDdAwdg.
6. "Frank Furness and Steve Young," YouTube, December 19, 2013. Accessed May 6, 2014. www.youtube.com/watch?v=kEQVV2B9hGw.
7. Simon Danaher, "Want to Be a Sales Commando?" International Adviser, April 10, 2014. Accessed May 6, 2014. www.international-adviser.com/news/sales-commando-a-former-devere-adviser.
8. Kanis Li, "Three-Year Suspension for Agent Who Mis-Sold ILAS Products," *South China Morning Post*, June 20, 2013. Accessed May 6, 2014. www.scmp.com/business/banking-finance/article/1264579/three-year-suspension-agent-who-mis-sold-ilas-products.
9. Interview with Chip Kimball. E-mail interview by author, April 20, 2014.
10. Interview with Jon Williams. E-mail interview by author, April 15, 2013.
11. . Interview with Alla Rao. E-mail interview by author, February 12, 2013.
12. Interview with Steve Batchelor. E-mail interview by author, September 15, 2013.
13. "Premier Advance," Friends Provident. Accessed May 6, 2014. www.fpinternational.com/common/layouts/subSectionLayout.jhtml?pageId=fpint%2FSitePageSimple%3Asavings_premier_advance.
14. Ben Steverman, "The Worst Deal in Mutual Funds Faces a Reckoning," Bloomberg.com, May 1, 2012. Accessed May 6, 2014. www.bloomberg.com/news/2012-04-30/the-worst-deal-in-mutual-funds-faces-a-reckoning.html.

15. Rudy Luukko, "Embedded Mutual Fund Commissions Hurt Investors," Thestar.com, June 15, 2013. Accessed May 6, 2014. www.thestar.com/business/personal_finance/investing/2013/06/15/embedded_mutual_fund_commissions_hurt_investors.html.

16. Interview with Lawrence Graham. E-mail interview by author, November 21, 2013.

17. "Pension Plans & Hidden Charges": "BBC *Panorama* P1—Who Took My Pension?" YouTube, October 11, 2010, accessed July 1, 2014, www.youtube.com/watch?v=rS36OlVCY5s; "BBC *Panorama* P2—Who Took My Pension?" YouTube, November 3, 2010, accessed May 6, 2014, www.youtube.com/watch?v=gajTHiHW8iA.

18. Meena Datwani, Hong Kong Monetary Authority, March 14, 2011. Accessed May 7, 2014. www.hkma.gov.hk/media/eng/doc/key-information/guidelines-and-circular/2011/20110314e1.pdf.

19. "Hong Kong Consumers Angry After Being Sold Complex Insurance Product ILAS," *South China Morning Post.* Accessed July 1, 2014. www.scmp.com/business/money/investment-products/article/1262327/hong-kong-consumers-angry-after-being-sold?page=all.

20. Adam Uren, "Expat Gets Pension Restored by This Is Money After It Fell £80,000," This Is Money, February 28, 2014. Accessed May 6, 2014. www.thisismoney.co.uk/money/pensions/article-2570171/Expat-gets-pension-restored-This-Money-fell-80-000.html.

21. Interview with Shawn Wong. E-mail interview by author, May 20, 2014.

22. Daniel R. Solin, *Does Your Broker Owe You Money?* (New York: Penguin Group, 2006).

23. "Vanguard Total Stock Mkt Idx Inv." (VTSMX), Fund Performance and Returns. Accessed May 6, 2014. http://performance.morningstar.com/fund/performance-return.action?t=VTSMX®ion=usa&culture=en-US.

24. "Protected Asset TEP Fund," Asset Fund Management. Accessed May 6, 2014. www.pdlinternational.com/products/protected-asset-tep-fund-plc/fund-price-history.aspx.

25. Interview with Susan Proctor. E-mail interview by author, June 28, 2013.

26. "Quantitative Analysis of Investor Behavior," Dalbar Group. Accessed May 6, 2014. www.qaib.com/public/default.aspx.

Chapter 7

Self-Appointed Gurus and Neanderthal Brains

T housands of years ago, a couple of your ancestors pushed their way through jungle foliage looking for their next meal. A tiger attacked from behind and ate one for lunch. The survivor told other villagers. One woman shared a similar story. So the villagers realized a pattern. Giant cats eat people. Better avoid them.

Another time, your ancestors discovered which berries were poisonous, which caused diarrhea, and which they could safely eat and enjoy. To survive and propagate, they learned patterns: which berries would kill, which would woo, and which could ruin a perfect picnic.

Humans are hardwired to seek such patterns. But while good for survival, these same pattern-seeking tendencies make us lousy investors. We figure if something is rising in price, it will keep rising. And if something drops in price, it will keep falling. But the stock market isn't a tiger or a jungle berry.

The best times to have invested in stocks would have been 1931, after the 1929–1930 stock market crash; 1973–1974, after the markets plunged more than 40 percent; October 1987, when a single-day market drop exceeded 20 percent; 2000 to 2002, when markets fell 40 percent; and 2008–2009, when global stocks were sliced in half. Instead of celebrating these discounts, however, many investors soiled their pants.

When stocks fall, many fear the market will never recover. So they don't invest. Others try guessing where the market will bottom out before buying. To them, purchasing plummeting stocks is like catching a falling knife.

Jason Zweig details such cognitive dissonance in his excellent book, *Your Money and Your Brain*.[1] You don't have to be a brain surgeon or neuropsychologist to understand the stock market. Just remember the *Rocky* movies. Global stock markets are a lot like Sylvester Stallone's character, Rocky Balboa. When you own diversified global stocks across a variety of geographic sectors, they get knocked to the canvas from time to time. But on aggregate, they *always* get up. Not only do they resume rising, they eventually hit new heights. Not every stock market responds immediately. But the biggest drops are usually followed by the biggest rewards. Sadly, few of us think about long-term history. Instead, our brains create short-term patterns, influenced by fear and immediate gratification.

Why Most Investors Should Hope for Falling Markets

Do you freak out when the stock market drops? If you're employed and in a position to buy stock market investments for at least the next five years, you should celebrate falling markets.

Warren Buffett, history's greatest investor, tries to educate the general public on stock market prices by offering the following quiz.

> If you plan to eat hamburgers throughout your life and are not a cattle producer, should you wish for higher or lower prices for beef? Likewise, if you are going to buy a car from time to time but are not an auto manufacturer, should you prefer higher or lower car prices? These questions, of course, answer themselves.

But now for the final exam: If you expect to be a net saver during the next five years, should you hope for a higher or lower stock market during that period? Many investors get this one wrong. Even though they are going to be net buyers of stocks for many years to come, they are elated when stock prices rise and depressed when they fall. In effect, they rejoice because prices have risen for the "hamburgers" they will soon be buying. This reaction makes no sense. Only those who will be sellers of equities [stock market investments] in the near future should be happy at seeing stocks rise. Prospective purchasers should much prefer sinking prices.[2]

The stock market is like a grocery store filled with nonperishable items. When prices fall, stock up on those products. Prices will inevitably rise again. If you like canned beans, and the store is selling them this week at a 20 percent discount, you have a choice. You can sit on your haunches and wonder whether they'll be selling even cheaper the following week, or you can stop being silly and just buy the beans. If the price drops further the following month, you can buy more of them. But if you sit on your butt and miss out on the sale (because you're speculating that beans will get even cheaper), well, you miss out on the sale.

A stock market drop is much the same. But most investors shun stock market discounts. Amateurs and professionals alike often dive out of stock investments when they forecast rough times ahead. Stock markets, however, are extremely unpredictable. If you (or an advisor) move money based on forecasts, your wealth will eventually suffer.

It's Not Timing the Market That Matters; It's Time in the Market

There are smart people (and people who aren't so smart) who think they can jump in and out of the stock market at opportune moments. It seems simple. Get in before the market rises and get out before it drops. This is referred to as "market timing." But most experts have a better chance of beating Usain Bolt in a footrace than effectively timing the market over an investment lifetime.

Vanguard founder John Bogle, named by *Fortune* magazine as one of the four investment giants of the twentieth century, says this about market timing:

> After nearly 50 years in this business, I do not know of anybody who has done it successfully and consistently. I don't even know anybody who knows anybody who has done it successfully and consistently.[3]

Warren Buffett, the world's greatest investor, states in a 1992 Berkshire Hathaway annual report, "We've long felt that the only value of stock forecasters is to make fortune tellers look good."[4]

Pundits try forecasting, of course. And they all sound logical spewing their theories in the *Wall Street Journal* or on CNBC. But predictions rarely jibe with future realities. Consider unemployment figures. If you've watched a bit of market-based TV, you've probably heard experts predicting rough times for stocks when unemployment figures rise. And it makes perfect sense, right? Wrong. Unfortunately, short-term market movements make no sense at all.

High Unemployment and High Stock Returns

In his excellent book *Markets Never Forget*, money manager Ken Fisher pokes our Neanderthal brains. He explains that, historically, high unemployment has been followed by high future stock returns.[5] No, I'm not suggesting keeping money out of the stock market until soup kitchens outnumber Starbucks coffee shops. Nor was Fisher. This is a random phenomenon, as likely to be repeated as not. But can you imagine the headline? *Stocks will surge next year because unemployment is getting close to hitting a new peak!*

If Table 7.1 inspires you to try predicting when we're six months from an unemployment peak, then you're missing the point. You can't predict such a thing any more than you can forecast the next zit on your nose. And the pattern won't likely perpetuate. Predicting a tiger would eat you in a one-on-one cage match is a pretty safe bet. But forecasting stock markets and zits is next to impossible.

But come on, surely experts can predict the stock market. Many would like you to think so. Yet five-year-old kids and house pets often

Table 7.1 High Unemployment and S&P 500 Returns

Six Months Before Unemployment Peaks	S&P 500 Returns in Following 12 Months
November 30, 1932	+57.7%
December 31, 1937	+33.2%
July 30, 1946	−3.4%
April 30, 1949	+31.3%
March 31, 1954	+42.3%
January 31, 1958	+37.9%
November 30, 1960	+32.3%
February 26, 1971	+13.6%
November 29, 1974	+36.2%
January 31, 1980	+19.5%
June 30, 1982	+61.2%
December 31, 1991	+7.6%
December 31, 2002	+28.7%
April 30, 2009	+38.8%
Average	**+31.2%**

SOURCES: Bureau of Labor Statistics; Global Financial Data Inc., S&P 500 total return as of 05/01/2011.

make them look foolish. In 2012, the British paper *The Observer* pit selected professional stock pickers against a group of children and a cat named Orlando in a one-year stock-picking competition. The feline purred to the top, gaining 10.8 percent, compared to a 3.5 percent gain for the professionals and a 2.9 percent loss for the kids. (Orlando made his picks by throwing a toy mouse at a grid of numbers allocated to different companies.)[6] How did Vanguard's British stock market index measure up? It beat them all, gaining 17.4 percent.[7]

In 2002, the *Financial Times* reported a stock-picking battle between a five-year-old kid, an astrologer, and a professional portfolio analyst. The winner was the child, beating the professional analyst by 52 percent.[8]

Ah, I can hear what you're thinking. Hallam is cherry-picking anomalies. Data-crunching firm CXO Advisory proves otherwise after putting dozens of the world's highest-profile financial forecasters to the test. When these so-called experts publicize their stock market predictions, the company tracks their accuracy. If you believe the talking heads

on CNBC or the experts profiled in the *Wall Street Journal* are worth
listening to, I'm sorry to disappoint you. Between 2005 and 2012, CXO
Advisory collected 6,584 forecasts by 68 experts. When predicting the
direction of the stock market, they were right just 46.9 percent of the
time. Coin flippers would rival them.[9]

On March 5, 2009, comedian Jon Stewart, of U.S. television's *The
Daily Show*, humiliated some of CNBC's highest-profile stock market
forecasters. His list of suffering victims included Jim Cramer, host of
CNBC's *Mad Money* program.[10]

Footage of Cramer's failed predictions gave plenty of video fodder
for the clever Jon Stewart.[11]

What Stewart didn't realize (and it would have made great viewing)
is that Cramer's long-term forecasting has been tracked by CXO Advisory. He has been correct just 46.8 percent of the time.[12]

Instead of following a guru's recommendation (or asking your house
cat) whether to buy U.S. stocks, British stocks, or Asian stocks, consider
owning them all. By doing so with index funds, you'll beat most professional investors.

What Can You Miss by Guessing Wrong?

In the previous chapter, I introduced you to two offshore pension investors (Steve Batchelor and Susan Proctor) whose investments sputtered compared to the results of the global stock market indexes. Not
only were Steve and Susan paying high fees; their advisors gambled on
what economic sectors they thought would thrive. And it cost these
expats dearly.

Predicting stock market movements, even with the benefit of hindsight, is next to impossible. Jeremy Siegel agrees. Author of *Stocks for the
Long Run* and professor of business at the University of Pennsylvania's
Wharton School, Siegel looked back at the biggest stock market moves
since 1885 (focusing on trading sessions where the markets moved by
5 percent or more in a single day) and tried connecting each of them to
a world event.[13]

Seventy-five percent of the time, he couldn't find logical explana-
tions. Yet he had the luxury of looking back in time and trying to match

the market's behavior with historical world news. If a world- renowned finance professor like Siegel can't make connections between world events and the stock market's movements with the benefit of hindsight, then how is someone supposed to predict future movements based on economic events—or the prediction of events to come?

If anyone tries convincing you to act on their short-term stock market predictions, ignore them. Doing otherwise could cost you plenty. For example, let's look at the U.S. stock market from 1982 through December 2005.

During this time, the stock market averaged 10.6 percent annually. But if you didn't have money in the stock market during the 10 best trading days, your average return would have dropped to 8.1 percent. If you missed the best 50 trading days, your average return would have been just 1.8 percent.[14] Markets can move so unpredictably, and so quickly. If you take money out of the stock market for a day, a week, a month, or a year, you could miss the best trading days of the decade. Neither you nor your broker can predict them.

A lucky guess or two (as exhibited by Orlando the cat) may be a curse. Like winning a few thousand dollars on your first trip to the casino, it could take plenty of beatings before realizing your skill was just luck.

Twice already, I've shown the damage of silly forecasting by examining Dalbar's research on investors' behavior. It shows how much the S&P 500 index made over 20 years compared to the average U.S. stock investor. We know these two decades were volatile, characterized by huge stock market booms (called bull markets) and busts (bear markets). Calm investors, contributing regular sums to a low-cost index, did well. But the average person didn't.

U.S. Stock Market versus Average U.S. Investor's Return, 1990–2010

Initial Investment	S&P 500 Grew To	Average American's U.S. Stock Market Investments Grew To
$10,000	$57,501	$21,205

This data is compelling. If you asked most investors whether their advisors (or their investment skills) were above average, many would say yes. It's much like asking a broad cross section of people whether they're smarter or better-looking than average. Optimism blinds.

Therefore, odds are 50–50 that if you invested $10,000 between 1990 and 2010, you would have earned even *less* than $21,205.

When Investors and Advisors Sabotage Their Rides

Imagine somebody at a fuel station letting half the air out of his car tires before a road trip. Next to the nut is a fruitcake pouring a liter of Coca-Cola into her fuel tank. Sound silly? Of course it does. The cars would limp and sputter. But most people do far worse to their investment accounts.

According to the fund-rating agency Morningstar, international funds averaged 9.95 percent per year for the recent decade. This was after fees. But the average investor *in those same funds* averaged just 6.84 percent.

Pointing fingers is embarrassing if they're aimed at us. So let's point them at John. He's a typical guy (2.2 kids, white picket fence, drives a Volvo). Let's assume he owned shares of an international stock market mutual fund from January 1, 2003, to January 1, 2013.

John or his advisor identified a fund with a solid track record in 2003. It gained rapidly from 2003 to 2007. They were pleased with its performance, so John kept adding money to it, ignoring some of his underperforming funds. This is perfectly normal behavior. But normal is disastrous.

From 2007 to 2009, John's fund starts to tank. The year before, John happily paid a higher price. But now that the stocks within the fund are on special, he doesn't want to buy. Such behavior is normal—but, once again, foolish. In 2009, the fund has a decent year. But John's a bit gun-shy, so he waits. Halfway through 2010, the fund's price jumps. Hardwired like a Neanderthal, John starts buying again.

This is how John's fund could have averaged 9.95 percent, with John earning 6.84 percent. He loved his fund when it was expensive, and shunned it when it was cheap.

Instead, if he had contributed the same monthly sum to the fund, he might have earned more than 9.95 percent. Consistent monthly investments purchase fewer fund units when prices are soaring, and more fund units when prices drop.

Most people don't add consistent sums to the same funds. They prefer chasing what's rising and shunning what's falling. Consequently, according to Morningstar, the average international mutual fund between 2003 and 2013 should have turned $10,000 into $24,782. But the average investor *in those same funds* turned $10,000 into just $19,379.[15]

Such performance gaps between what funds earn and what investors make are prevalent across every major asset group. People jump onto bandwagons. And it costs them plenty.

John Bogle explains how much money we burn in the May/June 2008 issue of the *Journal of Indexes*. His article, "The Yawning Gap between Fund Returns and Shareholder Returns," examines a broad sample of 200 popular U.S. funds from 1996 to 2005. The typical fund earned an average of 8.9 percent per year. But the average investor in those same funds earned just 2.4 percent per year.[16]

If a financial advisor ever suggests an investment product because "it's performing really well right now," don't walk from the bozo—run! Recent past results rarely indicate a strong future. In most cases, the opposite holds true. As detailed in Chapter 5, most mutual funds earning top ratings as superb performers eventually fall from their mantels, underperforming the typical fund in the years ahead. Winning geographic sector funds often do likewise.

Take the countries with the best-performing stock markets in 2011. As reported by *Business Insider*, nine of the top 11 were developing countries.[17]

They were Venezuela, Mongolia, Panama, Jamaica, Tehran, Tanzania, Trinidad and Tobago, Botswana, and the Philippines, averaging a gain of 25 percent for 2011. Pattern seekers likely salivated after seeing these published returns. Many investors loaded up on emerging stock market exposure *after* their great performance run. Doing so, instead of just keeping a diversified portfolio of global stock markets, would have been silly.

In the 20 months after the *Business Insider* article was published, the average global stock outperformed the emerging stock index by 25 percent.[18]

Popular Stocks Underperform

Some investors try picking their own stocks. But their odds of beating a low-cost index fund are remote. Over the short term (a period of 10 years or fewer), anyone could get lucky. But over time, destiny favors indexes. Some people may scoff, believing if they buy large, established companies they could beat a simple index. Unfortunately, it's easier said than done.

Consider the 10 largest companies in the United States. As of August 2013, here they were in order of size.

America's Largest Publicly Traded Businesses
1. Apple Inc.
2. Exxon Mobil Corporation
3. Google Inc.
4. Microsoft Corporation
5. Berkshire Hathaway
6. Johnson & Johnson
7. General Electric
8. Wal-Mart Stores
9. Chevron Corporation
10. Wells Fargo & Company

At first glance, it's a list of hurricane-proof businesses that would satisfy even the most conservative investor. But the 10 biggest stocks change all the time. And those betting on the biggest firms as a group have always reaped weak returns. Between 1926 and 2006, the 10 biggest stocks in the United States underperformed the average U.S. stock by 2.9 percent the subsequent year. After three years, they lagged by 11.1 percent; after five years, by 17.7 percent; and after 10 years they were 29.4 percent behind the S&P 500. During the 81-year study, the largest 10 companies have never, as a group, outperformed the S&P 500 in subsequent years. As an expatriate, you can't afford such underperformance.

The study in question ended in 2006. On average, seven out of 10 of these company leaders underperformed the average U.S. stock. I wanted to check the performance of the biggest stocks since 2007, and compare their aggregate performance with the S&P 500 index. Of the 10 largest businesses in 2007, seven of them were lagging the market by early April 2013. The only index beaters were Wal-Mart, Procter & Gamble, and Chevron. Will these winners continue to beat the average stock? Odds suggest otherwise.[19]

How About the Next Big Thing?

When I first moved to Singapore, a Canadian woman cornered me at a business function to whisper about a great new investment opportunity. "There's a new cell phone company in China," she said. "It's run by a guy who used to work for Nokia, and I have an opportunity to buy shares as soon as the stock start starts trading on the exchange next month."

This is called an initial public offering (IPO). When a private company goes public, offering its shares on a stock exchange for the first time, it relies a great deal on hype. Stockbrokers flaunt its potential, creating breathless men and women (like the lady I met) salivating over the stock's supposed prognosis.

It's easy to get wrapped up in the hype. Many consider how much money they could have made with Microsoft's IPO in 1986. Such investors became quick multimillionaires.

But successful investors consider probabilities. Breathlessly jumping onto a hot IPO is usually a bad idea.

In June 2012, I wrote an article, "Facebook IPO Buyers Deserved to Lose," for *Canadian Business* magazine. I explained why hot new offerings are usually disastrous. At the time, Facebook investors were feeling the burn. Filled with hype, many viewed its IPO as a red-hot ticket. But like most investors gunning for the next big thing, they were immediately scorched by the stock. It dropped 30 percent shortly after the opening bell. Those investing $10,000 in Facebook stock had lost $5,000 just two and a half months later.

Here's an excerpt from the article:

University of Florida finance professor Jay Ritter has studied IPO performances for years. His findings suggest that IPO buyers are like rock climbers with frayed ropes. Examining 1,006 IPOs from 1988 to 1993, he found that the median IPO underperformed the Russell 3000 index of small-cap stocks [the average American small stock] by 30 percent during the three years after the offering. At the end of that period, 46 percent of the stocks were below their IPO price. Piper Jaffray, working for U.S. Bancorp, conducted a similar study, looking at 4,900 IPOs from May 1988 to July 1998. This 10-year period was great for the market: the S&P 500 gained 472 percent. But new IPOs didn't keep pace. Fewer than one-third of the newly public businesses were trading above their IPO price by the decade's end.

Some might assume that IPO winners easily offset the losers. There's the story of Microsoft, up nearly 31,000 percent since its 1986 IPO. Then there's Google, which, according to Morningstar, has gained more than 400 percent since its 2004 public debut. But dreamers believing that blockbuster IPOs are the tickets to financial freedom need to examine the bigger picture.

Outsized IPO gains, according to Wharton Finance professor Jeremy Siegel, are rare. In a study covering 1968 to 2003, Siegel found that IPOs underperformed the small-cap stock index [an index of small company stocks] 29 out of 33 years. In his book *The Future for Investors,* he argues, "investing in IPOs is much akin to playing the lottery." After tracking the performance of nearly 9,000 IPOs, he concluded that they're a great deal for the investment banks that underwrite them but usually a terrible deal for regular investors.

This is a long-term trend. Siegel notes that 80 percent of IPOs during the period he studied underperformed the small-cap index since their IPO date. In fact, IPO investors lagged the S&P 500 by 2 percent to 3 percent per year. What's more, the worst performing initial public offerings tended to be those companies on which investors pinned the highest hopes.

The fact is, the world's most profitable IPOs weren't storybook stocks like Microsoft or Google, but dull businesses that didn't open at silly prices. Fastenal, for example, provides building supplies. Since its 1987 IPO, which occurred a year after Microsoft's, its shares have gained about 1,000 percent more than Bill Gates's company.

So when the next overhyped IPO comes along, should you bother? I don't think so. Not unless you like scaling shale walls with frayed ropes.[20]

When Genius Fails

Most individual stock pickers possess a false sense of skill. Any time investors pick individual stocks and underperform the relevant stock market index, they're giving up proceeds for nothing. Consider the typical investment club, where groups of like-minded friends research stocks and pool their money.

Brad M. Barber (professor of finance at the University of California at Davis) and Terrance Odean (professor of banking and finance at UC Berkeley's Haas School of Business) used data from a large brokerage to study the performance of 166 investment clubs from February 1991 to January 1997. They published their findings in the January–February *Financial Analysts Journal*, proving that the typical investment club underperformed the S&P 500 index by 4.4 percent per year after trading costs.[21]

The results of the Mensa Investment Club are even more amusing. Mensa is a large, well-known society of geniuses. To qualify, members must have recorded IQ scores in the top 2 percent. Reported in the June 2001 issue of *Smart Money* magazine, the Mensa Investment Club averaged just 2.5 percent over the previous 15 years, losing nearly 13 percent each year to the S&P 500 index.[22]

If you're building a stock and bond market portfolio for your retirement, you probably shouldn't gamble with individual stocks. Nor should you heed a stock market prediction. Follow a disciplined approach. The book's following chapters will show exactly how.

Notes

1. Jason Zweig, *Your Money and Your Brain: How the New Science of Neuroeconomics Can Help Make You Rich* (New York: Simon & Schuster, 2007).
2. Warren E. Buffett, "1997 Chairman's Letter," Berkshirehathaway.com. Accessed May 6, 2014. www.berkshirehathaway.com/letters/1997.html.

3. John C. Bogle, *Common Sense on Mutual Funds: New Imperatives for the Intelligent Investor* (Hoboken, NJ: John Wiley & Sons, 2010), 28.

4. Warren E. Buffett, "Chairman's Letter—1992," Berkshirehathaway.com. Accessed May 6, 2014. www.berkshirehathaway.com/letters/1992.html.

5. Kenneth L. Fisher and Lara Hoffmans, *Markets Never Forget (but People Do)* (Hoboken, NJ: John Wiley & Sons, 2012).

6. Mark King, "Investments: Orlando Is the Cat's Whiskers of Stock Picking," *The Observer*, January 13, 2013. Accessed May 7, 2014. www.theguardian.com/money/2013/jan/13/investments-stock-picking.

7. "Vanguard UK Equity Index," Vanguard UK. Accessed May 7, 2014. https%3A%2F%2Fwww.vanguard.co.uk%2Fuk%2Fmvc%2FloadPDF%3Fdoc Id%3D2034.

8. Daniel R. Solin, *Does Your Broker Owe You Money?* (Bonita Springs, FL: Silver Cloud, 2004), 141.

9. "Guru Grades," CXO Advisory RSS. Accessed May 7, 2014. www.cxoadvisory .com/gurus/.

10. "About *Mad Money*," CNBC.com. Accessed May 7, 2014. www.cnbc.com/id/100000946.

11. Jon Stewart, "CNBC Financial Advice," *Daily Show*. Accessed May 7, 2014. www.thedailyshow.com/watch/wed-march-4-2009/cnbc-financial-advice.

12. "Guru Grades," CXO Advisory RSS. Accessed July 1, 2014. www.cxoadvisory .com/gurus/.

13. Jeremy J. Siegel, *Stocks for the Long Run: The Definitive Guide to Financial Market Returns and Long-Term Investment Strategies* (New York: McGraw-Hill, 2008), 217–218.

14. Kenneth L. Fisher, Jennifer Chou, and Lara Hoffmans. *The Only Three Questions That Count* (Hoboken, NJ: John Wiley & Sons, 2007), 279.

15. Morningstar.com, February 4, 2013. Accessed May 7, 2014. http%3A%2F% 2Fnews.morningstar.com%2Farticlenet%2Farticle.aspx%3Fid%3D582626.

16. John Bogle, "The Yawning Gap between Fund Returns and Shareholder Returns," *Journal of Indexes*, May/June 2008; *JOI* Articles, April 30, 2008. Accessed May 7, 2014. www.etf.com/publications/journalofindexes/joi-articles/4040-bogles-corner.html.

17. Eric Platt, "The 11 Best Performing Stock Markets of the Year," *Business Insider*, December 27, 2011. Accessed May 7, 2014. www.businessinsider.com/11-best-performing-stock-markets-2011-2011-12?IR=T&op=1#!J4p9R.

18. "Vanguard Emerging Markets Stock ETF," Morningstar.com. Accessed May 7, 2014. http%3A%2F%2Fquote.morningstar.com%2FETF%2Fchart.aspx%3Ft% 3DVWO%26region%3Dusa%26culture%3Den-US%26ops%3D%26cur%3D USD%26lan%3Den-US%26productcode%3DCOM.

19. Andrew Hallam, "With Stocks, Bigger Isn't Better," *Canadian Business*, October 15, 2013. Accessed May 7, 2014. www.canadianbusiness.com/investing/with-stocks-bigger-isnt-better/.

20. Andrew Hallam, "Facebook IPO Buyers Deserved to Lose," *Canadian Business*, June 11, 2012. Accessed May 7, 2014. www.canadianbusiness.com/investing/facebook-ipo-buyers-deserved-to-lose/.

21. Brad M. Barber and Terrance Odean, "Too Many Cooks Spoil the Profits," *Financial Analysts Journal*, January–February 2000. Accessed May 7, 2014. http://faculty.haas.berkeley.edu/odean/Papers%20current%20versions/FAJ%20JF00%20Barber%20and%20Odean.pdf.

22. Larry E. Swedroe, *The Quest for Alpha: The Holy Grail of Investing* (Hoboken, NJ: John Wiley & Sons, 2011), 53.

Chapter 8

An Employer's Greatest Challenge

Erica Holt Fursova is the human resources director at the Anglo-American School of Moscow and the Anglo-American School at St. Petersburg. She's among many expatriate leaders encouraging financial education among her staff. "We're planning to develop financial awareness," she says. "I'm proposing that we start a staff 'wealth accumulation' club as an Employee Wellness Activity for next school year; basically it would be a group of interested staff who want to research (like a book club) and discuss investment strategies."[1]

Erica has also headed committees to examine financial services providers for staff. But such decision making is tough. Some of the staff are American, while others aren't. Investment firms generally cater to one or the other. Then there's the question of cost. Investment firms usually sell themselves as low cost and transparent. But most are anything but.

Non-Americans at the Anglo-American School of Moscow choose between the Generali Vision Plan (an offshore pension) and the Meridian family of mutual funds.

Low cost is key. Generali Vision's charges are high and murky. Based on telephone discussions I've had with sales reps, even they have trouble explaining the fees. Investors, it appears, struggle in quicksand.

> The first 100 percent of regular premium unit allocations during the initial period are set aside in order to fund the administration fees due over the duration of the premium payment term. The exact period for this funding is shown on the Plan Statement and depends on the premium payment term of your Plan.[2]

Got that? Sure you do. The company then provides a table, indicating how many months of investor deposits go toward initial fees. Those investing for 25 years see their first 23 deposits disappear into the cost monster's mouth. Those investing for 25 years feed Generali Vision for 28 months.

Would the company have its fill by then? Not even close. According to the firm, there's an additional 2 percent administrative fee payable up to the 10th year of the "plan anniversary." After the 10th year, this fee drops to 0.3 percent. The firm also sites a 1.5 percent administrative charge "deducted on the units to the Plan annually." What about actively managed fund costs? We can't forget about those. They cost up to an additional 2 percent per year. As a result, investors with Generali Vision could pay (on average) more than 4 percent per year in fees.[3]

Those wishing to redeem shares early get whacked with a bamboo stick. In typical offshore pension fashion, early redemption fees can swallow large portions of the proceeds.

Let's create a scenario with an uber-generous employer. Assume your employer gave you a 20 percent bonus on every investment deposit. You could invest $48,000 for the price of $40,000 (see Table 8.1).

This sounds great, unless you're paying 4 percent in annual investment costs. Here's how the math plays out with two comparative examples:

Investor 1: Pays 1 percent in fees, receives no bonus.
Investor 2: Pays 4 percent in fees, receives 20 percent bonus on every deposit.

Table 8.1   Does the Bonus Ease the Pain?

	Investor 1: No Bonus	Investor 2: With 20% Bonus
Invests per year	$40,000	$40,000
Bonus	$0	$8000
Annually invested	$40,000	$48,000
Market returns	9%	9%
Total fees	1%	4%
Investment returns after fees	8%	5%
Time period invested	20 Years	20 Years
End value	$1,976,916	$1,666,524

As you can see, the 20 percent bonus wouldn't mitigate those seemingly small annual fee differences. In such a case, investors earning a 20 percent bonus on deposits (but paying 3 percent more in fees) would end up with $310,392 less after 20 years.

Fortunately, the Anglo-American School of Moscow also offers a cheaper option to non-American expats: the MFS Meridian series of funds. Teachers purchase the company's B-series products, so they don't pay commissions to invest. But there are back-ended loads for those wanting to redeem a fund's proceeds before the end of a six-year period. Such redemption fees, however, are peanuts compared to those typically charged by offshore pension plans.

MFS Meridian funds' costs can be found at Morningstar UK. Most of its stock market funds cost roughly 2 percent a year. Meridian's European Core and U.S. Growth funds each cost 2.05 percent; its Global Concentrated fund costs 2.9 percent, while its U.S. Value fund costs 1.19 percent.[4]

Fees—How Much Is Too Much?

Many U.S.-based companies offer employees investment plans, called 401(k)s. Employers often match investors' contributions, up to a certain percentage of their salary. If the plan fees are low and the matching contributions are generous, 401(k)s can be an excellent deal.

Some plans, however, are under fire for charging too much. Experts suggesting fees are too high at a given threshold set a precedent for

financially aware, global employers. So, what are fair charges for investment services?

Wall Street Journal writer Kelly Greene published "401(k) Fees:
How Much Is Too Much?" in October 2013.[5] She reported that a San
Francisco–based company, Personal Capital, has an online 401(k) plan
analyzer. It allows Americans to determine whether they're paying too
much in annual fees for their corporate-sponsored retirement plans.

Costs are categorized into zones and include mutual fund expense
ratios, commissions, and platform costs. Fees totaling less than 1 percent
earn Personal Capital's green zone designation. That's good. Investors
paying between 1 percent and 1.99 percent annually are in the yellow
zone—much like a moderate forest fire warning. Charges exceeding
2 percent are clearly in the red zone: Nobody light a match.

Mike Alfred, a chief executive at Brightscope, a financial information firm in San Diego, was quoted in the *Wall Street Journal* article
suggesting that when total investment costs are 2 percent or more, "It's
really going to be hard to accumulate assets."[6]

MFS Meridian funds, as offered to teachers at the Anglo-American
School of Moscow, cost far less than the typical offshore pension. But do
they offer a good deal?

Remember the premise about fees, published by Nobel economic
sciences laureate William F. Sharpe. On aggregate, professional investors
earn the market's return before fees. After fees, they lose in direct proportion to the fees charged.[7] Some funds buck the trend for a while. But
when it comes to an entire portfolio, low costs beat high costs.

Five-year returns of the MFS Meridian funds provide an example
(see Table 8.2). They have five stock market funds we can compare directly with Vanguard index funds representing the same asset classes:
Emerging Markets Equity, European Core, Global Equity, U.S. Growth,
and U.S. Value. Measured in U.S. dollars to April 30, 2014, four of the
five MFS Meridian funds underperformed their lower-cost counterparts. Investing equally into each of Vanguard's lower-cost funds would
have given the index investor a 17.6 percent advantage over just five
years. Over time, such an advantage would only grow.

Such comparisons reveal no coincidences: Lower-cost portfolios
usually outperform higher-cost portfolios in direct proportion to the
fees charged. In the example, MFS Meridian's funds cost nearly 2 percent

Table 8.2   Five-Year Performance Comparison

MFS Meridian Funds versus Vanguard's Indexes
Measured in USD to April 30, 2014

Asset Class	MFS Meridian	Vanguard
Emerging Markets Equity	+8.60%	+10.49%
European Core	+18.02%	+15.60%
Global Equity	+16.09%	+17.52%
U.S. Growth	+14.60%	+18.03%
U.S. Value	+14.66%	+20.21%
Average Annual Return	+14.39%	+16.37%
Total Return	+95.8%	+113.4%

SOURCES: Morningstar UK; MFS Meridian; Vanguard U.S.

more each year than Vanguard's. The cost discrepancy, as you can see, mirrors the performance.

Writing for Canada's national paper, the *Globe and Mail*, I revealed the same reality. I compared 10-year returns of actively managed funds from Fidelity, the Royal Bank of Canada, Toronto Dominion Bank, Canadian Imperial Bank of Commerce, IA Clarington, and Manulife, testing how they performed against their low-cost indexed counterparts.

As expected, lower-cost index fund portfolios outperformed their actively managed counterparts by an amount almost identical to the fee differences charged.

So What's the Solution for Global Employers?

Global employers should demand more. Offshore pensions offered by Friends Provident, Zurich International, Generali, Aviva, and Royal Skandia are poor options, as are any investment platforms costing 2 percent or more.

Better solutions exist. Firms like U.S.-based AssetBuilder already offer low-cost index fund options to companies with expatriate American employees. An international school or workplace would simply have to call them. Such employees could then invest like economics professors, instead of sales-led zombies. Total costs per employee would be less than 0.7 percent.

Raymond James Financial (see Chapter 12) will build portfolios of index funds for clients who specifically insist on them—but only for American international teachers. Such portfolios cost slightly more than 1 percent.

How about The Alexander Beard Company? Well . . . not so fast. This is a British-based business offering, among other products, expatriate investment solutions. "We believe that the total costs of our plan over any given period are lower than those of other offshore pension providers," says Janet Jenkinson, divisional director.[8]

The firm offers six portfolios comprising globally diversified actively managed funds. French-based La Mondiale Group constructs and rebalances Alexander Beard's portfolios. Models range from conservative to high risk.*

Alexander Beard's platform costs are 1.5 percent per year, not including a 5 percent commission charge for each purchase. Investors also pay a $500 (U.S.) start-up fee. Those opting to sell their investments midstream to buy a house, car, or boat are out of luck unless they suffer some kind of permanent disability before retirement. "Ordinary members cannot access their accounts before reaching the age of 55," says Jenkinson.

AssetBuilder's globally blended portfolios are far cheaper. Unlike Alexander Beard, AssetBuilder doesn't charge commission or start-up fees. Nor do they stop investors from selling before a pre-determined date.

Comparing the companies' five-year returns between June 2008 and June 2013 is an interesting test. In June 2008, global stocks suffered a precipitous plunge. Did the pricier Alexander Beard portfolios earn better five-year returns from this devastating starting point? Or did the cheaper AssetBuilder portfolios win out?

Costs, as always, are key. Those investing $10,000 with Alexander Beard during one of history's darkest moments earned no reprieve. Commissions swallowed $500. Start-up costs ate another $500. Starting $1,000 behind the eight ball, Alexander Beard's investors couldn't catch up. In fact, the lower-cost funds offered by AssetBuilder furthered the performance gap. After fees, all six Alexander Beard portfolios underperformed their lower-cost AssetBuilder counterparts. As you can see in Table 8.3, the race wasn't even close.

---

* Americans purchasing such non-U.S. domiciled funds can face severe tax implications or penalties from the U.S. government.

Table 8.3   Five-Year Returns of Investment Platforms Assuming $10,000 Invested

AssetBuilder versus Alexander Beard/La Mondiale Funds
June 2008–June 2013

Alexander Beard/ La Mondiale Funds	AssetBuilder Funds	Alexander Beard/ La Mondiale Funds	AssetBuilder Index Funds
Short Term (Conservative)	Model Portfolio 7 (Conservative)	$10,737 +7.3%	$13,155 +31.55%
Medium Term (Defensive)	Model Portfolio 8 (Defensive)	$11,367 +13.67%	$13,212 +32.12%
Medium Long Term (Cautious)	Model Portfolio 9 (Cautious)	$11,079 +10.79%	$13,267 +32.67%
Long Term (Balanced)	Model Portfolio 10 (Balanced Growth)	$10,863 +8.63%	$13,157 +31.57%
Very Long Term (Balanced)	Model Portfolio 12 (Balanced Growth)	$10,512 +5.12%	$13,303 +33.03%
Maximum Term (Adventurous)	Model Portfolio 14 (Aggressive Growth)	$10,242 +2.4%	$13,405 +34.04%

Returns measured in U.S. dollars, net of commission fees, fund costs, platform charges, and start-up fees

SOURCES: La Mondiale Group; Alexander Beard; AssetBuilder.

AssetBuilder is currently available to American expats only. By 2016, however, it will likely service expats from every nationality. "Just like we did in the United States," says CEO Kennon Grose, "we want to disrupt the high costs and bring our simple investing model to expatriate investors."[9]

Regardless of what financial service platform an employer chooses, the employer shouldn't force workers to invest in it. Human resource personnel making such decisions may not understand how the products work. They might also be unclear of how they compare with other providers. Those offering bonuses for investing in specific platforms may want to reconsider. If they don't, financially educated employees may resent them for it.

Employers offering to match a portion of a worker's savings should do so regardless of the platform chosen. Proof of investment deposits should be all that's required, whether or not an investor uses a financial advisory firm or invests the money on his or her own.

If you're considering investing without an advisor, you'll be surprised to learn how simple it is. Committing just a few minutes each year will allow you to spank the returns of those investing expensively. But to be an effective investor, you shouldn't follow your gut. Nor should you pay attention to the media's market gurus. Sure, it sounds counterintuitive. But read on. I'll prove it.

Notes

1. Interview with Erica Holt Fursova. E-mail interview by author, May 24, 2014.
2. "Generali Vision," Generali. Accessed July 2, 2014. www.generali-intl.com/media/28546/gi_vision_brochure_final_26_11_13.pdf.
3. Ibid.
4. "Share Prices | Fund Prices and Data | Morningstar," Morningstar UK. Accessed July 2, 2014. www.morningstar.co.uk/uk/.
5. Kelly Greene, "401(k) Fees: How Much Is Too Much?" Total Return, *WSJ*. Total Return RSS, October 1, 2013. Accessed July 2, 2014. http://blogs.wsj.com/totalreturn/2013/10/01/401k-fees-how-much-is-too-much/.
6. Ibid.
7. William F. Sharpe, "The Arithmetic of Active Management," *Financial Analysts Journal* 47, no. 1 (January/February 1991): 7–9. Accessed July 2, 2014. http://web.stanford.edu/~wfsharpe/art/active/active.htm.
8. Interview with Janet Jenkinson. E-mail interview by author, June 5, 2014.
9. Interview with Kennon Grose. E-mail interview by author, July 1, 2014.

Chapter 9

Couch Potato Investing

I magine a couch potato for a moment. A beer resting on his gut, he lies on the sofa watching football. The only time he perks up is when the home team scores or when a streaker (why are they always men?) races across the turf.

It might be hard to believe, but an investment strategy inspired by sloth runs circles around most professionally managed portfolios. Practitioners of the strategy spend less than an hour each year on their investments. They don't have to follow the economy, read the *Wall Street Journal*, subscribe to online investment publications, or hire an advisor. This champion slacker is called the Couch Potato portfolio.

Devised by former *Dallas Morning News* columnist Scott Burns, the original Couch Potato portfolio is an even split between a stock and a bond market index. It's easier to manage than a crew cut. If you invest $1,000 per month, you would put $500 into the stock index and $500 into the bond index. After one year, you would see whether you had more money in stocks or more in bonds. If you had more in stocks, you would sell some of the stock index, using the proceeds to buy more of

the bond index. Doing so realigns the portfolio with its original allocation: 50 percent stocks, 50 percent bonds. Scott Burns says anyone who
can fog a mirror and divide by two can pull this off.

Don't Bonds Tie You Down?

Many investment cowboys think bonds are boring and unprofitable, and
have no place in a portfolio. It's a good thing such Wild West throwbacks
(even if they're bull-riding studs) aren't running government pensions,
corporate pensions, or university endowment funds. Responsible individual and professional investors understand the importance of bonds in
a diversified portfolio.

Short-term first world government bonds or short-term, high-
quality corporate bonds don't pay scorching interest, but they're safe.
The easiest way to buy a basket of them is through a bond market index.

Is It More of a Fling Than a Real Relationship?

You might wonder why anyone would choose an index of short-term
bonds over those with longer terms. If you buy a long-term bond paying
4 percent annually over the next 10 years, inflation could always erode
its purchasing power. The bond may pay 4 percent annually, but if you're
buying fuel for your car that increases in price every year by 6 percent,
you're losing to a tank of gas.

For this reason, buying indexes of bonds with shorter maturities
(such as one- to three-year bonds) is usually wiser than buying indexes
with longer-term bonds. When a bond within a short-term index ma-
tures, it gets replaced. If inflation rises, the newly purchased bond will offer higher interest yields, allowing investors in short-term bond indexes
to exceed inflation over time.

Over long periods, bonds aren't as profitable as stocks. But they
stabilize portfolios. And despite what many think, bonds sometimes
outperform. Check out the decade between 2000 and 2009 shown in
Table 9.1.

U.S. stocks bled for the decade. Bonds averaged a 7.7 percent return per year. Not only did Couch Potato investors have skin in the

Table 9.1   U.S. Stocks and Bonds, 2000–2009

Asset Class	Annualized Return
Stocks	−1.0%
Bonds	+7.7%

SOURCE: Craig Rowland and J. M. Lawson, *The Permanent Portfolio: Harry Browne's Long-Term Investment Strategy* (Hoboken, NJ: John Wiley & Sons, 2012), 89.

better-performing asset class (bonds) but, as always, they bought low and sold high. Recall how this works (three steps):

1. Once a year, investors look at their portfolios.
2. They identify whether they have more money in stocks or more in bonds.
3. If stocks beat bonds that year, they sell some stocks to buy bonds; or if bonds beat stocks, they sell some bonds to buy stocks.

By rebalancing once a year, Couch Potato investors sell a bit of what's hot and buy a bit of what's not. They manage money much like disciplined government-held pension systems. Most other investors do the opposite: they buy high and sell low. With a Couch Potato portfolio and a bit of discipline, investors avoid such lunacy.

Because stocks outperform bonds over time, having bonds in a portfolio reduces returns—but not by as much as you might think.

In Table 9.2, you can see the results of the U.S. Couch Potato portfolio compared to the S&P 500 index between 1992 and 2013.

Table 9.2   U.S. Couch Potato Portfolio, 1992–2013

	Couch Potato Portfolio 50% Stock Index/50% Bond Index	S&P 500 Index 100% Stocks
Number of years with annual losses	3 Years	4 Years
Biggest annual loss	−16% (2008)	−37% (2008)
Biggest annual gain	+27.25% (1995)	+34.9% (1995)
Average annual gain	+8%	+9.3%

SOURCE: Morningstar.com.

Table 9.3   U.S. Couch Potato (75 Percent Stocks/25 Percent Bonds) versus S&P 500 Index, 1992–2013

	Couch Potato Portfolio 75% Stock Index/25% Bond Index	S&P 500 Index 100% Stocks
Number of years with annual losses	4 Years	4 Years
Biggest annual loss	−26.5% (2008)	−37% (2008)
Biggest annual gain	+31.4% (1995)	+34.9% (1995)
Average annual gain	+8.98%	+9.3%

SOURCE: Morningstar.com.

The Couch Potato portfolio is effective for two reasons: It's both diversified and cheap, costing as little as 0.1 percent per year.

It's also an insult to Wall Street. Most hedge fund managers (known as the smart money to the gullible) underperformed the Couch Potato portfolio every year between 2002 and 2013.

The premise is also adaptable. Investors taking slightly higher risk can build a Couch Potato portfolio with 75 percent stocks and 25 percent bonds (see Table 9.3). Long-term returns have been higher than with a portfolio split evenly between stocks and bonds (see Table 9.2).

Potatoes Growing Globally

The original Couch Potato portfolio is simpler than a ham-and-cheese sandwich: diversify between stocks and bonds, and rebalance. Further diversification, however, sometimes enhances returns and reduces volatility.

The founding editor of *MoneySense* magazine, Ian McGugan, won a national magazine award for adapting the Couch Potato for Canadians. He included two stock market indexes instead of just one. McGugan suggested investors split their money into three equal parts: a Canadian government bond index, a U.S. stock index, and a Canadian stock index. Back-tested to 1976, rebalancing such a portfolio would have beaten the returns of a pure Canadian stock index, and with far less volatility.

Here's how it works. An investor puts 33 percent of her money into bonds, 33 percent into the U.S. stock index, and 33 percent into the Canadian stock index. If by year's end, her bonds now represent

40 percent of her total portfolio's value (which would occur if stocks had fallen), she would sell some of her bond index, adding the proceeds to one or both of her stock indexes. Doing so realigns her portfolio with its original allocation.

She could also rebalance with monthly or quarterly investment purchases without selling anything. If her bonds rise above 33 percent of her total, she could add fresh money (from her salary) into one or both of her stock indexes. If her U.S. stock index rises the next month, while her Canadian stock index and bonds remain flat, she could add money (again, from her salary) to either Canadian stocks or bonds. The idea is to keep the portfolio aligned with the goal allocation.

In Table 9.4 you can see how a Canadian Couch Potato portfolio would have performed between 1976 and 2013 with no fresh money added.

Depending on the time period, sometimes rebalancing with stocks and bonds enhances returns, compared to a pure stock portfolio. Other

Table 9.4   Growth of $10,000 Invested in the Canadian Couch Potato Portfolio with No Money Added, 1976–2013

Year-End	Couch Potato Portfolio	Canadian Stock Index
1976	$11,835	$10,014
1977	$12,546	$12,097
1978	$14,501	$15,570
1979	$17,211	$22,366
1980	$20,945	$28,878
1981	$19,546	$25,711
1982	$24,314	$26,561
1983	$29,842	$36,189
1984	$32,322	$35,041
1985	$41,832	$43,481
1986	$47,521	$46,999
1987	$48,222	$49,365
1988	$52,546	$54,402
1989	$63,354	$65,511
1990	$60,074	$53,366
1991	$73,000	$61,528
1992	$79,342	$60,162
1993	$96,715	$79,122

(continued)

Table 9.   (*continued*)

Year-End	Couch Potato Portfolio	Canadian Stock Index
1994	$95,648	$78,353
1995	$118,430	$89,030
1996	$143,034	$113,373
1997	$176,435	$129,326
1998	$204,874	$126,258
1999	$230,713	$165,003
2000	$239,507	$175,821
2001	$226,772	$152,475
2002	$206,497	$132,434
2003	$231,829	$166,514
2004	$251,659	$189,122
2005	$232,912	$272,507
2006	$316,345	$318,887
2007	$333,184	$349,340
2008	$256,019	$234,232
2009	$309,481	$314,948
2010	$348,135	$369,308
2011	$348,209	$336,698
2012	$377,915	$359,986
2013	$432,977	$405,638
Average Annual Return	10.42%	10.23%

SOURCES: Ian McGugan, Duncan Hood, and Ian Froats, "Classic Couch Potato Portfolio: Historical Performance Tables," *MoneySense*. Accessed May 7, 2014. http%3A%2F%2Fwww.moneysense .ca%2Finvest%2Fclassic-couch-potato-portfolio-historical-performance-tables; "IShares ETF Performances," iShares Canada, April 5, 2006. Accessed May 7, 2014. http://ca.ishares.com/product_info/fund/performance/XIC.htm.

times it lags. But two things are certain. Diversified, rebalanced portfolios increase stability over pure stock portfolios. And if investment costs are low, they distribute good long-term returns.

Bonds Relative to Age and Risk

There's a rule of thumb suggesting your bond allocation should reflect your age. While it's a broad generality, it holds merit. As a 44-year-old, my personal portfolio has roughly 40 percent in bonds.

But consider your personal circumstance. If I were working in Canada and eligible for a school district's defined benefit pension, I would prefer to have only 25 percent of my money in bonds. I could afford to take higher risks, assuming my pension would have bondlike stability.

What If You're Falling Behind?

Investors arriving late to the investment game or trying to recover from the ravaging fees of an offshore pension sometimes consider taking higher risks to recoup lost time. But they shouldn't.

Assume an investor shuns bonds. If she retired at the end of 2007 with a U.S. stock portfolio, her money would have fallen 37 percent in 2008. A portfolio split evenly between U.S. stocks and bonds (for example) would have fallen just 16 percent.

Stock market drops are great for young people. But they're nightmares for undiversified retirees. While young investors can capitalize on falling stock markets by investing at lower prices, retirees must do the opposite. They require their investment proceeds to cover living costs. So they're selling.

If global stock markets collapse and remain low for years—which can certainly happen—retirees without bonds could be selling at a loss, year after year. Increasing a portfolio's risk to compensate for lost time is hardly worth the gamble.

Profiting from Panic—Stock Market Crash 2008–2009

When stock markets fall, many people panic and sell, sending stocks to lower levels. Dispassionate investors, however, lay foundations for future profits. My personal portfolio was far larger just two years after the financial crisis, compared with its level before the crisis scuttled the markets. Keeping my portfolio aligned with my desired allocation of stocks and bonds was the key.

I started 2008 (before the stock market crash) with bonds representing 35 percent of my total portfolio. When stocks fell I was thrilled, continuing to add monthly salary savings to my stock market indexes.

Unfortunately, despite buying stocks every month during the crash, I still couldn't get my stock allocation back to 65 percent of my total. By early 2009, my portfolio had far more allocated to bonds than to stocks.

As a result, I sold bonds in early 2009, realigning the portfolio to my desired allocation.

Naturally, I hoped the markets would remain low. But they didn't. As the stock markets began recovering later that year, I switched tactics again and bought nothing but bonds for more than a year. I was low on bonds because I had sold bonds to buy stocks, and my stocks were leapfrogging in value. Before long, my stock allocation dominated the portfolio. At that point, I even had to sell some of my stock indexes to add to my bonds.

This kind of rebalancing is common practice among university endowment funds and pension funds.

There's no magic formula to rebalancing a portfolio; don't get sucked into minutiae. Frequent rebalancing won't necessarily earn better returns than rebalancing annually on Elvis's birthday. Choose a date to rebalance and stick to it.

Owning the World

Purchasing a global stock market index provides the world's broadest stock exposure. Such products are fabulous portfolio building blocks comprising stocks weighted by global capitalization. Imagine, for example, owning every single stock on the planet. You're the grand poobah owning everything. If you sold every stock in 2013, you would have had $54.6 trillion in cash. What percentage of that money would have come from each country's stock market?

Answering this question provides a global capitalization breakdown. The United States represents roughly 48 percent of global capitalization, meaning 48 percent of the proceeds you would receive (after selling every stock on the planet) would come from the United States.

Vanguard's global stock market exchange-traded index fund (which I'll show how to buy in later chapters) comprises 48 percent U.S. stocks and roughly 13 percent emerging market stocks, with the remainder split among other developed world markets in proportion to their global capitalization.

Owning the world through a global index might make you feel like Julius Caesar, but you shouldn't neglect your own backyard. The Canadian stock market, for example, makes up less than 5 percent of global capitalization. Consequently, a global index has very little Canadian exposure. But if you'll eventually repatriate to Canada (or any other country), exposure to your home country market is important. After all, it represents the currency in which you'll pay your future bills.

Where Do You Plan to Retire?

Americans should have a nice chunk of U.S. exposure if they plan to retire in the United States. Canadians, Australians, Brits, Europeans, Singaporeans, or any other nationality with an established stock market should do likewise with their home country market.

Keeping it simple, you could split your stock market money between your home country index and a global index.

For example, a 30-year-old British investor could have a portfolio consisting of 30 percent government bonds, 35 percent global stock index, and 35 percent British stock index.

An American's portfolio composition would be different: 30 percent bond index and 70 percent global stock index.

You may be wondering where the U.S. stock market fits into the 30/70 portfolio. A truly global stock index contains roughly 48 percent U.S. stocks. As a result, no separate U.S. index would be required.

If you're making monthly investment purchases, you need to look at your home country stock index and your global stock index, and determine which one has done better over the previous month. You'll know by looking at your account statement and comparing it with the previous month's report. When you figure it out, add newly invested money to the index that hasn't done as well, to keep your account close to your desired allocation. Remember that if each stock index soared over the previous month, you would add fresh money to your bond index.

What do most people do? You guessed it. Metaphorically speaking, they sign long-term contracts to empty their wallets each morning into the trash bin—buying more of the high-performing index and less of the underperforming index. Over an investment lifetime, such behavior can cost hundreds of thousands of dollars.

Please note that I'm not talking about chasing individual stocks or individual foreign markets into the gutter. For example, just because the share price of company Random X has fallen, this doesn't mean investors should throw good money after bad, thinking it's a great deal just because it has dropped in value. Who knows what's going to happen to Random X?

Likewise, you take a large risk buying an index focusing on a single foreign country, such as Chile, Brazil, or China. Who really knows what's going to happen to those markets over the next 30 years? They might do really well. But it's better to spread your risk and go with a global stock market index (if you want foreign exposure). With it, you'll have exposure to older world economies such as England, France, and Germany, as well as younger, fast-growing economies like China, India, Brazil, and Thailand. Just remember to rebalance. If the global stock market index outperforms your domestic index, don't chase the global index with fresh money. If your domestic stock index and the global stock index both shoot skyward, add fresh money to your bond index.

Investors with portfolios tilted heavily toward emerging markets (e.g., India, Brazil, China) take massive global capitalization risk. Emerging markets make up roughly 13 percent of global market value. So it makes little sense for most investors to have more than 13 percent of their portfolios in emerging market stocks.

If you're convinced such markets will provide massive future returns based on their economic growth, temper those expectations. As mentioned in Chapter 3, data on emerging market returns reveal they've underperformed developed markets since 1985. They don't underperform every year or every decade. But since records have been kept, their less than stellar performances have surprised many.

So why bother with emerging market stocks? The future is always uncertain; performance from emerging market stocks may eventually overtake their developed market counterparts. They have had plenty of time to do so, and have largely disappointed. But anything can happen.

The Chinese market is an interesting example. At times, its results are scorching, gaining hundreds of percentage points over short periods. But it usually follows with flame-throwers to investors' butts.

While emerging market stocks could do very well in the future, it's important not to reach too far beyond their globally capitalized footprint. Therefore, maximize their exposure to 13 percent (or less) of your portfolio's total value.

Are You Retiring in an Emerging Market Country?

Those retiring to an emerging market country should remember a few things. Emerging markets tend to be volatile. Their stocks can fall dramatically. Inflation in such countries can run like a pack of Kenyans. Depending on economic stability, currencies can plummet. For this reason, if you plan to retire to a developing country, consider lighter exposure to its stock market. Here's an example for a 30-year-old who plans to retire eventually in Thailand:

30% bond index
50% global stock index
20% Thai (or Southeast Asian) stock market index

And another, for someone choosing Brazil:

30% bond index
50% global stock index
20% Brazilian (or Latin American) stock market index

Here are some sample portfolios for 60-year-old investors retiring in the following countries. Note the increased bond allocations, closely reflecting the investors' age.

Retiring in China
55% bond index
30% global stock index
15% Chinese stock index

Retiring in Malaysia
55% bond index
30% global stock index
15% Malaysian (or Southeast Asian) stock index

Whatever the allocation you choose, be consistent. Each year, rebalance to the goal allocation, increasing the bond allocation as you age.

Does This Sound Too Good to Be True?

When something sounds too good to be true, it usually is. Such is the case with the Couch Potato portfolio. While simple to administer, few people have the willpower. Human nature works full-time to derail sound investing plans. Nowhere is this more evident than with the questions I receive on my blog.

Sometimes after making an investment purchase, I write a post explaining what I bought and why. I follow a simple Couch Potato strategy: maintaining 40 percent bonds and 60 percent global stock indexes. But a consistent theme rings true. Many of my readers are tempted to speculate based on an expert's opinion online, on television, in the newspaper, or on the radio.

"I read that it's a bad time to invest in bonds."
"Some guy on CNBC says U.S. stocks are going to crash."
"I just read a report suggesting emerging markets are set to soar."
"Why invest in a global index when Europe's in the poop?"

Most forecasts prove wrong. Without capacities to ignore financial puffery, many investors fail. Financial news agencies and journalists are always looking for a piece to pen. Journalists failing to promote urgency jeopardize their jobs.

Because the media tries pulling you by the privates, successful investing requires a strong anesthetic. You're better off blind, deaf, and numb. By rebalancing a portfolio on a predetermined schedule, you'll always be buying a little when others are selling, and selling a little when others are buying.

If you're still up to the emotional challenge, super. There are, however, two additional strategies worth considering before taking the plunge. Much like the Couch Potato portfolio, they use low-cost indexes. They also utilize rebalancing. The first, based on back-tested studies, may be the world's most stable portfolio. It exceeded 9 percent a year from 1972 to 2013; its worst performance was a mere drop of −4.1 percent in 1981. It's called the Permanent Portfolio. And it's outlined in the following chapter.

Chapter 10

The Permanent Portfolio: Growth without Risk

Many myths were once accepted: The earth is flat. Touching a toad will give you warts. Gold is a great investment.

I hope the last one caught your attention. Because gold once served as a trading currency, many people think it's a great money-maker. Imagine your great-grandfather having a hoard of gold equal in value to the purchase price of his house back in the 1920s. He wills the cache to a future great-grandchild: the one most resembling Gertrude Stein. Fortunately (or not) your family declares you the spitting image.

You accept the nomination, figuring if your great-grandfather had enough gold to purchase a house in the 1920s, you could likely buy a small town with the proceeds today. It's good this story isn't true. If it were, you couldn't buy a single home with the proceeds. Despite its lore, gold is a pathetic long-term investment, underperforming stocks, real estate, and bonds, not to mention (perhaps) Gertrude Stein's first editions.

Gold in Isolation Is a Total Loser

According to Wharton Business School professor Jeremy Siegel, if $1 were invested in gold in 1801, it would be worth roughly $55 by 2014.

The same $1 invested in the average U.S. stock would exceed $11 million.[1]

Okay—so gold's a butt dragger. But it's more stable than stocks, right? Perhaps not. Between 1971 and 2014, gold's price fell during 16 calendar years. U.S. stocks, in contrast, dropped just 10 times. Gold had eight annual plunges exceeding 10 percent; stocks had six.[2]

Does this mean you shouldn't buy gold? Unfortunately, most pundits and advisors recommend the stuff before a big gold crash. It intoxicated investors in 1979, rising 125.6 percent. Two years later it plunged—taking nearly 25 years to fully recover. Many hapless folks bought gold in late 1979 and in 1980, just because it had recently risen.

Most people (including many financial advisors) follow crowds, predictions, and recent performers. Gold became the asset du jour in 2011 as well, shortly after its price increased 24 percent in 2009 and 29.3 percent in 2010. The average investor, however, boarded gold's rocket ship while it ran on fumes.[3] Institutional investors sold, dropping gold 37 percent just two years after its 2011 high.

Woeful tales from the average investor sound much like a country western song where the guy loses his pickup, his girl, and his dog. But with a disciplined strategy taking less than an hour each year, you could build what might be the most stable portfolio in the world. It's called the Permanent Portfolio. And ironically, gold is one of its building blocks.

A Disco-Era Brainchild from a Twentieth-Century Socrates

The Permanent Portfolio had just three losing years between 1972 and 2012. The worst drop was −4.1 percent in 1981. It averaged 9.6 percent per year over the 40-year period and would have turned $10,000 into $429,041 by 2013. Created by the late Harry Browne, it's a disco-era brainchild from a twentieth-century Socrates.

Socrates wandered around ancient Athens interviewing people in search of wisdom. But he found none. Intelligent people existed, yes, but what they didn't know far exceeded what they did know. Browne announced something similar in the 1970s. When trying to predict investment directions, nobody knows squat. Based on studies of financial forecasts (annually compiled by CXO Advisory), the guy was right.[4]

The Permanent Portfolio comprises four asset classes in equal proportions: gold, bonds, cash, and stocks. In later chapters, I'll show how to invest this way using exchange-traded funds (ETFs). But first, have a look in Table 10.1 at how $10,000 would have grown if invested in the Permanent Portfolio between 1971 and 2012.

This Great Portfolio Will Never Be Popular (But It Should Be!)

This portfolio has never been popular. And it never will be. No matter when you're reading this, there will always be reasons not to split your money evenly among cash, stocks, bonds, and gold. Perhaps gold will be too high, or stocks will be mired in a decade-long slump, or bond yields will be scraping the ocean floor.

In 1980, for example, gold hit nearly $850 an ounce. Putting a quarter of a portfolio in gold (which had climbed 2,025 percent in the prior

Table 10.1   The Permanent Portfolio Growth, 1971–2012

Year	Annual Returns of Permanent Portfolio	Growth with Permanent Portfolio
1971		$10,000
1972	18.6	$11,860
1973	14.4	$13,563
1974	14.4	$15,517
1975	6.8	$16,578
1976	11.8	$18,530
1977	5.1	$19,468
1978	11.9	$21,781

(continued)

Table 10.1   (*continued*)

Year	Annual Returns of Permanent Portfolio	Growth with Permanent Portfolio
1979	39.3	$30,334
1980	14.2	$34,636
1981	−4.1	$33,206
1982	23.6	$41,033
1983	3.5	$42,457
1984	3.1	$43,783
1985	20.2	$52,625
1986	18.1	$62,162
1987	6.4	$66,167
1988	4.2	$68,972
1989	12.9	$77,900
1990	1.6	$79,138
1991	13.0	$89,398
1992	4.3	$93,274
1993	12.7	$105,124
1994	−2.6	$102,407
1995	19.6	$122,526
1996	4.8	$128,387
1997	7.4	$137,875
1998	10.6	$152,506
1999	4.4	$159,159
2000	3.0	$163,997
2001	0.4	$164,643
2002	7.2	$176,451
2003	13.9	$200,948
2004	6.3	$213,584
2005	8.0	$230,735
2006	10.7	$255,522
2007	13.3	$289,500
2008	−0.7	$287,415
2009	10.5	$317,651
2010	14.5	$363,655
2011	10.5	$401,903
2012	6.8	$429,041
Average	**9.6%**	

SOURCE: Craig Rowland, "Permanent Portfolio Historical Returns," *Crawling Road.* Accessed May 7, 2014. www.crawlingroad.com/blog/2008/12/22/permanent-portfolio-historical-returns/.

nine years) might have looked crazy. But that's what the Permanent Portfolio allocates. Investing another 25 percent in U.S. stocks looked equally futile for the opposite reason. The S&P 500 index was lower than it had been 15 years previously. Many pundits said stocks were for suckers.

Nobody *knew* gold was going to plunge. Nor did they know that stocks would soar. Those investing in the Permanent Portfolio didn't have to worry; they owned a slice of each: gold, stocks, bonds, and cash. Whatever soared would eventually be sold; whatever plunged would eventually be bought.

The Permanent Portfolio prevailed with plucky returns for the decade. It averaged 10.36 percent between 1980 and 1989.

By 1990, stocks were rocketing. The Permanent Portfolio, in contrast, looked out of step. With 75 percent in bonds, cash, and gold (and only 25 percent in stocks), it resembled a relic from a paranoid era.

But in the decade ahead, to 1999, it averaged 7.7 percent. It doubled in value and dropped just once: down 2.6 percent in 1994.

Few again would have given the Permanent Portfolio serious consideration in 2000. Stocks had soared the previous two decades. Most investors thought they would continue to do so. Cash offered paltry interest, and gold had lost 70 percent of its value since 1980. But the following decade (2000–2009) saw Harry Browne's creation average nearly 7 percent a year. It followed with a 14.5 percent encore in 2010, 10.5 percent in 2011, and 6.8 percent in 2012. The portfolio recorded just one losing year between 2000 and 2012. It lost 0.7 percent in 2008, when the S&P 500 dropped 37 percent.

Here's a sample $100,000 portfolio:

$25,000 Bonds
$25,000 Stocks
$25,000 Gold
$25,000 Cash
$100,000 Total

As Craig Rowland and J. M. Lawson explain in their excellent book, *The Permanent Portfolio* (John Wiley & Sons, 2012), the investments would normally require rebalancing once every couple of years. The back-tested results in Table 10.1 came from rebalancing back to the original allocation only when one asset class exceeds 35 percent of the total, or when one slips to 15 percent of the portfolio's total composition.

For example, if gold drops, bonds stagnate, and stocks soar, the portfolio might look like this after a couple of years:

> $25,000 Bonds (23.36% of total)
> $38,000 Stocks (35.51% of total)
> $18,000 Gold (16.82% of total)
> $26,000 Cash (24.29% of total)
> **$107,000 Total**

In this case, one of the asset classes (stocks) would exceed 35 percent of the total. To realign the portfolio with the original allocation, some stocks and cash would need to be allocated into gold. While simple enough, commentators in newspapers and on the Internet (if you go searching) will be announcing gold's funeral. "Buying gold now, after its recent decline, would be like getting into bed with a corpse." Yuck, gross, and scary.

Their reasoning will always sound logical, of course. And you'll have a choice: to follow the Permanent Portfolio platform, which has historically worked, or to succumb to a method that typically doesn't—following the media's expert du jour.

If you're a working expatriate, you'll be adding regular sums to your portfolio each year, so you may not have to manually rebalance. As with the Couch Potato portfolio, you could simply add money from your monthly savings to the underperforming asset. To figure this out, all you need is your brokerage statement. Here's an example:

Account Statement: February 1, 2017
> $98,000 Bonds (25% of total)
> $98,000 Stocks (25% of total)
> $98,000 Gold (25% of total)
> $98,000 Cash (25% of total)
> **$392,000 Total**

One month later, your portfolio might look like this.

Account Statement: March 1, 2017
$99,000 Bonds (25.56% of total)
$89,000 Stocks (22.98% of total)
$101,000 Gold (26.08% of total)
$98,200 Cash (25.36% of total)
$387,200 Total

Because stocks would have been your worst-performing asset class the previous month, you would add fresh money to stocks. Don't worry if your purchase nudges your stock allocation slightly above the 25 percent threshold. Just consistently purchase the worst-performing asset class each month.

If all four asset classes have fallen in price (which isn't likely), purchase what fell the most.

Why Does It Work?

The Permanent Portfolio works because it's diversified across asset classes that often move in opposite directions. And like the Couch Potato portfolio, its rebalancing allows investors to be greedy when others are fearful. It won't make money every year, but almost—if history is an indicator.

Economically, just four configurations exist:

1. Prosperity
2. Deflation
3. Recession
4. Inflation

Prosperity is great for stocks and bonds. Characterized by rising productivity and optimism, prosperity leads many investors to pour money into the markets, perceiving even greater times ahead. Gold, in contrast, performs poorly under such circumstances. Popular among hoarders expecting to trade gold bars for bread during catastrophic economic meltdowns, gold buyers hibernate when the economy hums.

Deflation is much better for long-term bonds and cash. Stocks usually underperform as corporate profits get squeezed. Cash is king, as purchasing power increases each year with falling product prices. Stocks usually stink during deflationary periods, as does gold.

Recessions dampen most asset classes. But they're often short-lived. As the economy contracts, interest rates often rise, causing bonds to perform poorly. Gold and stocks often disappoint, leaving cash once again the portfolio's salvation.

Inflation is great for gold. When currency values diminish, fears for paper assets mount. Sometimes stocks do well under such conditions; sometimes they don't. But historically, gold has offered the greatest purchasing power protection when inflation rears its head.

While four economic conditions exist, you'll never predict what's coming next. Nor, with any degree of consistency, will anyone else. Owning everything, and lightening the load on a scorching asset class, has produced extremely stable results over time.

Note the comparative chart in Figure 10.1, showing the performance of the Permanent Portfolio versus U.S. stocks, bonds, cash, and gold. From 1971 to 2011, its performance compared favorably with stocks. But it wasn't nearly as volatile.

These results utilize a U.S. index for stocks. But investors could diversify further with a global stock index. Those from other countries may also want to utilize their own stock markets.

What Has It Done for Me Lately?

If you invest in the Permanent Portfolio and stocks soar 30 percent the following year, your money will lag the stock market's return. Even someone languishing in an expensive offshore pension could beat you for the year.

"I've made a mistake!" you might shriek. At this point, if you venture into the slippery world of stock market prognostications, almost certain failure lurks. You'll read about some hot new mutual fund earning triple-digit returns. You'll see scorching predictions for stocks ahead. And you'll read the "How I got rich on a single stock" stories seducing you to toss diversification into the gutter.

But fight such temptations. Whether you choose the Permanent Portfolio or the Couch Potato platform, stick to your plan. Jumping

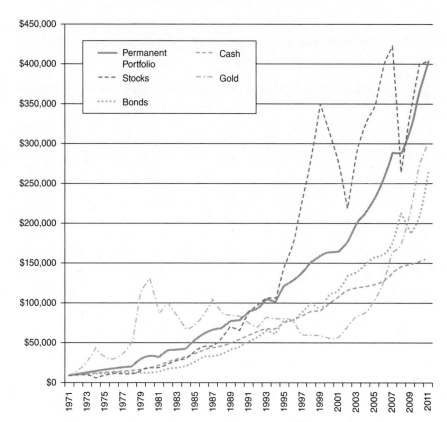

Figure 10.1 Permanent Portfolio Performance, 1971–2011

Source: Craig Rowland, "Permanent Portfolio Historical Returns," *Crawling Road*. Accessed May 7, 2014. www.crawlingroad.com/blog/2008/12/22/permanent-portfolio-historical-returns/. Reprinted with permission.

from one strategy to the next (and back when fortunes reverse) could have the same detrimental effects as buying high and selling low.

Before explaining exactly how to build such portfolios, I'll introduce you to one more strategy. It's a Couch Potato portfolio with a twist, using a concept called Fundamental Indexing.

Notes

1. JeremySiegel.com. Accessed July 2, 2014. http%3A%2F%2Fwww.jeremysiegel
   .com%2F.

2. Craig Rowland, "Permanent Portfolio Historical Returns," *Crawling Road*. Accessed May 7, 2014. www.crawlingroad.com/blog/2008/12/22/permanent-portfolio-historical-returns/.
3. Ibid.
4. "Guru Grades," CXO Advisory RSS. Accessed May 7, 2014. https://www.cxoadvisory.com/gurus/.

Chapter 11

Fundamental Indexing: Can We Build a Better Index Portfolio?

S ome academics suggest that traditional index funds can be beaten—not with actively managed funds (no professor is that nutty), but with fundamental indexes. (Fundamental Index is a registered trademark I'm using with permission from the firm Research Affiliates.)

Don't let the term *fundamental* freak you out. These indexes don't blow things up for heavenly harems. But they contrast with traditional indexes, which are capitalization (cap)-weighted. I'll explain the differences between each type of index with a basketball analogy.

Like Top Basketball Players Getting the Most Court Time

Imagine a basketball coach choosing which of his players will spend the most time on the court. He must utilize every player in each game, so he comes up with a simple solution: the biggest players get the most court time. Most of these players are also the best shooters and rebounders, so the simple strategy has merit.

If such a coach had a second career as an S&P 500 index fund builder for Vanguard, he would use a similar strategy, building an index that's cap-weighted. This means the largest stocks (many of which are also the most profitable) would be most emphasized. In other words, the money invested in a cap-weighted index fund would be allocated by quantity into the largest businesses by descending order of size.

Now imagine another basketball coach using the same players differently. Instead of giving the most court time to the biggest players, he objectively measures a combination of shooting accuracy, rebounding ability, and the highest percentage of muscle mass to coincide with playing time. Although he also has to use each player, he pushes the most court time onto players best fulfilling these metrics.

If this guy were given the role of building a fundamental index fund of S&P 500 stocks, he would ignore size, and put more of the fund's money into stocks with the greatest profits, dividends, and book values (business assets minus liabilities). Many of these companies would also be the largest, but not all of them. Instead of creating a cap-weighted index, his would be a fundamental index.

Cap-weighted and fundamental indexes are both based on mathematical formulas, in contrast to actively managed funds, which rely on speculating or forecasting.

But if a cap-weighted index emphasizes stocks in order of size, how do we measure how large or small a stock is? It's based on how much dough you would need if you were to buy every share of the whole business. In investment-speak, this total price is known as market capitalization. To determine it, we multiply a stock's share price by the number of shares available.

As I write, Walmart trades at $75 per share. When multiplying its share price by the number of shares existing, we get $244 billion. This is how much money you would need if you were to pay cash for the stock of the entire business.

To find out Exxon Mobil's total price, you would again multiply all of its shares by the share price. If Exxon Mobil trades at $97 and we multiply this by all available shares, we get a business value exceeding $400 billion. You would need $156 billion more to buy every share of Exxon Mobil, compared to every share of Walmart. Both companies are massive, but Exxon Mobil is larger, so it would get more playing exposure in a cap-weighted index.

Now assume you were a company like Vanguard. To build a cap-weighted S&P 500 index fund, you would need to put more money into stocks that were larger (with a higher market capitalization) than you would into companies that were smaller. Similar to your emphasis on big basketball players, you would put more money in Exxon Mobil than Walmart. Here's how each respective company's stock price movement would affect the index.

Assume 499 of the S&P 500's stocks didn't budge in price this week. If Exxon Mobil shares rose 50 percent over the duration, the index would slightly rise.

If Walmart, instead of Exxon Mobil, rose by 50 percent, with all remaining 499 stocks stagnant, the index would also rise—but not as much as if Exxon Mobil had risen 50 percent instead.

The S&P 500 weights its stocks in direct proportion to their market capitalization. The bigger the business (Exxon Mobil is bigger than Walmart), the higher the influence on the index's price level.

But the basketball coach turned fundamental index fund builder wouldn't want Exxon Mobil as his most emphasized stock unless it were also the most profitable, based on measurements of profitability, dividends, and book values.

Consider Apple when it first became the United States' biggest company in 2012. Was it also the country's most profitable business? It wasn't. Yet it would have cost more money to buy the entire company (share price × total shares) than to buy any other U.S. company. In a cap-weighted S&P 500 index, more of the money would have been resting on Apple than on any other individual stock. But this wouldn't be the case with a fundamentally constructed index. The most profitable business (not the largest) would most influence the index.

Cap-weighted indexes are top-heavy in popular stocks. Unfortunately, blind popularity often drives prices to unwarranted levels. During popular runs (which could last many years), a hip stock's price could rise faster than its business earnings. Eventually, this spells trouble, and the share price either stagnates or falls to realign itself with its true economic level.

Usually, a country's 10 largest businesses go on to underperform the average stock—like big basketball players tending to become slower and less effective on the court over time.[1] Fundamental indexes, however, are different. Their most heavily weighted stocks are rarely the largest or the most popular. Instead, they're shooting above their pay scale.

Index Funds That Appear to Beat the Market

Researchers Robert D. Arnott, Jason C. Hsu, and John M. West reported in their book, *The Fundamental Index* (John Wiley & Sons, 2008) that from 1962 to 2007, the S&P 500 averaged 10.3 percent per year, compared to a back-tested result of 12.3 percent for a fundamental index containing the same stocks, but in different proportions.[2] Compounded over a 45-year period, such a difference with $10,000 invested would exceed a million dollars.

$10,000 invested at 10.3 percent would grow to $823,944.
$10,000 invested at 12.3 percent would grow to $1,848,647.

Investment Legend Likens Them to Witchcraft

But fundamental indexes cost more, so not everybody loves them. John Bogle, the Vanguard Group's founder and father of index investing, argues the higher costs associated with maintaining a fundamental index would hurt investment returns.[3] He even likened them to witchcraft, where product marketing has triumphed over substance.

Australian researchers Anup K. Basu and Brigitte Forbes disagree. They published a study taking issue with Mr. Bogle's assertion. After cost estimates, they found that fundamental indexes beat the cap-weighted Australian index during every rolling five-year period between April

1985 and March 2010. The fundamental index advantage, over a cap-weighted index varied between 2.63 percent and 4.88 percent annually.[4]

Would fundamental indexing work in your home country market? Arnott, Hsu, and West would likely say yes. They compared cap-weighted index returns with fundamentally weighted counterparts from 1984 to 2007. Comparing returns in 23 countries, only one case existed (Switzerland) where the fundamental index fell short. The annual results are shown in Table 11.1.[5]

Just as interesting is what the researchers discovered about international market indexes. If a fundamental index containing S&P 500 stocks

Table 11.1   Fundamental Indexes versus Cap-Weighted Indexes, 1984–2007

Country	RAFI Fundamental Index	MSCI Cap-Weighted Index
Australia	16.3%	14.0%
Austria	17.8%	12.5%
Belgium	15.5%	14.0%
Canada	13.4%	10.7%
Denmark	12.7%	11.2%
Finland (starting 1998)	15.8%	14.7%
France	16.9%	12.9%
Germany	13.8%	10.9%
Greece (starting 1989)	21.0%	19.1%
Hong Kong	22.2%	18.6%
Ireland (starting 1998)	17.6%	9.6%
Italy	15.4%	13.1%
Japan	7.1%	4.3%
Netherlands	14.0%	12.8%
New Zealand (starting 1998)	7.2%	6.8%
Norway	17.5%	13.3%
Portugal (starting 1989)	13.2%	9.2%
Singapore (starting 1989)	13.1%	9.6%
Spain (starting 1989)	16.8%	13.7%
Sweden	17.1%	15.0%
Switzerland	11.6%	12.0%
United Kingdom	15.0%	12.1%
United States	14.4%	12.4%
23-Country Average	**16.5%**	**13.9%**

SOURCE: Robert D. Arnott, Jason C. Hsu, and John M. West, *The Fundamental Index: A Better Way to Invest* (Hoboken, NJ: John Wiley & Sons, 2008), 123.

can outperform its cap-weighted equivalent, could a fully international fundamental index do the same?

Global Fundamental Indexes Might Shelter Us from Bubbles

For example, as with individual stocks, some markets grow far faster than their economic footprint should warrant. Japan serves as a prime example. In the late 1990s, its stock market index was as high as a junkie at a cocaine carnival. At its peak, it represented 51 percent of the total developed world market capitalization. Did Japanese businesses create 51 percent of first-world product sales? Not even close. The country rode the wave of a ridiculous bubble—one it has yet to fully recover from.

A fundamental world stock market index wouldn't weight countries in proportion to their market capitalizations. So it wouldn't suffer traumatically if an individual country's index (as in the case of Japan) got hammered back to Earth. Instead, a fundamental global index would weight and rebalance itself in proportion to the strength of each country's business metrics. The more profitable the businesses are, based on their global impact, the more weighting that country's market would have on such an index.

Although no such index existed when Arnott, Hsu, and West published their book, they guessed such a product would boost returns by an additional 3.3 percent each year over a cap-weighted equivalent. So they created one for retail investors.

Called the PS FTSE RAFI All-World 3000 index, they launched it in December 2007. Its five-year return averaged 14.98 percent to December 2013. Its cap-weighted counterpart averaged 12.47 percent.[6]

Emerging Markets Show the Greatest Difference

Arnott and company found even greater differences comparing back-tested results of fundamental indexes versus their cap-weighted equivalents in emerging markets. Such markets can be extremely volatile. Consequently, many fall in price far below their economic footprint. Others defy gravity like helium balloons. Such misalignments don't last forever. As with individual stocks, disparities get corrected by invisible hands, forcing prices to realign with economic footprints.

From 1994 to 2007, Arnott, Hsu, and West found that a fundamental emerging market index would have averaged 19.4 percent per year, compared to just 8.7 percent annually for a cap-weighted equivalent. With $10,000 invested, the difference would be huge.

$10,000 invested at 19.4 percent for 13 years would grow to $100,243.

$10,000 invested at 8.7 percent for 13 years would grow to $29,579.

But back-tested results are one thing. How about a purchasable product?

Russell Investments provides such an index. Its 10-year return averaged 16.95 percent (measured in U.S. dollars) to October 31, 2013.[7] In contrast, the iShares emerging market index averaged 12.25 percent for the period.[8]

Fundamental indexes, however, won't always win. For example, iShares offers a Canadian market fundamental index (among others). Between its February 2006 inception and November 2013, it gained a total of 56.74 percent, lagging the 64.86 percent for Canada's iShares S&P/TSX cap-weighted index.[9]

Aren't These Just Actively Managed Products?

You might think fundamental indexes are just cheaper versions of actively managed funds. They aren't. They're dispassionately rebalanced based on measurements of economic footprints—profits, book values, and dividends. Active managers speculate. They guess which company shares are ready to rock, and such managers command very high salaries for doing so. Unfortunately, their salaries aren't justified. The vast majority underperform their benchmark indexes.

While slightly more expensive than traditional indexes, fundamental products are still cheap compared to actively managed funds. And they've reaped impressive results.

In the chapters ahead, I'll show how people of different nationalities could invest in such products. But choose your method of investing first.

Will it be a traditional Couch Potato portfolio, a Permanent Portfolio, or a Couch Potato portfolio with a fundamental twist? All three strategies should work well over time. But, as mentioned throughout this book, don't try one out for a time before committing.

Never get influenced by the current performance du jour. Choose a methodology based on reason, evidence, and your personality. One-year, three-year, or five-year historical performances aren't predictive of the future. So don't be influenced by them.

Notes

1. Andrew Hallam, "With Stocks, Bigger Isn't Better," *Canadian Business*, October 15, 2013. Accessed May 7, 2014. www.canadianbusiness.com/investing/with-stocks-bigger-isnt-better/.
2. Robert D. Arnott, Jason C. Hsu, and John M. West, *The Fundamental Index: A Better Way to Invest* (Hoboken, NJ: John Wiley & Sons, 2008), 19.
3. "Arnott Index Derided by Bogle as Witchcraft Beats Vanguard Fund," Bloomberg.com, June 2, 2011. Accessed May 7, 2014. www.bloomberg.com/news/2011-06-02/arnott-index-derided-by-bogle-as-witchcraft-beats-vanguard-fund.html.
4. Anup K. Basu and Brigette Forbes, "Does Fundamental Indexation Lead to Better Risk-Adjusted Returns? New Evidence from Australian Securities Exchange," *Accounting & Finance Journal* (January 2013). Wiley Online Library. Accessed July 2, 2014. http://onlinelibrary.wiley.com/doi/10.1111/acfi.12016/full.
5. Arnott, Hsu, and West, *Fundamental Index*, 123.
6. FE Trustnet Offshore. Accessed July 2, 2014. www.trustnetoffshore.com/Factsheets/Factsheet.aspx?fundCode=B5FO8&univ=E.
7. Russell Fundamental Index Series | Russell Investments. Accessed May 7, 2014. www.russell.com/indexes/americas/indexes/fact-sheet.page?ic=D41459.
8. iShares ETF Performance. Accessed May 7, 2014. www.ishares.com/us/products/239637/ishares-msci-emerging-markets-etf.
9. Andrew Hallam, "Is It Worth Making the Shift to Fundamental Indexes?" *Globe and Mail*. Accessed May 7, 2014. www.theglobeandmail.com/globe-investor/investment-ideas/strategy-lab/index-investing/is-it-worth-making-the-shift-to-fundamental-indexes/article11446205/.

Chapter 12

Capable Investment Advisors with a Conscience

C ome on, admit it—you're better looking than the average person, right? If you drive a car, you probably think you drive better than most behind the wheel. Chances are you also think you're smarter than average. Unfortunately, peer-assessed reviews of your desirability, car-driving ability, or intelligence could burst your bubble.

Likewise, many people overestimate their ability to manage a portfolio of index funds. Don't get me wrong. It's a simple thing to do. But most people can't do it effectively.

When the world is high on a profitable asset class, most mortals have a tough time selling portions when it's time to rebalance. Equally difficult is embracing a reeking asset class when the rest of the world is shunning it. I'm not going to lie. Controlling emotional reactions to a gyrating portfolio is an investor's greatest test.

Ask yourself whether you really have what it takes.

Most index investors underperform the returns of the very indexes they hold. It's a bizarre paradox. They buy what's hot, shun what's not, and don't rebalance. After sourcing data from Morningstar, Dalbar, and the Bogle Financial Markets Research Center, investment management firm Index Fund Advisors (IFA) found that the average index investor without an advisor earned just 82.7 percent of what the investor should have made over a 30-year period. In this case, if a diversified rebalanced portfolio of index funds should have grown to $1 million, the typical index investor would end up with $827,000 instead. Caving to internal and external pressures would cost them $173,000 (see Figure 12.1).[1]

The same research suggests those using actively managed funds do worse, earning just 36.75 percent of what a disciplined portfolio of indexes would earn over three decades. So that's a leaking bucket. Fortunately, investors can hire financial advisors to build portfolios of index funds for them.

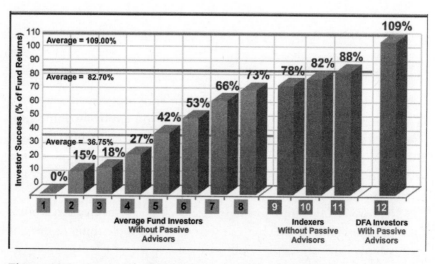

Figure 12.1   Percentage of Market Returns Earned by Actively Managed Mutual Fund and Index Investors, with and without Advisors

SOURCE: Index Fund Advisors (IFA), using data from Morningstar, Dalbar, *Money* magazine, and the Bogle Financial Markets Research Center.

Do You Have a Ninja's Discipline?

If you're emotionally wired like a ninja warrior, you shouldn't have any problem managing your own portfolio of indexes. But consider the following questions:

- Do you ever overeat?
- Did you binge drink in college because your friends did?
- Have you ever tried a cigarette?
- Do you eat foods you know aren't healthy?
- Do you worry about stock market crashes?
- Do you ever consider acting on financial predictions?

If you answered yes to any of those questions, congratulations—you're normal. But investors capable of rebalancing a portfolio of index funds are anything but. Don't feel misled. The process *is* simple. But when markets gyrate or plunge, it's a tough challenge.

Qualities of a Great Financial Advisor

For this reason, scrupulous advisors building and managing a client's indexed portfolio can easily be worth the fees they charge. Unfortunately, such advisors are a bit like ninjas themselves. They exist, according to legend, but you've probably never seen one.

They won't stomp into your place of employment or cold-call you looking for business. Most don't advertise. They're stealthlike.

I can hear what you're thinking. Why would any financial advisor bypass massive commissions or mutual fund kickbacks to do the right thing? We shouldn't have to ask. Not every financial advisor succumbs to the dark side.

Some scrupulous advisors charge consultation fees, providing direction for a one-time cost. Others charge a low percentage of the portfolio's assets each year.

The Advisor Shouldn't Be Compensated by Commissions

Advisors charging commissions contend with a conflict of interest. Instead of providing the best products for clients, they may climb into bed with firms that satisfy their own needs. Some deal exclusively with a single mutual fund company for this very reason. One such company, Tie Care International, sells the American Fund family of actively managed products. To be fair, this firm is like Mother Teresa compared to the typical offshore pension seller. Tie Care doesn't charge annual account fees. The expense ratios (on the American Fund family products) are also very low. But by being charged 5.75 percent commissions on every investment purchase, investors must earn 6.1 percent the following year just to break even on the previously invested sum.

As Princeton economics professor and *Random Walk Down Wall Street* author Burton Malkiel says, "In no event should you ever buy a load fund (a fund with a commission fee). There's no point in paying for something if you can get it free."[2]

The Advisor Shouldn't Purchase Individual Stocks for Your Portfolio

Some advisors shun actively managed mutual funds, but claim they can pick individual stocks to beat the market. Don't fall for that. Most stock pickers underperform indexes over time. Remember, 70 percent of actively managed corporate pensions underperform the market.[3] I'm not talking about the offshore donkeys sold by firms like Generali and Friends Provident. Instead, I'm talking about stallions: corporate pensions unavailable to retail investors, charging razor-thin costs to firms like General Electric. If they can't beat the market, how can your high-cost retail broker?

Not only do stock-picking brokers underperform, but most fail to adequately diversify. Larry Swedroe, CBS MoneyWatch columnist and coauthor of *Think, Act, and Invest like Warren Buffett*, suggests that investors require at least 50 individual large-cap American stocks just to provide enough U.S. large-cap diversification.[4] That doesn't include midsize or small companies. According to Vanguard, its total U.S. stock market index contains more than 3,600 stocks, including large, medium-sized, and small company stocks (known as large cap, mid-cap, and small cap).

Full diversification, of course, isn't just limited to stocks of different sizes. It also includes international exposure. Unless your broker is going to add hundreds of foreign stocks, you won't receive a broad representation of the global markets. And because your advisor can't predict the movements of hundreds of different stocks from multiple countries, you're better off with indexes.

The Advisor Should Charge No More Than 1.25 Percent Each Year

Ensure that your prospective advisor charges 1.25 percent (or less) each year to manage your indexed portfolio. If an advisor charges as much as 1.25 percent, you should demand exceptional ongoing service. This would be a $1,250 annual charge on a $100,000 portfolio. As you've seen, costs add up. Paying 1.5 percent instead of 1.25 percent could cost tens of thousands of extra dollars over time when calculating the effects of compounding interest.

The Advisor Shouldn't Gamble

Speak to prospective advisors about their investment philosophy. Avoid advisors who alter portfolios based on economic predictions. They may sound sophisticated while referencing soothsaying economists, but don't fall for it. If forecasting (whether the advisor's or the firm's) is the order of operation, plug your ears and walk. Most economic predictions are wrong—making them very costly indeed.

The Advisor Shouldn't Buy High-Cost Indexes

Advisors can choose from a variety of index fund providers from which to build your portfolio. But insist they do so from Vanguard, Schwab, Dimensional Fund Advisors (DFA), or T. Rowe Price only. If they're using exchange-traded index funds (ETFs), insist on Vanguard, Schwab, iShares, Horizon, BetaShares, or PowerShares. A few other low-cost providers exist, but if your advisor can't build a portfolio with the ones I've named, you're dealing with a charlatan.

Investment Professionals worth Considering

Here are a few advisory firms that meet all of the aforementioned standards. It's a short list. But if you research further, you may find others.

Index Advisors for American Expats

Company Name: Noto Financial Planning
Minimum Account Size Requirement: $150,000 (U.S. dollars)
Contact E-mail: info@notofp.com
Tel. #: +1 (808) 638-2475

Years ago, the Campbell Soup Company stuck a boy's face on each of its cans. He represented wholesome goodness, and even today I can't get his image out of my mind when tucking into a bowl of mushroom soup.

Spend 10 minutes with Tony Noto and you might think you've found the adult manifestation of Campbell's wholesome image.

Tony Noto became a Certified Financial Planner (CFP) while living in Shanghai, China. He's also a CFA (Chartered Financial Analyst), making him one of the most financially educated expatriate advisors available. "When I began advising expats in Shanghai on their finances in 2008," says Tony, "all of the companies focused on selling insurance-linked investments. I started Noto Financial Planning to provide expatriates with an alternative: financial advice free from commission bias."

After living in China for eight years, he relocated to Hawaii, where he continues to specialize in expatriate financial planning for Americans. He accepts clients with a minimum of $150,000, charging 1 percent per year for investment management and financial planning. All portfolios utilize index funds. Tony charges less when account values exceed $750,000.

Unlike most financial advisors, he keeps his client base small. Doing so allows him to provide the highest level of personal attention. He meets with clients in person or via teleconferencing two to six times each year. His annual fee covers all aspects of financial planning: insurance, investment needs, U.S. tax planning, goal setting, and tuition for children's education.

For those not signing on as regular clients, he also offers consultations for expats. Many advisors offer a watered-down version for free. But such promises are often guises, snaring unwary investors into commission-driven products. Tony doesn't receive compensation from offshore pension firms, insurance companies, or mutual funds. With his expatriate experience, integrity, and credentials, he's a very sought-after advisor.

Company Name: Creveling & Creveling: Private Wealth Advisors
Minimum Account Size Requirement: $750,000 (U.S. dollars)
Website: www.crevelingandcreveling.com/
Contact Tel. #: (66) 2661 2716

Chad and Peggy Creveling are cut from the same solid cloth as Tony Noto. Based in Bangkok, the American couple both carry the Certified Financial Planner (CFP) designation. They're also Chartered Financial Analysts (CFAs) and previously worked as equity research analysts. "We mentor clients on an ongoing basis," explains Peggy, "usually communicating monthly during the first six to 12 months."

Instead of building a large client base, the Crevelings focus on a high level of continuing service. "Our client base is relatively small," says Chad, "but full-service planning is extremely time intensive."

"Many expats have partners of different nationalities," explains Peggy. "We keep abreast of international tax regulations, ensuring our clients can legally maximize their financial potential."

Chad says many expats also require coaching in order to save enough money. "Not only do we build indexed portfolios for our clients, but we assist them with a comprehensive plan. We help them monitor their income, expenditures, tax planning, and future retirement needs."

As of 2014, the Crevelings charge 1.2 percent on assets for accounts between $750,000 and $1 million. Above that threshold, fee percentages drop. In contrast, most offshore pensions cost three to four times that amount. Those selling such products are typically less qualified, and offer a diluted level of professional service.

Most of the Crevelings' clients are American. But they also offer consultations for clients of other nationalities.

Company Name: MASECO Private Wealth
Minimum Account Size Requirement: $1,000,000 (U.S. dollars)
Website: www.masecoprivatewealth.com
Contact Tel. #: (44) 207 043 0455
Limitation: For American expats in Great Britain

Americans living in Europe sometimes languish in a tax vice. Those in the United Kingdom, for example, must pay British and U.S. taxes on their American investments, once they've lived abroad for seven years or longer. UK-based Americans often marry spouses of different nationalities, complicating tax matters. MASECO specializes in such issues as it builds investment portfolios and provides full-service financial planning for American expats in Great Britain.

It's a niche market, for sure, but one with massive followings. Co-founder Josh Matthews explains: "We started the business in 2008, figuring demand would be high. In six years we've accumulated $870 million under management." Most of the firm's clients have between $1 million and $10 million invested.

The complicated tax structures involved when coupling the regulations of the United States and Great Britain have drawn a huge client following for the 30 employees and eight financial advisors at MASECO. Josh explains that many larger U.S.-based investment firms came to the United Kingdom to do much the same thing. But they soon abandoned that idea after recognizing the tax complexities. "It's a great marketplace, but very complicated. It's a disaster [for clients] if you don't get it right."

Fortunately, MASECO, which invests in DFA indexes for clients, does have it right.

MASECO charges a maximum 1.25 percent on assets for the first $500,000 invested, dropping its fees for subsequently larger sums. Those hoping to use the firm require a minimum $1 million investment.

Company: Index Fund Advisors, Inc. (IFA)
Minimum Account Size Requirement: $100,000 (U.S. dollars)
Website: www.ifa.com
Contact E-mail: info@ifa.com
Contact Tel. #: (1) 949-502-0050
U.S. Toll Free: 888-643-3133

Index Fund Advisors (IFA) has been advising clients and building index portfolios since 1999. The company had $2.2 billion in assets under management as of December 31, 2013. It stresses that investors should always seek fiduciaries that avoid conflicts of interest. As such, they recommend that members of your financial team should be independent of each other: a registered investment advisor (like IFA), an independent estate planning attorney, an independent CPA, and an independent insurance advisor. And it makes sense. Investment advisors, for example, who also act as insurance salespeople can be tempted to sell various financial products that pay them the most—while their clients get the shaft.

IFA founder Mark Hebner and the 40 employees at IFA service their clients and provide unique investor education through videos, articles, and books. IFA has designed a series of portfolios providing 86 years of simulated returns, which it demonstrates with calculators, tables, and dynamic charts.

IFA's investment strategy is based on academic research, including the work of Eugene Fama (2013 Nobel Prize in economics), Harry Markowitz (1990 Nobel Prize in economics), and highly respected academic Kenneth French. Its advisory fee starts at 0.9 percent annually for the first $500,000, with lower fees charged for larger accounts.

Company Name: RW Investment Strategies
Minimum Account Size Requirement: None
Contact E-mail: robert@rwinvestmentstrategies.com
Tel. #: (1) 443-896-4123

Robert Wasilewski may be one of the world's most unusual investment advisors. His goal is to ultimately fire himself. And most of the time he does.

Believing that anyone can build and maintain a portfolio of low-cost exchange-traded index funds (ETFs), he works as an advisor and educator. "I offer three services: hourly consulting at $150 an hour, investment management, and investment management with the goal of the client taking over investment management after three months or six months. I charge 0.4 percent to manage assets less than $1 million, and 0.3 percent for assets above that. There's an additional $150 quarterly charge for accounts I manage."

Of course, some of his clients want him managing their money forever. "They're sometimes too busy to do it themselves," he says, "or they're mathophobic." Wasilewski started his career as an advisor to the trustees of a multibillion-dollar multi-employer pension plan—the United Mine Workers of America (UMWA) Health & Retirement Funds. He became a managing director of one of the largest money management firms in the Washington, D.C., area and retired in 2000.

Unable to stay out of the money management industry for long, he began working with retail clients for another investment firm. "At one public presentation, the president of the company suggested I tell the audience that if they invested with our firm, we would beat portfolios of index funds. I had two problems with this. First, the Securities and Exchange Commission doesn't allow this kind of statement. Second, the firm's portfolios were not beating index funds! That's when I decided to leave."

Soon after, he started his own investment firm. "A lot of people have badly wrecked finances because of fast-talking Wall Street types. Wall Street brokers are formidable foes with their fancy charts and promises. I just want to help people avoid messes created by self-serving brokers."

Company Name: AssetBuilder
Minimum Account Size Requirement: $50,000 (U.S. dollars)
Website: http://assetbuilder.com/contact_us.aspx
Tel. #: +1 (972) 535-4040

AssetBuilder's cofounder, Scott Burns, is the man who created and popularized the original Couch Potato portfolio in 1991. Back-tested studies prior to 1991 revealed that a combination of stock and bond indexes, rebalanced just once a year, would trounce most investment professionals. When Burns first published his claim, brokers balked.

"Brokers lie," says Burns, in a 2012 interview with Dan Bortolotti. "That's one of the things we just have to deal with: the sell side lies. Their education, by and large, is a marketing education. They get trained in arguments that are totally untrue."

After 1991, the Couch Potato strategy continued to embarrass professional advisors everywhere. Many investors wanted to take the plunge themselves—but struggled. They feared investing without an advisor. So in 2006, Scott and Kennon Grose created AssetBuilder. They built a series of Couch Potato–like portfolios utilizing Dimensional Fund Advisors' indexes. For expatriate Americans, AssetBuilder uses Schwab's low-cost ETFs. Clients select an asset allocation suiting their risk level with help from an AssetBuilder representative.

Portfolios utilize a strategy called mean variance optimization. Influenced by economic sciences Nobel Prize laureates William Sharpe and Harry Markowitz, AssetBuilder's portfolios contain a variety of indexed asset classes, including small stocks, large stocks, value stocks, growth stocks, international stocks, emerging market stocks, real estate investment trusts, and government bonds. The goal is to maximize returns while minimizing risk. The portfolios are rebalanced annually. Such realignments aren't influenced by forecasts. Instead, the company simply brings each portfolio back to its original allocation at the end of each year.

AssetBuilder's services don't include estate planning, goal setting, or other broad financial planning needs. But its annual fees are low, its rebalancing is disciplined, and it plans to offer a similar service for non-Americans soon.

Full Disclosure: I write for AssetBuilder's website.

AssetBuilder's Fee Schedule

Account Size	Annual Fees Charged
$50,000 to $249,999	0.45%
$250,000 to $599,999	0.43%
$600,000 to $999,999	0.40%
$1,000,000 to $3,999,999	0.30%
$4,000,000 to $19,999,999	0.25%
$20,000,000 and above	0.20%

SOURCE: AssetBuilder.com.

Company Name: Raymond James Financial Services
Minimum Account Size Requirement: $20,000 (U.S. dollars) for an indexed portfolio
Web Page: www.raymondjames.com
Contact E-mail: lara.yates@raymondjames.com
Tel. #: 1 (703) 406-8440
Limitation: For international teachers only

Before my wife and I were married, she had an account with Raymond James Financial Services. I pored over her account prospectus in 2006. Using the Morningstar database, I then looked up the costs of her funds. Adding her 1.75 percent annual account fee to her average fund cost, I was mortified to discover she paid more than 3 percent per year in fees. We promptly moved her money to Vanguard.

In 2011 my neighbor, Mark, wanted to know what he paid in fees for his Raymond James Freedom Account. Taking his account statements and once again using Morningstar, I found his total costs also exceeded 3 percent annually: 1.75 percent paid to Raymond James for the account's annual fee plus 1.3 percent for his account's mutual fund expenses. Could Raymond James offer a cheaper service?

In 2014 I e-mailed Lara Yates, one of Raymond James's financial advisors. "Would you be willing to build portfolios of index funds for American expatriates," I asked, "charging no more than a 1 percent annual fee?" I knew it was a tall order. But if she acquiesced, American expats might have another low-cost investment option with a financial advisor. Such portfolios would cost 1.2 percent or less (including index fund expense ratios), which is nearly two-thirds lower than what my wife and neighbor were paying when they invested with the firm.

Lara was excited by the idea, getting back to me a couple of weeks later. "I can do it for international teachers," she said, "and the firm's other international advisors say they can, too." This is a huge step. And it could be great for American expats. But investors should be vigilant.

Raymond James has historically rewarded bonuses for advisors who generate high fees for the company. Bruce Kelly, writing for New York–based *InvestmentNews* in 2007, explained: "In an effort to charge up its top registered representatives and financial advisers, **Raymond James Financial Services Inc.** is giving bonuses to its biggest-producing brokers."

Kelly added, "The new deferred-compensation program this year [2007] gives a bonus of 1 percent to affiliated reps who produce $450,000 in fees and commissions, a 2 percent bonus for $750,000 producers, and 3 percent for reps and advisers who produce $1 million . . . topping out at 10 percent for reps who produce $3.5 million in fees and commissions."[5]

Raymond James Financial is a publicly traded company. People can buy its shares on the New York Stock Exchange. In 2008, Louis Lowenstein and Neil Barsky, in their book *The Investor's Dilemma: How Mutual Funds Are Betraying Your Trust and What to Do about It,*[6] urged readers to avoid using publicly traded investment firms, suggesting that the primary loyalties of those firms are to shareholders. No, a shareholder isn't someone using Raymond James's services; shareholders own company stock. Raymond James shares (as with any stock) rise or fall over time in proportion to the company's profits. If the company generates consistently higher income (through fees) for its investment services, the share price follows. According to Morningstar, from August 1983 to April 2014 Raymond James's stock price soared 8,000 percent.[7] Few other businesses came close to generating such high shareholder profits.

Fees are a tricky concept for many investors because few bother to calculate their impact.

Here's a little quiz: Which investor will pay more in fees? An investor in actively managed funds paying 5.75 percent sales commissions per purchase, or an investor not paying sales commissions, but paying 1.75 percent annual fees based on account size?

The truth might surprise you. After all, 5.75 percent is a much bigger number than 1.75 percent.

Tie Care International usually sells the American Funds family of actively managed funds to its clients. The firm doesn't charge annual fees, but does charge a 5.75 percent purchase commission. A Raymond James Freedom Account investor in actively managed funds wouldn't pay sales commissions but would pay up to 1.75 percent per year in annual account fees. Table 12.1 is a side-by-side comparison revealing how they might stack up over 25 years if their respective funds averaged 8 percent returns annually.

Table 12.1   Tie Care's 5.75 Percent Purchase Commission versus Raymond James's 1.75 Percent Wrap Fee

Assuming $1,200 Invested over 25 Years

	Tie Care International— with American Funds	Raymond James—with Freedom Account
Amount invested per year	$1,200	$1,200
Amount invested after 5.75% sales commission (applicable to Tie Care)	$1,131	$1,200
Annual return before wrap fee (where applicable)	8%	8%
Annual return of funds after 1.75% wrap fee (applicable to Raymond James)	8%	6.25%
Total value after 25 years	$89,297.44	$72,465.34

If fund returns were equal, wrap fees of 1.75 percent per year would be far more damaging than 5.75 percent sales commissions.

One Raymond James representative, however, suggested the wrap fees (which are lower for larger accounts) are justified. She e-mailed me to explain: "Raymond James is the only firm in the industry to use forward looking capital markets assumptions. The economic information is purchased from a third party firm called Mercer Investments." In other words, Raymond James believes the firm it hires helps it strategically speculate about which sectors or asset classes to purchase: crystal ball kind of stuff.

Personal finance columnist Jason Zweig, in his excellent book *Your Money and Your Brain*, figures such firms should be held to an ancient standard: "The ancient Scythians discouraged frivolous prophecies by burning to death any soothsayer whose predictions failed to come true. . . . Investors might be better off if modern forms of divination like market forecasts and earnings projections were held to biblical standards of justice."[8]

Evidence suggests that forecasting is more salesmanship than substance. In his 1992 letter to Berkshire Hathaway shareholders, Warren Buffett said, "We've long felt that the only value of stock forecasters is to make fortune tellers look good."[9]

The late economist John Kenneth Galbraith, a Harvard economics professor for half a century, was the president of the American Economic Association. His career also included serving as editor of *Fortune* magazine from 1943 to 1948. "We have two classes of forecasters," he said, "those who don't know—and those who don't know they don't know."[10]

The broadest evidence, perhaps, is the ongoing data provided by CXO Advisory: "To investigate [market predictions] during 2005 through 2012 we collected 6,582 forecasts for the U.S. stock market offered publicly by 68 experts, bulls and bears employing technical, fundamental and sentiment indicators."

CXO Advisory found that just 46.9 percent of the forecasts proved accurate. Odds are better flipping coins.[11]

Those investing with Raymond James, however, now have a choice. As Lara Yates explains, "Investors with at least $20,000 to invest can have portfolios of index funds." And the firm would charge just a 1 percent wrap fee (excluding fund expense ratios).

How would such a platform stack up against a portfolio of Tie Care's American Funds, where investors are charged a 5.75 percent sales commission?

Actively managed mutual fund performance, in aggregate, is equal to the market's performance before fees. After fees it's a different story. On average, active funds underperform by an amount proportional to the fees charged. If Raymond James built portfolios of index funds with expense ratios, averaging 0.2 percent per year, and Tie Care's actively managed American Funds average expense ratio costs of 0.7 percent per year, then odds are high that the index portfolio (over the long term) would outperform the active fund portfolio, long term, by roughly half a percentage point annually.

Assuming a 0.5 percent average annual performance difference, how would a Raymond James portfolio of Vanguard indexes (with a 1 percent wrap fee) stack up against an American Funds portfolio charging a 5.75 percent commission per purchase? We'll assume a market return, before fund expense ratio costs, of 9 percent per year. As you can see in Table 12.2, the race gets tighter.

We can't forecast, of course, which portfolio would truly outperform. But lower fees increase odds of better performance. In this case, the battle is close, with Tie Care edging Raymond James in this hypothetical

Table 12.2 Tie Care's American Funds versus Raymond James's Index Fund Portfolio

	Tie Care International—with American Funds	Raymond James—with Index Funds
Amount invested per year	$1,200	$1,200
Amount invested after 5.75% sales commission (applicable to Tie Care)	$1,131	$1,200 (no sales commission)
Assumed market return	9%	9%
Annual return after fund expense ratio costs	8.3%	8.8%
Annual return after 1% wrap fee (applicable to Raymond James)	8.3% (no wrap fee cost)	7.8%
Total value after 25 years	$93,566	$91,851

example. But there's one important element that would likely tip the winning odds in Raymond James's favor.

The actively managed products of the American Funds family have higher taxable turnover than their index counterparts because a fund manager's job is to trade stocks. An index fund is different. Its low (nearly no) turnover creates a more tax-efficient vehicle in a fully taxable account. As such, the Raymond James portfolio, after taxes, would likely win.

Raymond James investors, however, should be vigilant. They may have to fight for their indexes. Tales from the United States' northern neighbors are worth heeding.

Most of Canada's banks offer index funds. But if you ask one of their advisors to build you a portfolio of index funds, you'll find they would rather kiss an ashtray. I've walked into enough banks with friends and family members to see this time and again. The banks' advisors pull out glossy charts, showing cherry-picked funds that have beaten the market. But yesterday's winning funds rarely maintain their winning ways. Canadian banks tout them because they're more profitable for the bank to sell. Their investors take the punch.

Will Raymond James representatives try steering clients away from index funds—even if clients ask for them? I'm not sure. Never forget how the firm makes money.

Investors should also be wary of expensive index funds. David Randall, writing for Reuters in 2014, reported that roughly a dozen index fund providers in the United States are charging more than the average actively managed mutual fund.[12] With broad availability of low-cost index funds in the United States, no American index investor should pay more than 0.35 percent per year for any stock market index fund. Vanguard, Schwab, Fidelity, and T. Rowe Price have solid, low-cost index funds. If you use a Raymond James advisor, ensure he or she sticks with these firms.

Finally, Raymond James clients should ask their advisors *not* to adjust portfolios based on speculation. Forecasting doesn't consistently work. As Ben Bernanke, then head of the U.S. Federal Reserve, said during a 2009 Boston College School of Law commencement address, "many smart people have applied the most sophisticated statistical and modeling tools available to try to better divine the economic future.

But the results, unfortunately, have more often than not been underwhelming."[13]

Instead, encourage your advisor to dispassionately rebalance Couch Potato style, just once a year.

So, is Raymond James still worth it? If they build you a portfolio of index funds, I think so. But keep your eyes wide open.

Index Advisors for Canadian Expats

Company Name: Objective Financial Partners Inc.
Certified Financial Planner: Jason Heath
Website: www.objectivefinancialpartners.com
Contact E-mail: info@objectivefinancialpartners.com
Tel. #: 1 (416) 691-8471

Jason Heath is in a tough business. He provides objective financial planning but doesn't receive a dime in commissions. The Markham, Ontario–based CFP and income tax specialist doesn't earn annual fees based on his client account sizes, either. So how does the guy make money?

Jason charges consultation fees for broad financial planning: everything from estate planning to budgeting to retirement goals and investment allocation. Because he doesn't benefit from investment purchases or client account sizes, he advises with no strings attached. His firm has an in-house accountant and an estate lawyer. And Jason isn't too proud to use external resources when it makes sense to do so.

"I was disillusioned by the mainstream financial industry," he says, "so I wanted to do something different." Few investment advisors could survive such a lean, transparent compensation structure. But Heath builds a client base through heaps of credibility. He writes a column devoted to financial planning for the *National Post*, one of Canada's two national papers. Such a platform gives him plenty of exposure.

"I have clients in Canada, Brazil, Europe, the United States, and Africa," he says. Jason's services are perfect for Canadian expats building portfolios of low-cost index funds. "If they open accounts with an offshore discount brokerage [like TD Direct International, Saxo Capital Markets, DBS Vickers] or a nonresident account with TD Waterhouse, I can assist them with portfolio allocation after providing comprehensive short-term and long-term retirement, children's education, and asset al-location strategies."

Heath spends plenty of time constructing financial planning goals with clients. He charges anywhere from $1,500 to $4,500 for a plan. "Some of my clients have relatively simple goals and asset distributions," he says. "But other individuals might have assets all over the place: a home in London, investment accounts in Asia, RRSPs [registered retirement savings plans] in Canada, college funds in an RESP [registered education savings plan]. My job is to negotiate strategies to best utilize these resources with tax efficiency, while aligning with the clients' goals. And as they invest each month, they can call me up and I'll ensure they stick to a logical investment allocation."

Jason's services are worth the money. Consider someone with a $100,000 portfolio paying 2.5 percent in Canadian actively managed mutual fund fees. That person would pay $2,500 each year ($2,500 is 2.5 percent of $100,000). Those with $500,000 portfolios would pay $10,000 a year in hidden expenses. Advisors stuffing client accounts with such products aren't objective. Canadian actively managed mutual funds are the world's most expensive. Those selling them benefit nicely. With Jason, however, investors could pay as little as $1,500 once, before getting on track with their plan and their ultra-low-cost portfolio of index funds.

Index Advisors for Australian Expats

Company Name: Global Index Investment Company
Minimum Account Size Requirement: $50,000 (U.S. dollars) or
    the willingness to make regular savings
Contact E-mail: info@giic.com.au, malcom@giic.com.au
Tel. #: 61 (0) 428 348 801

Malcom Lewis and Scott Burton formed Global Index Investment Company in 2014 to work predominantly with Australian expats or British expats planning to one day move to Australia. Both founders grew frustrated by the international investment firms they previously worked with. "We found that fees, charges, and other high-cost penalties were really taking away from clients' investment returns," explains Malcom. So they decided to start their own firm.

Malcom and Scott strongly advocate index investing. But for them, other factors are equally important. "We believe budgeting, cash flow, and debt management are just as important as investing," says Malcom. "There's little point investing until these areas are in order, and if your advisor doesn't examine this for you, then you need to ask yourself why not."

The team runs a variety of fee models, with the typical investor paying roughly 1.2 percent each year for investment management. Such costs include client goal setting, budgeting, cash flow management, debt management, tax minimization, and advice on wills and insurance.

"We ensure that clients have clear financial goals and that their budget and cash flow are in order. We then help them prepare for retirement through sensible saving and investing," says Malcom.

All clients complete specific budgets with Malcom and Scott's guidance. The advisors also regularly review their clients' status to ensure they're on track with their budgets and financial goals.

Index Advisors for British Expats

Company Name: Satis Asset Management
Minimum Account Size Requirement: £500,000
Contact E-mail: info@satisuk.com
Tel. #: 44 (0) 20 3272 0120

Many expatriates feel betrayed by those selling them expensive off-shore pension schemes. They may wonder whether there truly are firms that shun commissions, embrace low-cost index funds, and provide high levels of personal financial planning. Fortunately, a few exist, such as Satis Asset Management.

Based in London, the firm was established by the chartered accountant and tax advisory firm Hillier Hopkins LLP in 2012. Today, Satis Asset Management provides investment and taxation advice to a modest number of wealthy families. As director Ben Sherwood explains, "We have a number of expatriate British clients. Although it's early days for our firm, business growth has exceeded our expectations. We are also one of only a handful of firms that have experience and competence to advise Americans residing in the UK."

Sherwood is a Certified Financial Planner and Chartered Financial Analyst. He also coauthored the book *The 7 Secrets of Money: The Insider's Guide to Personal Investment Success* (SRA Books, 2nd ed., 2013). In it, he emphasizes the importance of low-cost investing and diversifying investments across a variety of asset classes. One of the key messages of the book is that investors should concentrate on factors within their control, such as taxes and fees.

For bond allocations, Satis Asset Management usually buys a combination of gilts (individual bonds) and bond funds for clients. For client equity allocations, the firm currently uses Vanguard and Dimensional Fund Advisors' indexes.

Clients wishing to open accounts with Satis must do so with a minimum £500,000.

Investment consultancy and wealth management charges are 0.9 percent per year for the first million pounds, dropping to 0.75 percent for the next £4 million, down to 0.6 percent for the next £5 million.

Conclusion

Glancing at Table 12.3, investors will realize two things: Most of the options are for Americans, and investors require a large amount of money to invest with most full-service index fund advisors.

Back in Canada, my friends and I enjoyed a comedy show called *This Hour Has 22 Minutes*. In one regular section, "Talking to Americans," reporter Rick Mercer went south of the border to ask questions about Canadian events. He convinced a bunch of Americans that VCRs were previously outlawed in Canada, and asked them to congratulate Canada on their legalization.

Another time, Mercer convinced a professor at Princeton University to sign a petition against restarting the Annual Toronto Polar Bear Hunt (Toronto and London, England, share similar latitude). When George W. Bush was running for president, Mercer convinced him that Canada's Prime Minister Jean Chrétien (who had been in power for seven years) was named Jean Poutine and that he was supporting Bush's candidacy.

But Canadians shouldn't be smug. When it comes to low-cost investing, financially educated Americans are light-years ahead. Demand for sensible investment options among Americans is high. As more global

Table 12.3 Firms Building Index Fund Portfolios for Expatriates

Advisory Firm	Nationality Serviced	Maximum Management Costs	Minimum Account Size	Includes Full-Service Financial Planning	Will Rebalance Portfolios of Indexes	Contact Information
Noto Financial Planning	Americans	1%	$150,000	Yes[a]	Yes	info@notofp.com Tel. #: 1 (808) 638 2475
Creveling & Creveling	Americans[b]	1.2%	$750,000	Yes[a]	Yes	www.crevelingandcreveling.com Tel. #: (66) 2661 2716
MASECO	Americans based in Great Britain	1.25%	$1,000,000	Yes[a]	Yes	www.masecoprivatewealth.com Tel. #: (44) 207 043 0455
Index Fund Advisors	Americans	0.9%	$100,000	Yes	Yes	info@ifa.com Tel. #: 1 (949) 502 0050
RW Investment Strategies	Americans	0.4%	No minimum	No	Yes	Robert@rwinvestmentstrategies.com Tel. #: 1 (443) 896 4123
AssetBuilder	Americans[c]	0.45%	$50,000	No	Yes	http://assetbuilder.com/contact_us.aspx Tel. #: 1 (972) 535 4040
Raymond James Financial	International teachers only	1%	$20,000	No[d]	Yes	Lara.yates@raymondjames.com Tel. #: 1 (703) 406-8440
Objective Financial Partners Inc. Jason Heath	Canadians	Consultations charges	No minimum	Yes	No	info@objectivefinancialpartners.com Tel. #: 1 (416) 691 8471
Global Index Investment Company	Australians	1.25%	$50,000	Yes[a]	Yes	info@giic.com.au, malcom@giic.au Tel. #: 61 (0) 428 348 801
Satis Asset Management	British Investors	0.9%	£500,000	Yes[a]	Yes	info@satisuk.com Tel. #: 44 (0) 20 3272 0120

[a] Includes multiple financial planning consultations each year.
[b] Will provide consultations for non-Americans.
[c] Soon to offer services to non-Americans.
[d] This service is offered for an additional consultation fee.

expatriates catch on, greater numbers of full-service index fund advisors should start popping up for those of different nationalities.

But why do such advisors usually limit their services to those with large amounts of money? They aren't greedy; they're practical. Many provide time-intensive customer service multiple times each year. For this reason, they can service only a small number of clients. Because they don't earn commissions or mutual fund kickbacks, their profit margins are also slim. As a result, many require large dollar entry points just to survive.

Expats investing without an advisor, of course, don't require large sums of money. I'll explain how to do it in the following chapters.

Those with modest sums who wish to qualify for a future full-service index fund advisor could build their portfolios on their own until their accounts grow large enough to qualify for a full-service firm.

Or those with a ninja's aptitude could fly solo. Doing so is cheaper—and potentially more profitable.

Notes

1. "Investor Success Capturing Fund Returns with and without Advisors," Index Fund Advisors, Inc. Accessed May 8, 2014. www.ifa.com/aboutus/.
2. Burton G. Malkiel, *A Random Walk Down Wall Street: The Time-Tested Strategy for Successful Investing*, 10th ed. (New York: W.W. Norton, 2003), 329.
3. Larry E. Swedroe, *The Quest for Alpha: The Holy Grail of Investing* (Hoboken, NJ: John Wiley & Sons, 2011), 133–134.
4. Larry E. Swedroe and Carl Richards, *Think, Act, and Invest Like Warren Buffett: The Winning Strategy to Help You Achieve Your Financial and Life Goals* (New York: McGraw-Hill, 2013), 68.
5. Bruce Kelly, "Raymond James Unit Gives Bonuses to Big Producers," *InvestmentNews*: Login. Accessed July 2, 2014. http://goo.gl/LD77fM.
6. Louis Lowenstein and Neil Barsky, *The Investor's Dilemma: How Mutual Funds Are Betraying Your Trust and What to Do about It* (Hoboken, NJ: John Wiley & Sons, 2008).
7. "Raymond James Financial Inc.," Morningstar. Accessed July 2, 2014. http://quotes.morningstar.com/stock/rjf/s?t=RJF.
8. Jason Zweig, *Your Money and Your Brain: How the New Science of Neuroeconomics Can Help Make You Rich* (New York: Simon & Schuster, 2007), 76.
9. Warren E. Buffett, "Chairman's Letter—1992," Berkshirehathaway.com. Accessed May 9, 2014. www.berkshirehathaway.com/letters/1992.html.

10. Dan Solin, "If You Want to Play the Game, You Better Know the Rules," *Huffington Post*, November 4, 2008. Accessed July 2, 2014. www.huffingtonpost.com/dan-solin/if-you-want-to-play-the-g_b_139953.html.

11. "Guru Grades," CXO Advisory RSS. Accessed May 9, 2014. https://www.cxoadvisory.com/gurus/.

12. David Randall, "Analysis: High-Priced Index Funds? The Worst Deal for Investors," Reuters, January 13, 2014. Accessed May 9, 2014. www.reuters.com/article/2014/01/13/us-indexfunds-costs-analysis-idUSBREA0C0N920140113.

13. Ben Bernanke, "2009 Boston College School of Law Commencement Address," Board of Governors of the Federal Reserve System, May 22, 2009. Accessed May 9, 2014. www.federalreserve.gov/newsevents/speech/bernanke20090522a.htm.

Chapter 13

Choosing Your Offshore Brokerage—For Non-Americans

I f you're capable of controlling your emotions, the cheapest and most profitable way to build an index portfolio is to do it yourself. Consider how much time you spend cutting your toenails each year. I'm not talking about sculpting them, just clipping them down once a month. Anyone spending more time maintaining an index fund portfolio is doing something wrong.

All you need is a discount brokerage account. Ensure you can open and manage the account regardless of where you happen to be living. Second, brokerage costs should be low. Ensure your account is located where the government is stable and where banking regulations are solid. Finally, if you live where offshore investments won't be taxed (confirm with a tax accountant), choose an offshore brokerage located where the authorities won't charge capital gains taxes.

Here are three such examples for non-American expatriates: DBS Vickers Securities, based in Singapore; TD Direct Investing International, based in Luxembourg; and Saxo Capital Markets, located in more than 20 worldwide locations, including Hong Kong, Singapore, Uruguay, and the United Arab Emirates.

DBS Vickers Securities Opens the Door to Everyone

Some brokerages discriminate against expatriates living in certain countries, not allowing them to open accounts. But Singapore's DBS Vickers isn't one of them.

"Any non-American expat can open an account as long as they meet the management subject of approval," says Madeline Chen, of DBS Vickers Client Services. So what does that mean? I pressed her to elaborate: "They must open a local POSB [POSB Bank Singapore] or DBS bank account [in Singapore] first. They must be above the age of 21; they can't be currently bankrupt; they can't be a delinquent. Nor can they be an ex-delinquent."[1] So if you flattened the tires of your teacher's Volvo as a 12-year-old (little deviant), don't tell the folks at DBS Vickers. Instead of qualifying for a brokerage account, you could earn a retroactive caning.

Those opening the account must pass a 20-question online multiple-choice securities quiz. DBS Vickers will send you the link.

Taking the quiz is free. You can also retake it as many times as necessary. Brenda Perkins, a Canadian teacher at the International School of Bangkok, opened her DBS Vickers account in 2012. "I didn't know anything about finance but studied the online quiz materials for a couple of hours. I scored 70 percent the first time (failing the test) but passed with 90 percent the second time."[2]

Accredited investors (defined as those with massive incomes or millions of dollars) are sometimes exempt from the quiz, as are individuals with formal educations in finance.

DBS Vickers Securities allows investors to trade online using the Hong Kong, Singapore, U.S., and Canadian markets.

Singapore's markets are limited. Canada and Hong Kong, on the other hand, provide a wide variety of exchange-traded index funds suitable for those of different nationalities.

Why not buy shares off the U.S. market? It's tempting—but avoid doing so. At some point you're going to die. And when the Grim Reaper knocks, the Internal Revenue Service (IRS) follows. The U.S. government doesn't care whether you or your heirs are U.S. citizens. When you die, they posthumously make you a patriot if you own more than $60,000 in American-traded shares. Your heirs get a condolence letter that looks, smells, and tastes (eating it won't help) like a U.S. estate tax bill. As stated by the IRS, "Deceased nonresidents who were not American citizens . . . are subject to estate taxation even though the nonresident held the certificates abroad or registered the certificates in the name of a nominee."[3]

I purchase off the Canadian market, where I face no such risk.

The Canadian market holds a wide range of exchange-traded funds (ETFs). They include total global indexes, as well as country-specific indexes representing the United States, Canada, India, and China, to name just a few.

DBS Vickers doesn't levy fees to open a trading account, nor is there an annual account charge. The firm does, however, charge purchase commissions. On the Canadian exchange, such costs total 0.5 percent of every purchase or $29—whichever is greater. For example, if you invested $2,000 in an S&P 500 ETF, you would pay $29 in commissions. Multiplying the commission (0.5 percent) by the amount invested would equal $10. But the minimum cost for a DBS Vickers trade is $29, so you would pay the greater sum. Investing $20,000 would cost $100 in commissions because 0.5 percent of $20,000 is $100.[4]

There's no need to file a Canadian income tax form. DBS Vickers simply sends 15 percent of each dividend to the Canadian government (as other brokers do, when you buy off the Canadian exchange). DBS Vickers does, however, charge a processing fee totaling 1 percent of the net dividend per quarter. There's a $4 minimum charge and a $40 maximum.[5]

For example, investors receiving $100 in a quarterly dividend pay the $4 minimum. Those receiving $1,000 would pay 1 percent of the $1,000, totaling $10.

I've held an account with DBS Vickers since 2003.

Why You Should Avoid E★Trade Financial

E★Trade Financial is a U.S.-based discount brokerage with offshore offices in locations such as Singapore and Hong Kong. Trading costs are low, just $9.99 per trade, regardless of purchase size.[6] You want to invest $100,000 all at once? It costs just $9.99. What if you wanted to invest $1 million? Again, you could do so for the price of a Big Mac, fries, and a Coke. With no annual account fees and no dividend processing costs, it's certainly tempting. But if you're a non-American expat, avoid this brokerage.

Investors pay 30 percent dividend withholding taxes because the brokerage trades solely on the U.S. market. Much worse, when investors float to their ultimate reward, their heirs pay U.S. estate taxes. Unless E★Trade begins to offer trading on non-American exchanges, global expats should avoid it.

TD Direct Investing International

Owned by Canada's TD Bank Group, TD Direct Investing International is a brokerage based in Luxembourg. According to Luxembourg-based PWC Tax Consulting, if shares are held for a period longer than six months, no capital gains taxes are levied when sold.[7]

The brokerage tempts clients with "several hundred of the best offshore mutual funds from the world's leading asset managers—carefully handpicked for you by TD Direct Investing International." There are no fees to buy such funds. But they are actively managed. Don't fall for their online sales rhetoric. Their expense ratios cost 1.5 percent or more each year.[8]

They want you to buy what's profitable for their firm. Instead, use TD Direct Investing International to buy low cost ETFs.

The brokerage allows investors to access 18 different stock markets, including the London, Dublin, Toronto, and Sydney exchanges. Accounts can be opened online.

TD International charges a 0.2 percent annual account fee. Commission charges (for buying or selling) increase based on the amount invested. Those investing less than €5,000 pay €28 per trade. Purchasing between €5,001 and €10,000 costs €35. Fees increase incrementally for those investing greater sums, with costs capped at 0.1 percent for trading €250,000 or more. Those investing a quarter of a million euros at once, for example, pay €250 in commissions.

Some investors, however, aren't eligible to open accounts with TD International. Expats living in Japan and Bangladesh are two such examples. Those living in Indonesia are also scratched from the party list.

One British investor currently residing in Indonesia contacted me recently in disappointment. "I was a client at TD International for five years, but they sent me an apologetic letter stating that Indonesian residents can no longer use their brokerage." Such restrictions sometimes relate to whether the brokerage feels it can trust the identity of the account holder.

Some brokerages ask for notarized certificates verifying investor identities before they can open accounts abroad. If the brokerage doesn't trust a country's notaries, they may restrict expatriates living in that country from opening accounts.

Saxo Capital Markets—A Jewel with Distractions

Saxo Capital Markets provides new account holders with a gift card for a casino. Okay, I'm lying. But there's some truth to the hyperbole. They want to addict you to rapidly trading stocks, futures, puts, and options. The online platform is like a 747 cockpit, when all you really need is a steering wheel, brake, throttle, and gearbox.

Brokerages make more money when investors trade feverishly. Investors taking advantage of up-to-the-second stock quotes and a myriad of exotic gambling options are dream clients. But you shouldn't aspire to be a dream client; aspire to be a rich one. The less you trade, the more money you'll make. According to researchers Brad M. Barber and Terrance Odean, "of 66,465 households with accounts at a large discount broker during 1991 to 1996, those that traded most earned an annual return of 11.4 percent, while the market [index] returned 17.9 percent."[9]

And what about Warren Buffett, the man deemed by many to be history's greatest investor? In his 1988 chairman's letter to Berkshire Hathaway shareholders, he wrote that his favorite holding period is forever.[10]

He also says, "If you aren't wiling to own a stock for ten years, don't even think of owing it for ten minutes."[11] The same should be said of an index fund.

Many brokerages want you to think that trading rapidly and staying on top of the latest stock market news is a sophisticated moneymaking strategy. And it is—for the brokerage.

So is Saxo Capital Markets a bad brokerage for tempting us to trade and for offering a giddy array of bells and whistles? No. Investing with Saxo is a bit like walking into a narcotics den. But as long as you avoid the little white powder and stick to buying and holding exchange-traded funds, you shouldn't fall into a crack.

To open a Saxo Capital Markets account, you won't have to visit branches in Hong Kong, Singapore, Uruguay, or the United Arab Emirates. All that's required is verification of identity with a notary. The account can be opened online once such documents are sent to the brokerage.

As with TD Direct Investing International, however, expats from some locations don't qualify. Those living in Japan, Bangladesh, and some African countries get shunned. Don't ask me why Japan is on the leper list. Perhaps a Sumo wrestler seduced a slew of global bankers' daughters. Fortunately, Japanese-based expats can still open accounts with Singapore's DBS Vickers.

Similar to TD International, Saxo Capital Markets allows trading access to a variety of global exchanges. Commissions vary depending on the exchange used. In 2014, Saxo charged 3 cents per share for Canadian-based exchange-traded funds or a minimum of $25. If, for example, an investor wanted to invest $10,000 in Vanguard's Canadian stock market ETF and the ETF price was $30 per share, the investor could afford 333 shares. At 3 cents a share for commission, this would amount to roughly $10. But with minimum trading costs of $25, investors would pay the greater sum.[12]

Saxo Capital Markets Costs

As of this writing, Saxo Capital Markets doesn't charge additional account fees. But according to Singapore's senior manager, Eoh You Loong, it may be rolling out a 0.2 percent annual charge sometime in 2014. This would align the brokerage costs similarly with TD Direct Investing International's. The fee, according to Mr. Eoh, would likely be waived on a "case-by-case basis." When I asked for further clarification, he suggested that accounts exceeding values of $500,000 would be exempt.[13]

So which brokerage is cheapest? It depends. Saxo Capital Markets offers low-cost commissions. But there's a flip side. Assume you get paid in euros, but you want to invest on a British exchange. To purchase ETFs on the London market, investors need to convert their euros into pounds (some ETFs on the UK market also trade in U.S. dollars). Those allowing Saxo Capital Markets to convert currencies pay a 0.5 percent exchange rate commission, above the spot rate. Investors looking for something cheaper should convert money into their desired currency before sending it to the brokerage.

Comparing Fees with International Brokerages

To examine long-term costs associated with each of the brokerages just discussed, I created four scenarios. In each case, the investor starts a portfolio with $10,000. The four investors then add either $12,000, $24,000, $60,000, or $120,000 per year. They build the same low-cost portfolio of ETFs. Expense ratios on the ETFs total 0.125 percent: easily achieved with a combination of Vanguard and iShares Canada ETFs.

Note in Tables 13.1 to 13.4 that DBS Vickers charges the highest purchase commissions but doesn't charge an annual account fee. Saxo Capital Markets has low trading costs, but hits investors with an exchange rate commission. And TD International hampers investors slightly with its 0.2 percent annual account charge.

Over 25 years, returns from each brokerage would be similar.

Table 13.1 Using DBS Vickers, TD International, and Saxo Capital Markets

Starting with $10,000 and Investing $1,000 per Month

	DBS Vickers	TD International	Saxo Capital Markets
Beginning value of account	$10,000	$10,000	$10,000
Annual investment/monthly purchase	$12,000 per year	$12,000 per year	$12,000 per year
	$1,000 per month	$1,000 per month	$1,000 per month
Total trading commissions paid assuming 12 purchases per year	$348	$360	$300
Currency exchange commissions	0	0	$120
Annual investment/monthly investment after trading commission costs	$11,652 per year	$11,640 per year	$11,700 per year
	$971 per month	$970 per month	$975 per month
Stock and bond market annual return	9%	9%	9%
ETF/fund annual expense ratio average	0.125%	0.125%	0.125%
Annual account fee as percentage of account value	0%	0.2%	0 to 0.2%
Dividend collection fees	0.02% (assuming 2% net dividend yield)	0%	0%
Annual return after fees	8.86%	8.67%	8.67% to 8.87%
Portfolio Value after 25 Years	**$1,135,822**	**$1,100,272**	**$1,105,532 to $1,142,012**

SOURCES: DBS Vickers; TD Direct Investing International; Saxo Capital Markets.

Table 13.2 Using DBS Vickers, TD International, and Saxo Capital Markets

Starting with $10,000 and Investing $2,000 per Month

	DBS Vickers	TD International	Saxo Capital Markets
Beginning value of account	$10,000	$10,000	$10,000
Annual investment/monthly purchase	$24,000 per year	$24,000 per year	$24,000 per year
	$2,000 per month	$2,000 per month	$2,000 per month
Total trading commissions paid assuming 12 purchases per year	$348	$360	$300
Currency exchange commissions	0	0	$120
Annual investment/monthly investment after trading commission costs	$23,652 per year	$23,640 per year	$23,580 per year
	$1,971 per month	$1,970 per month	$1,965 per month
Stock and bond market annual return	9%	9%	9%
ETF/fund annual expense ratio average	0.125%	0.125%	0.125%
Annual account fee as percentage of account value	0%	0.2%	0 to 0.2%
Dividend collection fees	0.02% (assuming 2% net dividend yield)	0%	0%
Annual return after fees	8.86%	8.67%	8.67% to 8.87%
Portfolio Value after 25 Years	**$2,553,586**	**$2,471,909**	**$2,466,650 to $2,551,394**

Sources: DBS Vickers; TD Direct Investing International; Saxo Capital Markets.

Table 13.3 Using DBS Vickers, TD International, and Saxo Capital Markets
Starting with $10,000 and Investing $5,000 per Month

	DBS Vickers	TD International	Saxo Capital Markets
Beginning value of account	$10,000	$10,000	$10,000
Annual investment/monthly purchase	$60,000 per year	$60,000 per year	$60,000 per year
	$5,000 per month	$5,000 per month	$5,000 per month
Trading commissions paid assuming 12 purchases per year	$348	$360	$300
Currency exchange commissions	0	0	$300
Annual investment/monthly investment after trading commission costs	$59,652 per year	$59,640 per year	$59,400 per year
	$4,971 per month	$4,970 per month	$4,950 per month
Stock and bond market annual return	9%	9%	9%
ETF/fund annual expense ratio average	0.125%	0.125%	0.125%
Annual account fee as percentage of account value	0%	0.2%	0 to 0.2%
Dividend collection fees	.02% (assuming 2% net dividend yield)	0%	0%
Annual return after fees	8.85%	8.67	8.67% to 8.87%
Portfolio Value after 25 Years	**$5,462,156**	**$5,307,846**	**$5,286,808 to $5,456,685**

SOURCES: DBS Vickers; TD Direct Investing International; Saxo Capital Markets.

Table 13.4 Using DBS Vickers, TD International, and Saxo Capital Markets
Starting with $10,000 and Investing $10,000 per Month

	DBS Vickers	TD International	Saxo Capital Markets
Beginning value of account	$10,000	$10,000	$10,000
Annual investment/monthly purchase	$120,000 per year $10,000 per month	$120,000 per year $10,000 per month	$120,000 per year $10,000 per month
Trading commissions paid assuming 12 purchases per year	$600	$444	$300
Currency exchange commissions	0	0	$600
Annual investment/monthly investment after trading commission costs	$119,400 per year $9,950 per month	$119,556 per year $9,963 per month	$119,100 per year $9,925 per month
Stock and bond market annual return	9%	9%	9%
ETF/fund annual expense ratio average	0.125%	0.125%	0.125%
Annual account fee as percentage of account value	0%	0.2%	0 to 0.2%
Dividend collection fees	0.02% (assuming 2% net dividend yield)	0%	0%
Annual return after fees	8.85%	8.67%	8.67% to 8.87%
Portfolio Value after 25 Years	**$10,849,657**	**$10,559,950**	**$10,519,978 to $10,856,810**

Sources: DBS Vickers; TD Direct Investing International; Saxo Capital Markets.

Is Interactive Brokers the Dark Horse Winner?

DBS Vickers, TD Direct Investing International, and Saxo Capital Markets aren't the only discount brokerages in the global game. Others exist. One such example is Interactive Brokers, a firm *Barron's* rated the best online brokerage in 2014.[14] The company website lists more than 200 countries from which people can invest. While many brokerages don't allow expatriates from such countries as Japan, Bangladesh, and Indonesia, for example, Interactive Brokers shows no such prejudice.

Investors can open accounts online, requiring a minimum of U.S. $10,000 (or equivalent) to start. Interactive Brokers aims for $10 to be generated in monthly trading commissions. The firm charges investors extra if they don't generate at least this sum.

For example, investors paying $5 in commissions for a given month would be charged an extra $5, providing the brokerage with a minimum $10 for the month. But such extra fees are waived for investors with more than $100,000 in their account. Trading costs depend on the exchanges used (Canadian, Australian, British, etc.), and they're typically much cheaper than those charged by DBS Vickers, Saxo, or TD International.

Before using Interactive Brokers, however, check with an international tax accountant. It's an American firm and holds all securities in North American accounts, regardless of the exchange from which they're purchased. As such, you'll want to be certain your heirs won't be liable for U.S. estate taxes.

After reading this, you'll probably still have questions. I address 16 commonly asked queries in the following chapter. And the chapters that follow provide the exact products investors of different nationalities should buy, whether investing in the Couch Potato, Permanent, or Fundamental Indexing model.

Notes

1. Interview with Madeline Chen. Telephone interview by author, May 4, 2014.
2. Interview with Brenda Perkins. E-mail interview by author, April 4, 2013.
3. "Some Nonresidents with U.S. Assets Must File Estate Tax Returns," Internal Revenue Service. Accessed May 9, 2014. www.irs.gov/Individuals/

International-Taxpayers/Some-Nonresidents-with-U.S.-Assets-Must-File-Estate-Tax-Returns.

4. "Fees: Schedules," DBS Vickers Securities. Accessed July 2, 2014. https://www.dbsvonline.com/english/Pfee.asp.

5. Ibid.

6. "Experience & Innovation: Welcome to E★Trade Financial." Accessed July 2, 2014. https://global.etrade.com/glp/sg/en/home.

7. "Luxembourg Income Taxes 2013: Guide for Individuals," PWC Luxembourg Tax Consulting. Accessed May 9, 2014. https://www.pwc.lu/en/tax-consulting/docs/pwc-publ-lux-income-taxes-2013.pdf.

8. "Offshore Investment Funds," TD Direct Investing International. Accessed May 9, 2014. http://int.tddirectinvesting.com/en-gb/investment-products/savings-and-investing/investment-funds/.

9. Brad M. Barber and Terrance Odean, "Trading Is Hazardous to Your Wealth: The Common Stock Investment Performance of Individual Investors," Social Science Research Network. Accessed May 9, 2014. http://papers.ssrn.com/sol3/papers.cfm?abstract_id=219228.

10. Warren E. Buffett, "Chairman's Letter—1988," Berkshirehathaway.com. Accessed May 9, 2014. www.berkshirehathaway.com/letters/1988.html

11. Warren Buffett and Lawrence A. Cunningham, *The Essays of Warren Buffett: Lessons for Investors and Managers* (Singapore: John Wiley & Sons (Asia) Pte, 2009), 117.

12. "Saxo Capital Markets: Commissions, Charges and Margin Schedule." Accessed July 2, 2014. http://sg.saxomarkets.com/prices/general/.

13. Interview with Eoh You Loong. Interview by author, February 3, 2014.

14. Theresa W. Carey, "The Best Online Brokers of 2014," *Barron's*, March 15, 2014. Accessed May 9, 2014. http://online.barrons.com/news/articles/SB50001424053111904628504579433251867361162.

Chapter 14

The 16 Questions Do-It-Yourself Investors Ask

1. What's the Difference between an Exchange-Traded Index Fund (ETF) and an Index Fund?

An exchange-traded index fund (ETF) and an index fund (also known as a tracker fund or indexed mutual fund) are much the same. If they track the same market and charge equivalent expense ratios, they should perform identically. For example, Vanguard's S&P 500 index fund holds the same 500 stocks that the iShares S&P 500 ETF holds. But the manner of purchasing an index fund and ETF differ. You buy index funds directly from a fund company. Doing so rarely incurs commission costs, and investors can often reinvest dividends for free.

In contrast, investors purchase ETFs directly from a stock exchange through a brokerage that usually charges commissions. As with regular index funds, investors also receive dividends. But there's rarely an option to reinvest those dividends automatically into additional ETF shares. Instead, dividend deposits (which come either monthly or quarterly) get lumped into the cash portion of the brokerage account. When you add new money to your account (from your savings) it also gets deposited into the cash portion of the account. You can use such cash to purchase an ETF holding, combining the money you deposited from your savings with any dividend cash in the account.

Non-expatriate investors in some countries can purchase commission-free index funds from a few select brokerages. But opportunities for expats to do likewise are limited. It's tempting for Canadian, Australian, or British expats to purchase index funds from their home country financial institutions. But doing so may generate higher taxable consequences.

Many expatriates (with Americans being an exception) can avoid paying capital gains taxes on investment profits if they invest with firms situated where they won't be charged capital gains taxes and if their resident country won't tax them on foreign earned investment gains. Legal tax havens for investments include locations such as Luxembourg, Singapore, Hong Kong, some of the British Isles, and the Cayman Islands.

2. Do Non-Americans Have to Pay U.S. Estate Taxes upon Death If They Own U.S. Index Shares?

The U.S. Internal Revenue Service (IRS) is crafty. Non-Americans buying ETFs off a U.S. stock market could end up paying estate taxes to the U.S. government at death if the investment holdings exceed U.S. $60,000.[1] Some people living *la vida loca* might enjoy stuffing their heirs with an American estate tax, but most expats would prefer to bequeath money to their family, not the U.S. government.

Table 14.1 shows four identical U.S. index funds that non-Americans could buy shares in through an offshore brokerage. The only differences are the expense ratio costs and where each product is domiciled.

3. What's a Sector-Specific ETF?

Hundreds of different ETF products exist, many of which are sector specific. That means you can buy exchange-traded funds tracking almost

Table 14.1   S&P 500 Indexes Available on Different Global Exchanges

ETF	Purchasing Symbol/ Quote/Ticker and Available Exchange	Expense ratio	Would U.S. Estate Taxes Apply?
State Street Global Advisors S&P 500 ETF	SPY: New York Stock Exchange	0.09%	Yes
Vanguard Canada S&P 500 ETF	VFV: Toronto Stock Exchange	0.15%	No
iShares UK S&P 500 ETF	SACC: London Stock Exchange	0.15%	No
iShares Australia S&P 500 ETF	IVV: Australian Stock Exchange	0.07%	No

Costs as of December 2013.

SOURCES: Vanguard USA; Vanguard Canada; iShares UK; iShares Australia.

anything: small company stocks, mining stocks, health care stocks, retail company stocks. Some of the ETFs flooding the markets are just plain wacky. An ETF focusing on the fishing industry is one.

Most exist to excite gamblers. Those thinking that mining stocks will surge this month may purchase a mining stock ETF, perhaps trading their health care ETFs to do so. Meanwhile, an even more backward stock market junkie might choose (and yes, it exists) an ETF specifically designed for its gut-wrenching volatility. The exchange-traded fund market is a bit like Bangkok. Anything goes.

Such an overflow of products also pleases brokerages, allowing them to charge fees on every intoxicating trade.

Stick to ETFs providing broad international exposure and broad exposure to your home country market. In the chapters that follow, I'll show various options for building a Couch Potato portfolio, a Permanent Portfolio, or a Couch Potato portfolio with a fundamental twist.

4. Should I Buy an Index That's Currency Hedged?

Not if you can help it. Some funds are hedged to a specific currency. When British investors buy, for example, a U.S. stock market index, the fund is subjected to U.S. dollar movements. When a fund company creates a currency-hedged version, it attempts to limit the foreign currency's influence on the fund.

But currency fluctuations are natural. If we accept that, we'll be better off than if we try engineering fixes for the problem.

To understand the problems with currency-hedged funds, it's important to recognize that currency fluctuations aren't always bad. If, for example, the British dollar falls against most foreign currencies, then investors could profit from a nonhedged international index, as the growing strength of foreign currencies against the pound juices the returns of a foreign stock index in British dollars.

Buying products that try to smooth these ups and downs through currency hedging involves an extra layer of costs—and those costs can hurt your returns.

In Dan Bortolotti's book *MoneySense Guide to the Perfect Portfolio*, he outlines the true cost of hedging using two U.S. S&P 500 indexes trading on the Canadian market. One was hedged to the Canadian dollar; the other was not. In theory, their returns in local currencies should be the same, but they're not even close. The currency hedging adds an extra cost of 1 to 3.5 percent per year.[2]

According to Raymond Kerzérho, a director of research at PWL Capital, currency-hedged funds get burdened with high internal costs, dragging down results. In a PWL Capital research paper, he examined the returns of hedged S&P 500 indexes between 2006 and 2009. Even though the funds were meant to track the index, they underperformed it by an average of 1.49 percentage points per year. Although less dramatic, he also estimated that between 1980 and 2005, when currencies were less volatile, the tracking errors caused by hedging would have cost 0.23 percentage points per year.[3]

The more cross-currency transactions that a fund makes, the higher its expenses—because even financial institutions pay fees to have money moved around. Consider the example of a currency exchange booth at an airport. Take a $10 Canadian bill and convert it into euros. Then take the euros they give you, and ask for $10 Canadian back. You'll get turned down. The spreads you pay between the buy and sell rates will ensure that you come away with less than $10.

Large institutions don't pay such high spreads, but they still pay spreads.

With indexes, it's best to go with a naturally unhedged product. Accepting currency volatility (instead of trying to hedge against it) will increase your odds of higher returns.

5. What's the Scoop on Withholding Taxes? (For Non-Americans)

Most stocks pay dividends, which are cash proceeds to shareholders. Indexes and exchange-traded funds do likewise because they comprise individual stocks. Regardless of whether your money is situated in a capital-gains-free zone, most investors are liable for dividend taxes.

I'll show a Canadian stock market ETF to demonstrate how much an investor would pay in dividend withholding taxes.

If you averaged a pretax return of 10 percent per year, roughly 8 percent of that growth would come from capital appreciation. Such growth reflects the rising value of the stocks within the index. Most stocks pay shareholder dividends as well, and ETF investors are entitled to their share. If dividends were 2 percent per year, then you would pay 15 percent tax on your 2 percent dividend. In this case, your 2 percent dividend would be reduced to 1.7 percent. As a result, if the pretax return on your ETF were 10 percent, your posttax return would be 9.7 percent.

How Withholding Taxes Affect Returns on a Canadian ETF or Stock

$$8\% \text{ from capital gains}$$
$$+2\% \text{ from dividends}$$
$$\overline{10\% \text{ pretax return}}$$
$$15\% \text{ tax on dividends } (2 \times 0.15 = 0.3)$$
$$= 10\% \text{ pretax return} - 0.3\% \text{ dividend tax}$$
$$\text{Net return: } 9.7\%$$

Non-American expats choosing to own individual U.S. stocks (Google, Microsoft, Coca-Cola, etc.) must fill out a W-8BEN form. It's officially known as a "Certificate of Foreign Status of Beneficial Owner for United States Tax Withholding." Brokerages mail the forms to investors every couple of years. Investors fill them out before mailing them back to the brokerages. The brokerage then sends them to the IRS.

ETF investors trading on non-U.S. stock exchanges don't have to fill out such forms. But there's one thing to remember. In most cases, they're still charged withholding taxes. The rate may differ, depending on the country's respective tax treaty, but if there are U.S. stocks within the index (for example), the U.S. government has a way of siphoning off money. You probably won't see it, so consider it a ghost tax.

Investors in offshore pension schemes also pay dividend withholding taxes. Unknowledgeable sales reps won't disclose this, but the company must. Here's an example on the Friends Provident International website, under "Investment Benefits":

> Virtually tax free accumulation of your savings (some dividends may be received net of withholding tax, deducted at source in the country of origin). . . . [4]

And once again, on the Royal Skandia offshore pension website:

> . . . certain investment income accruing to a fund may be subject to a tax deduction at source which is withheld in the country where the investment is situated. [5]

When investing offshore using ETFs, you can see the tax machinery under the hood. Other costs of the financial industry also become apparent. Many can't be avoided, but it's good to know what they are.

6. Will You Have to Pay Currency Conversions?

If an investor earning a salary in Malaysian ringgit buys a mutual fund of Southeast Asian stocks, she'll get dinged on a currency conversion. Investors earning Australian dollars and buying a global stock market mutual fund will pay likewise. There's no way around this. You might not see the cost of such a transaction, but that doesn't mean it doesn't exist.

For instance, if your salary is in Indian rupees and you buy an Indian stock or shares in an Indian stock market mutual fund, you won't pay a currency conversion fee. However, if the same Indian-based investor bought an Indian-based mutual fund focusing on U.S. stocks, some kind of currency spread would take a nibble from the fund's returns. The Indian fund manager would need to convert Indian rupees to purchase the fund's U.S. stocks.

You'll never see such costs on your statement, of course, but they're an unavoidable cost of doing business.

When investing in ETFs from a brokerage, you'll likely see such nibbling fees. It's much like driving a car with a transparent hood. If your salary is in Singapore dollars and you buy a global ETF off the Canadian stock market, your money will be converted to Canadian dollars. Like a money exchange at an international airport, the banks are going to take a bite. Don't let anyone convince you otherwise.

Such hidden banking costs occur only during transactions. And they're negligible, compared to high ongoing mutual fund costs or account fees.

7. Should I Be Concerned about Currency Risks?

Many investors think that if they buy an exchange-traded fund priced in a foreign currency, their money is subject to that foreign currency's movement. This isn't the case. For example, assume a Spanish expatriate buys an ETF tracking the Spanish market. If he buys it off a British stock exchange, the investor will see the price quoted in British pounds. However, the movement of the English currency has no bearing on the Spanish ETF.

Imagine the following scenario:

- An investor buys a Spanish ETF trading at 20 pounds per unit on the British market.
- Spanish stocks slide sideways for one year after the investor purchases the ETF.
- The British pound falls 50 percent against the euro during that year.

The British pound's movement wouldn't affect the investment itself. In this case, despite the fact that the Spanish market didn't make money, the ETF purchased at 20 pounds per unit would now be priced at 40 pounds per unit. The British currency crash would affect the ETF's listed price in pounds, but its overall value in euros would be entirely dependent on the movement of the Spanish stock market.

Likewise, a New Zealander buying a global stock market ETF off the Australian market wouldn't be pegged to the value of the Aussie dollar. While the ETF may be priced in Australian dollars, its holdings reflect the currencies of the stock markets it tracks. If the Australian dollar dropped 90 percent compared to a basket of global currencies, a global stock market index trading on the Aussie market would shoot skyward in price. Australian dollar currency movements wouldn't affect its true value.

8. Do the Unit Prices of ETFs Show Which Are Expensive or Cheap?

I often receive e-mails from investors asking me about the prices associated with certain exchange-traded funds. For instance, an American might see a Vanguard S&P 500 ETF trading at $90 per share, and an iShares S&P 500 ETF trading at $180 per share. Although Vanguard and iShares are different providers, their respective ETFs are still tracking the same 500 large American stocks. Their values are identical.

In the same vein, five one-dollar bills aren't worth less than one five-dollar bill. The quoted price difference between two ETFs tracking the same market is a mirage.

That said, one ETF is actually cheaper than another if its expense ratio is lower. If Vanguard's S&P 500 ETF has an expense ratio of 0.09 percent per year and the iShares S&P 500 ETF carries costs of just 0.07 percent, the iShares ETF would be cheaper, based on its lower annual fee.

9. If I Have a Lump Sum, Should I Invest It All at Once?

Most stock market investors add monthly or quarterly to their investments. Such a process is called dollar cost averaging. Doing so ensures that they pay less than an average cost over time. If they invest a constant, standard sum, they'll purchase more units when prices are low and fewer units when prices are high.

But what if you found $100,000 on the street? You report it to the local police, nobody claims it, and you become the happy (or paranoid) recipient of a drug dealer's spoils. Should you invest it all at once, or divide your purchases over many months or quarters?

Much depends on your psychology. If you invest the entire amount and the markets crash 20 percent the following day, how would you feel? If it wouldn't bother you, consider the lump-sum investment. This is based on findings by University of Connecticut finance professors John R. Knight and Lewis Mandell. In a 1993 study spanning a variety of time periods, they found that investing a windfall up front beat dollar cost averaging most of the time.[6]

Odds will be in your favor if you invest the money as soon as you have it.

10. I'm in Some Expensive Products, but They're Currently Down in Value. Should I Sell Now or Wait?

Selling investments at a loss is like a kick to the groin. But if your money is languishing in a high-cost account, making a switch is usually best. Don't wait until the account recovers. Here's why:

Rising and falling markets influence most investment portfolios. If a well-allocated, actively managed portfolio gets hammered in a given year, a well-allocated index portfolio would have done likewise. The opposite applies during years when the markets roar: A rising tide raises all boats. This is one of the reasons you can't congratulate yourself (or your advisor) for gaining 15 percent, 20 percent, even 25 percent in a single year. The big question should be: How did an equally allocated portfolio of index funds perform in comparison?

Here's another example putting the same concept in perspective.

Imagine you bought a house for $100,000. It drops in value to $80,000. You're interested in buying the house next door, but you would need to sell your own house in order to do so. Should you wait for your house to rise in value, back to the $100,000 you paid, before buying the house next door? If you do, you're nuts. The same factors increasing the price of your home would do likewise for the neighborhood.

The same premise applies with the stock and bond markets. If you're trading one diversified portfolio for another, you'll make a market-to-market switch. If stock markets are on a low and you sell your high-cost account to build an index portfolio, you'll likely be selling and buying on a low as well. If markets are on a high, you'll be selling high to buy high. Whatever you do, don't time your sales or purchases based on where you or someone else thinks the markets are headed. That's a fool's errand.

11. How Do I Open a Brokerage Account and Make Purchases? (For Non-Americans)

You might discover that your local offshore bank offers a low-cost brokerage, and that you could open such an account to purchase ETFs. But be careful. Don't wander down to the bank without a clear mission. Banks exist to make money. If you aren't forceful, they might rob you: trading currencies on your behalf, bleeding you with an offshore pension, or cajoling you into their favorite actively managed unit trust.

You're looking for gems in an ogre's den. Be clear about what you want. Don't let anyone sway you.

Tell the financial institution you want to open a brokerage account providing access to a variety of different markets. No, you don't want their advice. No, you don't want their super-duper market research. No, you don't want a free trip to expense-ville.

Ask to open a no-frills, low-cost brokerage trading account.

Here are the steps to follow:

Know what you want to buy.

Each ETF has a ticker symbol or quote that you can locate either from the website of the ETF provider or with a Google search. If, for example, you want a Canadian stock index trading on the Toronto market, you could find such a symbol at Vanguard Canada or iShares Canada.

Vanguard offers its FTSE Canada All Cap Index constituting 245 Canadian stocks of various sizes. It charges a paltry 0.12 percent a year. A quick search on the iShares site shows that the iShares S&P/TSX Capped Composite index ETF comprises roughly the same number of stocks, but its expense ratio is a barrel-scraping 0.05 percent per year. Which would you buy? Considering that both track the same market and the same number of stocks, it pays to go with the iShares product because it's cheaper. Its trading ticker symbol is XIC.

If you were purchasing off the British or Australian stock exchanges, you would do much the same thing. Determine what you want, then do a comparative search using at least two large providers. Vanguard UK and iShares UK work well for Brits and Europeans. Vanguard Australia and iShares Australia suit Aussies. Asians or South American expats could take their pick from ETF providers based in Canada, the United Kingdom, Australia, or Hong Kong.

Determine how many units you want.

You'll know how much money you want to invest, but you'll need to find out how many units of the ETF this will buy. With some online brokerages, you'll be able to find your desired product's unit price. If it's unavailable on the brokerage site, you could use a variety of online searches instead. Let's assume you want to invest $10,000.

If you wanted the iShares Canadian index (XIC), you could use Ya-hoo! Finance to look up its current price.

Near the top of the Yahoo! Finance page, enter the quote or sym-bol. In this case, because it trades on the Toronto stock exchange, you would enter XIC.TO. Figure 14.1 shows how the page would look.

The price per unit is $23.87 CDN. So if you have $10,000 CDN to invest, you can afford to buy 418 units ($10,000 divided by $23.87 per share = 418.94). You'll only be able to purchase whole shares, and, while $10,000 would buy 418 units at $23.87, market prices could change slightly before the transaction is completed. There's also a purchase commission to consider. For these reasons, order a conservative number, like 400 units.

If you're getting paid in a currency other than Canadian dol-lars, remember to convert the currency to the denomination of the ETF. You won't have enough money, for instance, if you try buying 400 units of this ETF with $10,000 Hong Kong dollars. The Cana-dian dollar (which the ETF is denominated in) is worth much more.

Make your purchase.

Regardless of the brokerage selected, steps to purchasing an ETF are similar. When you can do it with one brokerage, you can do it with almost any. I'll use examples from three separate brokerages.

When your account is set up and the cash is ready to go, sim-ply log in. Select "trade" or "order entry" to make the purchase.

iShares S&P/TSX Capped Composite (XIC.TO) - Toronto ★ Follow

23.86 ↑ 0.02(0.08%) Jun 20

Prev Close:	23.84	Day's Range:	N/A - N/A
Open:	N/A	52wk Range:	18.51 - 23.93
Bid:	23.75	Volume:	0
Ask:	23.87	Avg Vol (3m):	101,078
NAV[1]:	21.20	P/E (ttm)[2]:	16
Net Assets[2]:	1.59B	Yield (ttm)[2]:	2.51
YTD Return (Mkt)[2]:	8.65%		

Figure 14.1 iShares S&P/TSX Capped Composite Index at Yahoo! Finance
SOURCE: Yahoo! Finance.

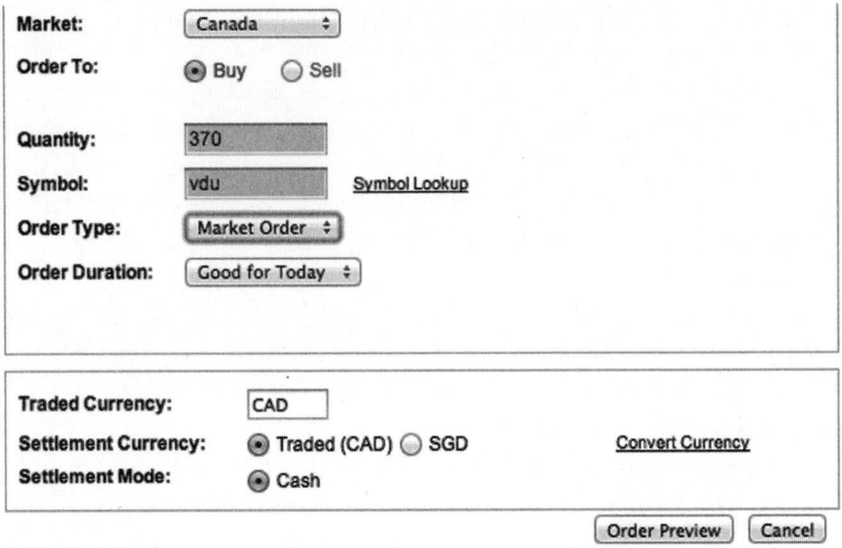

Market: Canada ⬍

Order To: ⦿ Buy   ◯ Sell

Quantity: 370

Symbol: vdu   Symbol Lookup

Order Type: Market Order ⬍

Order Duration: Good for Today ⬍

Traded Currency: CAD

Settlement Currency: ⦿ Traded (CAD) ◯ SGD   Convert Currency

Settlement Mode: ⦿ Cash

Order Preview   Cancel

Figure 14.2   Purchasing 370 Shares of Vanguard's International Developed World Index
SOURCE: DBS Vickers.

Figure 14.2 shows how it looks with DBS Vickers when purchasing 370 shares of Vanguard's international developed world index.

The same purchase is just as simple using TD International's brokerage in Luxembourg. Figure 14.3 is a screen shot of the same order.

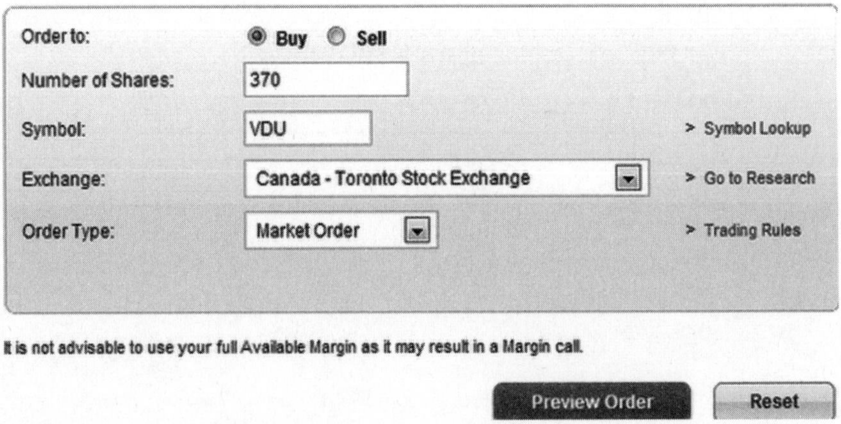

Order to: ⦿ Buy   ◯ Sell

Number of Shares: 370

Symbol: VDU   > Symbol Lookup

Exchange: Canada - Toronto Stock Exchange ▾   > Go to Research

Order Type: Market Order ▾   > Trading Rules

It is not advisable to use your full Available Margin as it may result in a Margin call.

Preview Order   Reset

Figure 14.3   Purchase Using TD International's Brokerage in Luxembourg
SOURCE: TD Direct Investing International.

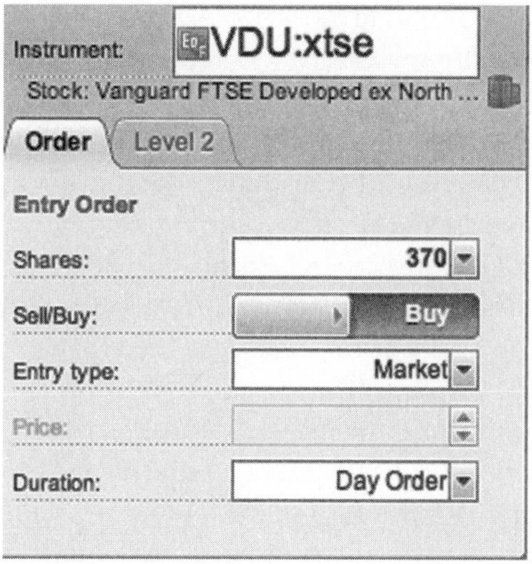

Figure 14.4   Purchase Using Saxo Capital Markets
SOURCE: Saxo Capital Markets.

And Figure 14.4 shows what the purchase screen looks like using Saxo Capital Markets. Note that this brokerage refers to the symbol as the "instrument."

Because the investors in these examples would be purchasing off the Canadian exchange, they would select "Canada" for the market/exchange.

They would select the order to "buy," then enter the number of shares they can purchase, before choosing the ETF symbol (VDU in this case). For order type there's usually an option to select "market" or "limit."

When selecting a market order, you're agreeing to pay the current price or (if the stock market is closed) the price at which the ETF trades when the markets reopen. During stock market trading hours, prices fluctuate. By choosing a market order, you may end up paying a slightly higher or lower price than the latest quote. The stock market doesn't have to be open when you make a purchase order. For example, Australians purchasing an Aussie stock index through TD International can do so even if the Australian markets are closed. The order would be processed once the markets reopened.

Instead of choosing market orders, some people prefer the limit order option. In this case, you could enter a price that represents the maximum you would pay for the day. If the price of the ETF drops to that price, the transaction goes through. If you enter a limit order at $26.28 per share (because that was the last quoted price of the trading session) and the ETF opens trading at $25 the following day, you'll pay $25 for the purchase, not $26.28.

If it doesn't drop to the price you select, the order won't go through. As with market orders, you can also place limit orders when the markets are closed.

Some brokerages don't allow for market orders, insisting you place limit orders instead. This can be troublesome. If you select a low limit order price for the day but the index rises, the trade won't finalize. You may have to place the order again the following day at a higher price. I guarantee this will quicken your pulse. You'll be frustrated, perhaps causing you to sweat or salivate. But this is exactly what the brokerage wants. Nervous Nellies trade more than bovine Buddhas.

For this reason, when given the option I prefer market orders. Sometimes it works in my favor. Sometimes it doesn't. But either way, it's usually just a hair-splitting contest. I would rather get on with my day than worry whether my order was accepted.

12. What If I Find a Higher-Performing Bond Index?

Some people may find better-performing bond indexes than what they originally start with. But always remember that the past is rarely repeated in the future. If a bond ETF pays a 4 percent yield today and a different bond ETF pays 2 percent, don't consider the yields to be carved in stone. Prices of the bonds themselves, as well as the ever-changing average yields (while new bonds replace old) can influence bond ETF returns. Rather than obsessing over past returns and current interest yields, here are the three most important considerations:

1. Ensure that your bond ETF comprises just first-world government or AAA-rated corporate bonds.
2. When possible, make sure it comprises short-term bonds (maturing in three or fewer years).
3. Ensure that the expense ratio charges 0.4 percent or less.

13. What If I Find a Cheaper ETF?

New ETFs are launched continuously. Be wary of trading. Moving from one ETF to another will cost a commission fee, and it might not be worth it. An ETF charging 0.15 percent per year costs just $15 for every $10,000 invested. Another ETF charging 0.12 percent would cost $12. Is it really worth saving $3 per year when it might cost as much as $50 to make a trade?

Brokerages want you to trade. But don't. Rapid trading equals more money for the brokerage, less for the trader. Many brokerages offer discounted commissions to frequent traders. But don't get sucked into the bank's web.

14. Should I Be Most Concerned about Commissions, Annual Account Fees, Fund Costs, or Exchange Rate Fees?

Hands down, ongoing fund costs and annual account fees are far more detrimental than commissions and exchange rate fees. Here are two scenarios. Joe pays 3 percent commissions on each of his purchases. Joe then pays 0.3 percent in hidden ETF expense ratio charges, with no additional account fees.

Julie doesn't pay any commissions to purchase her investments, but her mutual fund expense ratios average 1.5 percent per year, and her account carries an additional 1 percent annual cost. As you'll see, annual costs on the account's total value are a far bigger drag on profits than commissions are.

If Joe and Julie each invested $10,000 per year, earning 8 percent per year before fees, Table 14.2 shows how their profits would compare.

Sure, purchase commissions and exchange rate costs are a pain. I liken them to doing a bike race, where once in a while your opponent leans over and flicks at your brake. But ongoing account fees and high fund charges are worse. They're like another rider holding your seat for the race's duration.

15. How Little Can I Invest Each Month?

Some brokerages, such as Vanguard for Americans, allow people to invest as little as $100 a month. But those using a discount brokerage (and paying commissions on each purchase) should consider only larger monthly sums.

Let's assume you're a non-American using TD Direct Investing International. Minimum commissions are 28 euros per trade. If you invest

Table 14.2 Joe's and Julie's Profits

	Joe	Julie
Invests per year	$10,000	$10,000
Commission paid on purchases	3%	0%
Amount annually invested after commissions	$9,700	$10,000
Annual return made before fees	8%	8%
Annual fund/account costs	0.3%	2.5%
Annual returns after fees	7.7%	5.5%
Investment duration	25 years	25 years
Money grows to	$731,066.88	$539,659.81

100 euros, you would be giving away 28 percent in commissions. To keep costs low, think of the 1 percent rule. Never pay more than 1 percent of your total invested proceeds in commissions.

You can't exactly strong-arm your brokerage into providing a better deal. But think strategically about how much you'll invest at any one time. Assume minimum commissions are 28 euros. By following the 1 percent rule, you would never invest less than 2,800 euros. If you don't have 2,800 euros a month, save for the investing occasion.

Perhaps you can save 500 euros monthly. In this case, keep the money in a savings account until you've accumulated 2,800 euros. Then make your purchase.

Don't be afraid to buy one index at a time. The first time you save 2,800 euros, perhaps you could buy an international stock index. A few months later, buy a bond index. Build your portfolio slowly, one index at a time. Don't worry about rebalancing until your portfolio hits roughly 50,000 euros. From that point, you could buy the underperforming index with each purchase, trying to align your portfolio with your goal allocation.

16. Stock Markets Are High. Should I Really Start Investing?

Finance writers and news media love writing headlines such as these: "U.S. Markets Hit Their Highest Point Ever!" "Are Stocks Ready for a Crash?" "Bonds Are Ready to Fall!"

Let me cut through the murk and give you the market certainties. Ready?

- Stocks will continue to hit new heights.
- Stocks will crash.

- Bonds will decline in value.
- Bonds will rise in value.

These four scenarios will occur over and over during your investment lifetime. Those trying to time their purchases and sales will almost certainly underperform a disciplined, rebalanced portfolio of stock and bond indexes. Sure, you might make a lucky prediction once or twice. But that would be a travesty. Much like the guy who wins big during his first trip to the casino, he's going to go back. And eventually the house will win.

When building your investment portfolio, forget about predictions. If you're adding a lump sum (because you happen to have the money), diversify it properly. Don't try to guess whether you should buy bonds, buy stocks, or sit on your rump waiting for a better deal. Investing isn't a sprint; it's an ultramarathon. You're not trying to race somebody else to the next telephone pole. The real finish line is many years ahead.

Always remember how the average investor performs. Fear, greed, and general speculation cause investors to buy high, sell low, and miss opportunities. Instead, put your calculating brain toward something more constructive: how to best wash the car, shave your face or legs, or get a whole pizza down your gullet in less than five minutes. Speculating with the stock market is a loser's game. If you can't restrain yourself, hire an advisor.

Let's Go!

If you can control your emotions, let's get this going. Jump to the chapter pertaining to your nationality. I'll explain exactly which ETFs to buy, whether you're choosing a Couch Potato portfolio, a Permanent Portfolio, or a Couch Potato approach with a fundamental twist.

Notes

1. "Latest Transfer Tax and FATCA Developments," International Law Office, February 14, 2013. Accessed July 2, 2014. www.internationallawoffice.com/ newsletters/detail.aspx?g=b3f9b11d-c117-47bc-9e09-da4b55975c32.

2. Dan Bortolotti, "*MoneySense* Guide to the Perfect Portfolio," *MoneySense*, November 29, 2011. Accessed July 2, 2014. www.moneysense.ca/uncategorized/moneysense-guide-to-the-perfect-portfolio-2.

3. Raymond Kerzerho, "Currency-Hedged S&P 500 Funds: The Unsuspected Challenges," PWL Capital White Paper, September 1, 2010. www.pwlcapital.com/pwl/media/pwl-media/PDF-files/Articles/Currency-Hedged-S-P500-Funds_The-Unsuspected-Challenges_2010_10_21.pdf?ext=.pdf.

4. "Zenith: Features and Benefits," Friends Provident. Accessed May 09, 2014. www.fpinternational.com/common/layouts/subSectionLayout.jhtml?pageId=fpint%2FSitePageSimple%3Asingle_zenith.

5. Skandia-Life.co.uk. Accessed May 10, 2014. https://www.skandia-life.co.uk/beacon/documentlibrary/pdf08/SK5895.pdf.

6. John R. Knight and Lewis Mandell, "Nobody Gains from Dollar Cost Averaging: Analytical, Numerical and Empirical Results," *Financial Services Review* 2, no. 1 (1993): 51–61. Accessed May 10, 2014. www.valueaveraging.ca/docs/Nobody%20Gains%20from%20DCA.pdf.

Chapter 15

Investing for
American Expats*

L et's say you're an emotional rock, think casinos and lotteries are
for suckers, and would like to stick it to the Wall Street types.
If so, you could make more money building your own indexed
portfolio, rather than paying an advisor to do it for you.

It's simple. And if you're doing it right, you'll spend more time on
the toilet in a week (especially if you read) than you'll spend managing
your portfolio in an entire year.

That said, it's not emotionally easy. You'll need to stick to your
game plan.

The world's largest index fund provider is Pennsylvania-based
Vanguard. It has more assets under management than any fund company

---

*American expats: Most of you probably invest with actively managed mutual funds. In this
chapter, I explain why buying index funds is better. I've also listed investment firms that
would build such portfolios for you: http://goo.gl/dI8AZ5.

in the world. Vanguard doesn't charge annual account fees, nor does it charge fees to enter or exit the funds.

Unfortunately, Vanguard hasn't allowed expatriates to open accounts since 2006. Since then, the only American expats who have done so have lied about their residency on the online application form (providing a U.S. address). They've also strategically failed to reveal their location when speaking on the phone to a Vanguard rep. They haven't broken any laws. But it's not exactly James Dean cool.

Vanguard isn't alone in its discrimination. In the *Wall Street Journal* on July 1, 2014, Laura Saunders wrote, "Fidelity Bans U.S. Investors Overseas from Buying Mutual Funds." She reports that a growing number of American firms are closing doors to U.S. expats.[1]

If you had an account with Vanguard before moving overseas, you're luckier than a gecko without a house cat. You can maintain the account as long as the firm has a U.S. address on record. Otherwise, you'll require a different investment brokerage.

Do You Currently Invest with Vanguard?

Vanguard's investors own the company.[2] No, I'm not blowing smoke up a dark crevice. If you own shares in a Vanguard mutual fund, whether it's an index fund or one of Vanguard's low-cost actively managed products, you're a company owner. It's much like a nonprofit. Owners are the people who purchase the funds. The same can't be said for folks owning funds with Fidelity, Goldman Sachs, T. Rowe Price, Wells Fargo, American Funds, or Morgan Stanley. In every other case (exceptions being nonprofits TIAA-CREF for educators and the Thrift Savings Plan for federal employees), American mutual fund companies have a conflict of interest.

Their first priority is making profits for their firm. Fund investors come second. Mutual fund companies earn profits from the expenses they charge clients, generating much of their business from misleading advertisements. They showcase top-performing funds du jour, while ignoring their laggards (many of which were yesterday's funds du jour).

In 2012, Bloomberg.com reported that the Johnson family (owners of the fund giant Fidelity) was worth $22 billion. Either way you slice it, they've made a colossal living.[3] While Fidelity is privately held, many fund companies trade on the public market.

As economics Nobel Prize winner Paul Samuelson said back in 1967:

> I decided there was only one place to make money in the mutual fund business as there is only one place for a temperate man to be in a saloon, behind the bar and not in front of it . . . so I invested in a management company.[4]

In contrast, Vanguard doesn't have any third-party overlords. The company makes money from its fund expenses, using proceeds to pay employees and business expenses. That's it. Over time, when profits mount, Vanguard lowers its fund costs. And it does so with impressive regularity. During the year I spent writing this book, I kept pace with Vanguard's expense ratio costs—many of which dropped below the levels I reported in the manuscript's first draft.

The same can't be said for the average U.S. mutual fund company. On an unweighted basis, the average U.S. mutual fund cost 0.77 percent per year in 1951. By 2010, costs were up to 1.54 percent.[5]

If you're considering moving overseas but have yet to take the plunge, open a Vanguard account online before leaving the United States at www.vanguard.com. (Remember that you can maintain the account as long as the firm has a U.S. address on record.)

Couch Potato Investing with Vanguard

The simplest way to own a hands-free Couch Potato–like portfolio (see Chapter 9) is with Vanguard's Target Retirement funds. They're cheap, costing roughly 0.17 percent per year. Each target fund is a fully diversified portfolio that gets automatically rebalanced. As fund investors age, bond allocations (as a percentage of each fund) increase.

Let's look under the hood of Vanguard's Target Retirement 2030 fund (see Table 15.1).

It comprises four indexes in a single fund: two stock indexes representing the U.S. and international markets and two bond indexes representing both U.S. and international government bonds. If U.S. stocks

Table 15.1   Vanguard's Target Retirement 2030 Fund: A Look under the Hood

Fund	Allocation
Vanguard Total Stock Market Index Fund	53.7%
Vanguard Total International Stock Index Fund	22.7%
Vanguard Total Bond Market II Index Fund	18.9%
Vanguard Total International Bond Index Fund	4.7%

SOURCE: Vanguard.com, January 31, 2014.

soar and international stocks sink, the fund shifts some money from U.S. to international stocks.

When both stock indexes fall, Vanguard takes money from the bond component, adding it to the stock indexes. Classic Couch Potato. No speculation. Vanguard rebalances the fund back to its original allocation.

Vanguard's Target Retirement 2030 Fund has 23.6 percent allocated to bonds (18.9 percent U.S. bonds, 4.7 percent international bonds) and 76.4 percent allocated to stocks (53.7 percent U.S. stocks, 22.7 percent international stocks). Despite its name, it may not necessarily be suitable for expats wanting to retire in 2030. Those wanting their bond allocation to roughly equal their age should choose the fund reflecting such an allocation.

Don't by fooled by the year in the fund's name. It's not a carton of milk with an expiration date. In 2014, investors could still purchase a Vanguard Target Retirement 2010 fund. It's just a name, not a "best before" warning.

Table 15.2 lists seven of Vanguard's Target Retirement funds, along with their identifying ticker symbols, respective allocations to stocks and bonds, and suitable approximate birth year ranges for investors. Note, for example, I recommend the company's 2010 fund for investors born between 1945 and 1955. The fund's bond allocation is somewhat aligned with these investors' ages.

Note: The stock and bond allocations per fund will shift to more conservative allocations over time. As a result, the suggested birth year range per fund will maintain its relevance. Investors born in certain years where the ranges overlap may choose to divide their money between two Target Retirement funds.

Table 15.2 Vanguard's Target Retirement Funds

Fund	Identifying Ticker Symbol	Rough Percentage in Stocks (2/23/2014)	Rough Percentage in Bonds (2/23/2014)	Hallam's Suggested Birth Year Range for Fund Investors
Vanguard Target Retirement 2010	VTENX	41%	59%	1945–1959
Vanguard Target Retirement 2015	VTXVX	55%	45%	1955–1969
Vanguard Target Retirement 2020	VTWNX	65%	35%	1969–1979
Vanguard Target Retirement 2025	VTTVX	70%	30%	1974–1984
Vanguard Target Retirement 2030	VTHRX	80%	20%	1984–1994
Vanguard Target Retirement 2035	VTTHX	85%	15%	1989–1999
Vanguard Target Retirement 2040	VFORX	90%	10%	1994–2004

SOURCE: Vanguard.com.

Couch Potato Investing with a Vanguard Stick Shift

Investors who want to build a Couch Potato portfolio without a Vanguard Target Retirement fund can purchase individual indexes instead. Such a process comes with benefits and drawbacks. The upside is you can build the portfolio at an even lower cost, especially once you qualify for Vanguard's Admiral Shares (more on that later).

And when managed with discipline, taxable turnover can be lower. Take Vanguard's Target Retirement 2020 fund as an example. Its taxable turnover is roughly 17 percent. When investing in taxable accounts, the lower the turnover, the better. Turnover is a percentage of the holdings traded within a fund during a given year. Each index within a target fund trades a very small number of its stocks annually. If an S&P 500 company goes bankrupt, for example, Standard & Poor's would likely give it the boot. In this case, a newly eligible stock would replace it. The low turnover of index funds makes them especially efficient in taxable accounts.

A Target Retirement fund generates turnover based on the trading occurring within each individual index coupled with the target fund's rebalancing. An investor purchasing his or her own indexes instead can buy the lagging index each month or quarter. By purchasing the lagging index, the investor may be able to keep the portfolio aligned within the goal allocation without selling anything. This decreases turnover. It might frustrate Uncle Sam's tax collectors. But it leaves you legally richer.

Those buying individual indexes require plenty of discipline: discipline most of them don't have. They're like folks who read about nutrition, fill their fridge with organic foods, but stuff themselves with Twinkies. Many index investors begin well—then binge on speculation.

When Investors Binge on Speculation

Norman Rothery, reporting for the *Globe and Mail*, showed returns for a variety of Vanguard funds during the 15-year period ending 2013.[6] The purpose of his article was to show what the funds earned, compared to what investors in those same funds made (see Table 15.3).

Fear, greed, and an unhealthy reliance on expert tips put fat around the organs.

The average investor in the S&P 500 earned only half of what he or she should have earned between 1998 and 2013. This is what I call a screwball.

Many such investors followed so-called sophisticated strategies, listening to CNBC, their gut, or their brother-in-law when committing their unfortunate market timing.

Investors in the European stock index did even worse. Thanks to the same silly behavior, their personal profits underperformed the funds they

Table 15.3 Fund Returns versus Investors' Returns, 1998–2013

Vanguard Fund	Total Fund Returns	Average Investor's Return
S&P 500 Index	+95.7%	+48.4%
European Stock Index	+98.3%	+13.0%
Total Bond Market Index	+107.0%	+77.0%
Total International Stock Index	+110.2%	+117.6%

owned by nearly 85 percent over 15 years. Even those investing in bonds relinquished 30 percent, buying and selling *strategically*.

Note, however, that the average investor in Vanguard's Total International Stock Index fund actually outperformed the fund itself. More of these investors may have deposited regular monthly sums, a process called dollar cost averaging. They would have bought more units when prices were low and fewer units when prices were high. Perhaps they shunned Twinkies, too.

Disciplined Couch Potato investors, however, are the true paradoxical pigs. When rebalancing, they always buy a little low and sell a little high, guaranteeing they never underperform their funds. Here are Vanguard's building blocks to such a portfolio.

Vanguard Global Couch Potato Portfolio Components
Sample Composition for a 40-Year-Old Investor
30% Vanguard Total Stock Market Index (VTSMX)
30% Vanguard Total International Stock Index (VGTSX)
40% Vanguard Short-Term Treasury Index (VFISX)

The funds' expense ratio costs are a lean 0.2 percent, 0.22 percent, and 0.17 percent, respectively. However, once an investor has $10,000 in one of these funds, the expense ratio for that particular fund will drop as the investor qualifies for Vanguard's Admiral Shares rates. Expenses on the Admiral Shares equivalents are a puny 0.05 percent, 0.16 percent, and 0.12 percent.

If you're purchasing the Admiral Shares for the first time (assuming an initial purchase of at least $10,000 per fund), the fund symbols are:

Vanguard Admiral Shares Total Stock Market Index (VTSAX)
Vanguard Admiral Shares Total International Stock Index (VTIAX)
Vanguard Admiral Shares Short-Term Government Bond Index (VSBSX)

Alternatively, investors could purchase Vanguard's Total World Stock Index for the stock component. It simply combines the holdings in the U.S. and international stock index funds. As such, the portfolio could look like this for a 40-year-old investor with less than $10,000 in each fund.

60% Vanguard Total World Stock Index (VTWSX)
40% Vanguard Short-Term Treasury Index (VFISX)

As of this writing, Vanguard's Total World Stock Index charges 0.3 percent. No Admiral Shares equivalent exists. But based on Vanguard's mandate to keep lowering costs, the company may introduce one soon.

Investors building a Permanent Portfolio (discussed in Chapter 10) or a Fundamental Index portfolio (a Couch Potato portfolio with a fundamental twist, discussed in Chapter 11) are better served using a discount brokerage. Vanguard's product scope doesn't include the required funds.

Charles Schwab Offers a Great Deal

I recommend Charles Schwab's online trading platform. As long as you have a U.S. address to put on the application (it could be your brother's, aunt's, or mother's), you should be able open an account.

The Charles Schwab Corporation offers an online trading platform that makes it cheap and convenient to invest in almost anything. If toasters traded on the U.S. market, Schwab would find a way to sell them. Best of all, Schwab offers its own brand of ETFs. As I write, they're the cheapest in the world.

And when purchasing Schwab ETFs from their own brokerages, investors don't pay commissions.

It's likely that Schwab loses money on the products, which are probably serving as a loss leader. It's much like a supermarket offering a sale on bananas, sometimes selling below the store's cost to do so. While the grocery store may lose money on bananas, people get drawn into the store. From there, shoppers usually pick up the rest of their needed groceries, from which the store profits.

Whether using Vanguard, Schwab, or any other U.S. brokerage, you'll need to wire your savings to a U.S. bank account first. From there, you can set up an automatic monthly transfer into your brokerage of choice.

Doing the Couch Potato with Schwab

Schwab's commission-free ETFs are a couch potato's buffet. Table 15.4 is a sample portfolio for a 40-year-old investor. The four funds average costs of just 0.09 percent. It's probably the world's cheapest investment meal.

Table 15.4   Couch Potato Portfolio with Schwab's ETFs

Allocation	ETF	Symbol	Expense Ratio
40% short-term U.S. government bonds	Schwab Short-Term U.S. Treasury ETF	SCHO	0.08%
30% U.S. stocks	Schwab U.S. Broad Market ETF	SCHB	0.04%
25% international stocks	Schwab International Equity ETF	SCHF	0.09%
5% emerging markets stocks	Schwab Emerging Markets Equity ETF	SCHE	0.15%

Charles Schwab's International Equity ETF comprises developed foreign markets only. As in the portfolio sample, those seeking further diversification could add Schwab's Emerging Markets Equity ETF.

Don't get carried away, however, by dreams of emerging market potential. Sure, I dream of every Chinese man, woman, and child buying a copy of this book (realistically, they'd get a photocopied version). But investors should remember that emerging markets are small—making up less than 13 percent of global market capitalization.

Using Vanguard's Total World Stock Index ETF (containing U.S. stocks, developed world international stocks, and emerging market stocks) allows for an even simpler way to gain global stock exposure. Investors could purchase this index through a Schwab account, but they would pay a small commission to do so. Table 15.5 shows what the simplified portfolio could look like for a 40-year-old investor. With just two moving parts, it would be a dream to manage.

As always, younger investors or those with a higher risk tolerance may choose a lower bond allocation. Older investors, or those who are risk averse, may prefer a higher allocation to bonds.

Table 15.5   Simplest ETF Couch Potato Model

Allocation	ETF	Symbol	Expense Ratio
40% short-term U.S. government bonds	Schwab Short-Term U.S. Treasury ETF	SCHO	0.08%
60% global stocks	Vanguard Total World Stock Index ETF	VT	0.18%

Table 15.6   The Permanent Portfolio with ETFs

Allocation	ETF	Symbol	Expense Ratio
25% short-term U.S. government bonds	Schwab Short-Term U.S. Treasury ETF	SCHO	0.08%
25% U.S. stocks	Schwab U.S. Broad Market ETF	SCHB	0.04%
25% long-term U.S. government bonds	Vanguard Long-Term Government Bond ETF	VGLT	0.12%
25% gold	iShares Gold Trust	IAU	0.25%

Permanent Portfolio Investing with Schwab

The Permanent Portfolio (explained in Chapter 10) is never going to be popular. But that doesn't mean it isn't smart. Between 1972 and 2013, it averaged more than 9 percent annually, with its worst-performing year recording a minor −4.1 percent drop in 1981.

Investors, however, need patience. Sometimes the portfolio sputters—especially during years when the stock market soars. In 2013, the S&P 500 gained 33.18 percent, but the Permanent Portfolio dropped 2.4 percent. Craig Rowland, coauthor of the *The Permanent Portfolio: Harry Browne's Long-Term Investment Strategy* (John Wiley & Sons, 2012), updates its performance on his blog, *Crawling Road*.[7]

Table 15.6 lists the ETFs you could use. By utilizing Schwab's brokerage, you could purchase its house brand products (the first two listed) without paying commissions. I've listed short-term government bonds as a substitute for cash.

Fundamental Indexing Magic in the Works

It's also easy to build a Fundamental Index portfolio (explained in Chapter 11) through any U.S. discount brokerage. But once again, Schwab feeds us nicely, offering its own commission-free fundamental ETFs.

Table 15.7 is a sample Fundamental Index portfolio for a 50-year-old investor. It could also be suitable for a younger investor with a low risk tolerance.

Nobody is going to know whether the Couch Potato portfolio, the Permanent Portfolio, or the Fundamental Index portfolio will perform

Table 15.7   Sample Fundamental Index Portfolio

Allocation	ETF	Symbol	Expense Ratio
25% U.S. stocks	Schwab Fundamental U.S. Broad Market ETF	FNDB	0.32%
25% international stocks	Schwab International Fundamental Large Company ETF	FNDF	0.32%
50% U.S. short-term government bonds	Schwab Short-Term U.S. Treasury ETF	SCHO	0.08%

best in the future. Just remember, if things aren't going well, it's not like switching spouses. Does marrying your strategy until death do you part make sense? Not to our Neanderthal-like brains.

If you choose a Fundamental Index strategy and it underperforms a market-capitalized Couch Potato portfolio for a few years in a row, you're going to want a divorce. Don't do it. It's entirely possible (probable, actually) for an underperforming portfolio during one five-year period to become the champion of the three portfolios during the following five years. If you jump on the bandwagon of one method after it stomps the other two, you'll be disappointed when the other portfolios leapfrog. Maintain loyalty to a single method. They're all cheap. They're all diversified. And over your lifetime, they'll outperform most professional investors.

Don't Contribute Illegally to Your IRA

In February 2014, my wife and I met an American expatriate who had been living in Spain for the past eight years. I'll call her Mary. In a casual conversation, she said she had been investing the maximum allowable ($5,500 per year) into her individual retirement account (IRA). Unfortunately, by doing so, she poked a sleeping giant.

The giant (also known as the U.S. government) didn't allow expatriates in 2013 to invest in an IRA if they earned less than $97,600 per year. Mary earned just $50,000.

All of her income qualified for the IRS foreign earned income exclusion. This dull legal label simply means (in her case) she didn't have to pay U.S. income taxes because her Spanish income wasn't high enough. If she earned more than $97,600, things would have been different.[8]

What Exactly Is an IRA?

An IRA is a tax-sheltered investment account. It isn't a portfolio itself. Instead, it's like a special classification. Many Americans have two types of accounts: a tax-advantaged IRA account and a non-IRA taxable account.

If Mary were living in the United States, she could invest a maximum of $5,500 in an IRA and receive some kind of tax-associated benefit. By depositing into a Traditional IRA, the government says, "Good for you, Mary. We'll give you a discount on your taxes this year. You can watch your investment grow. And we won't tax you on its growth until you pull it out."

Mary could withdraw the money without penalty once she reaches 59½. And she must start withdrawing money by the time she's 70½. This would all be fine—if she were living in the United States or making more money as an expat.

The foreign earned income exclusion was $99,200 in 2014. If Mary earned $120,000 while living in Spain, she probably would be eligible to add money to a Traditional IRA. In 2014, allowable contribution limits were $5,500 per year for investors under the age of 50, and $6,500 for investors over the age of 50.[9]

If her foreign earned income above $99,200 were taxable (check online IRS updates[10]) and Mary's earnings exceeded $120,000 for the year, she would have to pay U.S. income taxes on the $20,800 difference. However, if she made a $5,500 Traditional IRA contribution, she could reduce her taxable income by $5,500, thus reducing her tax bill.

Once investors start withdrawing from their Traditional IRAs, withdrawals are taxed at ordinary income tax rates.

Roth IRAs Are Different

There are, however, two types of IRAs: Traditional and Roth. Unlike investing in a Traditional IRA, Roth IRA contributions aren't tax deductible. However, the Roth IRA grows tax-free. When the money is withdrawn during retirement, the principal and the investment gains aren't taxed. There's also added flexibility, considering investors don't have to start liquidating their Roth IRAs at 70½.

As with the Traditional IRA, you can't contribute to a Roth IRA as an expatriate unless you make enough money. Ineligible contributions to an IRA are known as "excess contributions." Excess contributions suffer a 6 percent penalty each year the excess money remains in the account.[11] In Mary's case, she earned $50,000 annually in Spain during 2012 and 2013. She shouldn't have contributed to an IRA because she didn't earn enough money.

Because Mary contributed to her IRA in 2012 and 2013, the government can penalize her. Assume that when we met Mary in February 2014 she hadn't yet filed her 2013 taxes. She would owe 6 percent on her 2012 contribution, but for the excess contribution in 2013 she would still have time to take the money out before filing her 2013 taxes. With such a withdrawal, she could avoid the 6 percent penalty. However, she would still owe taxes and penalties for any profits those contributions earned, determined by an IRS-provided formula.

Keep in mind, however, that taxable situations differ among individuals. An expatriate tax specialist may be worth the money. Many exist, including firms like Greenback Expat Tax Services, American Tax Service, and American Expat Tax Services.

While Americans may moan about paying U.S. taxes on worldwide income, their expat plight isn't all doom and gloom. American expats have access to the lowest-cost financial services companies in the world. Most of the planet's cheapest ETFs are also U.S. based. With discipline, American expats can use such products to slowly grow wealthy.

Notes

1. Laura Saunders, "Fidelity Bans U.S. Investors Overseas from Buying Mutual Funds," *Wall Street Journal*, July 1, 2014. Accessed July 3, 2014. http://online.wsj.com/news/article_email/fidelity-bans-overseas-investors-from-buying-mutual-funds-1404246385-lMyQjAxMTA0MDAwMjEwNDIyWj.

2. "Why Ownership Matters," About Vanguard. Accessed May 9, 2014. https://about.vanguard.com/what-sets-vanguard-apart/why-ownership-matters/.

3. Brendan Coffey, "Hidden Johnson Billionaires Found in Fidelity Fund Empire," Bloomberg.com, September 21, 2012. Accessed May 9, 2014. www.bloomberg.com/news/2012-09-19/hidden-johnson-billionaires-found-in-fidelity-fund-empire.html.

4. John C. Bogle, *The Battle for the Soul of Capitalism* (New Haven, CT: Yale University Press, 2005), 177.

5. John C. Bogle, *Don't Count on It!: Reflections on Investment Illusions, Capitalism, "Mutual" Funds, Indexing, Entrepreneurship, Idealism, and Heroes* (Hoboken, NJ: John Wiley & Sons, 2011), 75.

6. Norman Rothery, "Stick with Buy-and-Hold: Don't Try Timing the Market," *Globe and Mail*, February 4, 2014. Accessed May 9, 2014. www.theglobeandmail .com/globe-investor/investment-ideas/strategy-lab/value-investing/stick-with-buy-and-hold-dont-try-timing-the-market/article16697904/.

7. Craig Rowland, "Permanent Portfolio Archives," *Crawling Road*. Accessed May 9, 2014. www.crawlingroad.com/blog/tag/permanent-portfolio/.

8. "Foreign Earned Income Exclusion," Internal Revenue Service. Accessed July 3, 2014. www.irs.gov/Individuals/International-Taxpayers/Foreign-Earned-Income-Exclusion.

9. "Retirement Topics—IRA Contribution Limits," Internal Revenue Service. Accessed May 10, 2014. www.irs.gov/Retirement-Plans/Plan-Participant%2C-Employee/Retirement-Topics-IRA-Contribution-Limits.

10. Ibid.

11. Kaye A. Thomas, "Excess Contributions to Roth IRAs," Fairmark.com, November 15, 2013. Accessed May 10, 2014. http://fairmark.com/retirement/roth-accounts/contributions-to-roth-accounts/excess-contributions-to-roth-iras/.

Chapter 16

Investing for Canadian Expats

S ammy Sellmore leans back in his business-class seat. With just an hour before landing in Kuala Lumpur, it's time to get to work. He calls over a flight attendant, orders a glass of champagne, and opens his laptop to scroll through his client files.

The Canadian financial advisor meets overseas clients a few times each year. To be good at what he does—really good—he needs to maintain relationships. His job, after all, is more about managing people than it is about managing money. It's much the same for every successful salesperson. In Sammy's case, he needs to remember his clients' names, their kids' names, and what subjects each of them favors in school.

He'll take the wealthier clients out for dinner, and make notes to remember birthday and Christmas cards. If he becomes a dear friend of the family, he'll never get fired. Sammy's a persona representing leagues of advisors whose clients are expats.

So is Sammy friend or foe? There's one acid test: Is he selling actively managed Canadian mutual funds? If so, cost-conscious investors would have to let him go.

Canadian Funds Earn an "F" for Costs

Fund rating company Morningstar publishes an annual "Global Fund Investor Experience" report. Each year that it has been doing so, actively managed Canadian funds earn an F grade on costs. According to Morningstar, "Canada is hampered by having the world's highest total expense ratios."[1]

Such high costs plunder investment returns. Writing for Canada's *Financial Post* in October 2013, Michael Nairne cited the S&P/Dow Jones Indices vs. Active Funds (SPIVA) Canada scorecard. The study from 2008 to 2012 revealed that Canadian investors in actively managed funds underperformed their benchmark indexes by an average of 2.85 percent per year across seven major categories.[2]

In the *Globe and Mail*, I wrote a 2014 article comparing 10-year returns for the Royal Bank of Canada (RBC)'s actively managed mutual funds versus indexes in equal asset classes.[3] Where RBC had multiple funds representing the same broad asset class, I averaged the returns of those funds and compared them with an equivalent stock market index.

RBC's results weren't pretty. A media-relations gentleman from a competing firm, Fidelity Canada, congratulated me: "Great job on that RBC mutual fund article. Most of our funds have beaten indexes. But it's great to see you calling out the poorly performing fund companies."

Before receiving his e-mail, I hadn't thought about comparing Fidelity's funds to indexes. After some research, I wrote an article about Fidelity.[4] As with RBC, their performances were poor. Shortly after it was published, the Fidelity gentleman e-mailed back, stating that most of the poorly performing fund managers had been fired the previous year. Hampered by high fees, their new managers will likely fare no better.

A few weeks later, a media-relations woman from Manulife Financial e-mailed. "If you choose to write an article about our funds," she asked, "please use our lower-cost products." Some firms offer two classes of funds: expensive and ridiculously expensive. To be honest, I hadn't thought about writing an article exposing Manulife's funds either. But it was fun doing so. Like RBC and Fidelity, their results lagged the market—and I did use the lowest-cost products Manulife had![5]

Enjoying the shake-up, I then wrote about funds from Canadian Imperial Bank of Commerce (CIBC),[6] Toronto-Dominion Bank,[7] and IA Clarington.[8] The company I chose made little difference. On aggregate, portfolios of funds with 10-year track records were walloped by the indexes.

What's worse, many advisors flog funds with back-end loads. In such cases, if you own a fund for fewer than six or seven years and you sell it, you get slapped with a penalty. Who pockets proceeds from the fine? Your friendly, jet-setting financial advisor.

Such advisors, however, are Boy Scouts and Girl Guides compared to those selling offshore pensions from firms like Friends Provident, Zurich International, Generali, and Royal Skandia. Owning Canadian actively managed funds is like suffering from a constant cold. Most offshore pensions are like malaria.

Brokerage Options for Expatriate Canadians

Building a portfolio of exchange-traded funds (ETFs) requires a brokerage. Some Canadians, such as Scott Rousseu, have opened nonresident accounts with Toronto-based TD Waterhouse.[9] Investors can open such accounts only in person, and they must provide proof they reside overseas.

The 44-year-old, originally from Vancouver, British Columbia, did so in 2000, two years after leaving Canada. He currently teaches English at a university in the United Arab Emirates.

As a Middle East resident, he doesn't pay capital gains taxes on his TD Waterhouse investment profits. His dividends are taxed at a flat 15 percent.

Scott is comfortable investing in a nonresident Toronto-based account. Many Canadian accountants suggest doing so won't jeopardize nonresidency status. In 2009, Canadian accountant Arun (Ernie) Nagratha spoke to a group of Hong Kong–based Canadians to alleviate such fears. The seminar, supported by the Canadian Expat Association, can be found on YouTube at the following link: http://goo.gl/JkpR4r.[10]

Brokerages for Canadians in Capital-Gains-Free Jurisdictions

Some expatriates fear Canada may change its tax laws, either closing or taxing nonresident investment accounts based in Canada. Such investors prefer keeping their assets offshore. Luxembourg, Singapore, and Hong Kong attract plenty of expatriate clients, based on their low-cost tax structure. Foreign-based brokerages tend to cost more than they do in Canada. But for some, it's a small price to pay for a sound night's sleep.

TD Waterhouse charges just $9.99 per trade.[11] Luxembourg-based TD Direct Investing International charges minimum commissions of roughly $41 CDN (28 euros), which increase with higher invested sums.[12] Table 16.1 is a cost comparison between TD Waterhouse and TD Direct Investing International, assuming investors add $40,000 annually through 12 purchases. TD International costs more, but the long-term impact is less than you might think.

The difference is also slightly overstated. TD International's annual "security custody fee" charges 0.2 percent, up to a maximum of 600 euros per year. When the account value exceeds 400,000 euros (and in the example, it would have), the drag on returns would be slightly reduced. For example, if an investor's portfolio were worth 1 million euros, the

Table 16.1   Toronto-Based TD Waterhouse versus Luxembourg-Based TD International

20-Year Comparison

Brokerage	TD Waterhouse (Toronto)	TD International (Luxembourg)
Amount invested annually	$40,000 CDN	$40,000 CDN
Commissions paid on 12 annual purchases	$119.88 CDN	$499.96 CDN
Annual investment made after commissions	$39,880.12	$39,500.04
Annual returns before account fees	8%	8%
Annual account fees	0%	0.2%
Annual return after account fees	8%	7.8%
Account value after 20 years	$1,970,992	$1,905,956

600-euro annual fee would ensure a security custody fee of 0.06 percent, instead of the 0.2 percent listed.

Building a Canadian Couch Potato Portfolio

Canadian expats without a family vendetta should avoid U.S.-traded stocks and ETFs. U.S.-domiciled holdings exceeding $60,000 incur the wrath of U.S. estate taxes when the account holder floats to his or her ultimate reward. So if you don't want to stiff your heirs with a U.S. tax bill, avoid U.S.-domiciled products.[13]

That doesn't mean you can't build a fully diversified Couch Potato portfolio of ETFs, including U.S. stock market exposure. If you choose ETFs domiciled in Canada, Uncle Sam's grim reaper doesn't knock for money.

My sample portfolios comprise low-cost ETFs that aren't hedged to the Canadian dollar. Hedging (which I discussed in Chapter 14) reduces returns over time. The ETFs in Table 16.2 are also broadly diversified.

Table 16.2   Canadian Cap-Weighted Couch Potato Building Blocks

Index	Ticker Symbol	Expense Ratio	Comprising
iShares S&P/TSX Capped Composite Index ETF	XIC	0.05%	249 Canadian stocks
Vanguard U.S. Total Market ETF	VUN	0.15%	3,613 U.S. stocks
Vanguard FTSE Emerging Markets Index ETF	VEE	0.33%	922 stocks, nearly 70% of which come from China, Brazil, South Africa, and India
Vanguard FTSE Developed (ex North America) Index ETF	VDU	0.28%	1,301 stocks, roughly 65% of which come from Japan, the United Kingdom, France, Germany, and Switzerland
Vanguard Canadian Short-Term Bond Index ETF	VSB	0.15%	254 short-term bonds maturing within one to five years (mostly Canadian government)

SOURCES: Vanguard Canada; iShares Canada.

Allocating percentages for these ETFs has much to do with your age, your risk tolerance, and where you plan to retire.

Take 40-year-old Ian Page and his 41-year-old wife, Bridget. Teachers at Singapore American School since 2002, they've also taught in Cairo and Switzerland after leaving Canada in 1997. They plan to retire in Canada, but won't be eligible for public school teacher pensions. Nor will they receive much from the Canadian Pension Plan (CPP) after a career overseas.[14]

Without pensionable income, Ian and Bridget can't afford to take large financial risks. As a result, they're making sure their bond allocation roughly equals their age. Table 16.3 shows how their Couch Potato portfolio might look.

Because Ian and Bridget hope to repatriate one day, they're keeping more than half of their money in Canadian dollars: 40 percent Canadian bonds, 20 percent Canadian stocks. It makes sense, considering they'll pay most of their future bills in loonies. The remainder is split between U.S. and international stocks.

Alternatively, Ian and Bridget could buy a single index comprising stocks from every one of the world's stock markets. Vanguard Canada, as of this writing, doesn't offer such a product. But iShares does. Its expense ratio is currently 0.47 percent.

Table 16.3   Canadian Couch Potato Portfolio

For a 40-Year-Old Investor

Allocation	ETF	Symbol	Expense Ratio
40% Canadian short-term government bonds	Vanguard Canadian Short-Term Bond Index ETF	VSB	0.17%
20% Canadian stocks	iShares S&P/TSX Capped Composite Index ETF	XIC	0.05%
20% U.S. stocks	Vanguard U.S. Total Market ETF	VUN	0.15%
15% international stocks	Vanguard FTSE Developed (ex North America) Index ETF	VDU	0.28%
5% emerging market stocks	Vanguard FTSE Emerging Markets Index ETF	VEE	0.33%

SOURCES: Vanguard Canada; iShares Canada.

Table 16.4   Three-Fund Couch Potato Model

For a 40-Year-Old Canadian

Allocation	ETF	Symbol	Expense Ratio
40% Canadian short-term government bonds	Vanguard Canadian Short-Term Bond Index ETF	VSB	0.17%
20% Canadian stocks	iShares S&P/TSX Capped Composite Index ETF	XIC	0.05%
40% global stocks	iShares MSCI World Index Fund ETF	XWD	0.47%

SOURCES: Vanguard Canada; iShares Canada.

If Ian and Bridget used such a fund, their Couch Potato portfolio could look like the one in Table 16.4.

Replacing the U.S., developing, and emerging market indexes for a global stock ETF wouldn't alter the portfolio's allocation. But with just three indexes instead of five, the portfolio may be easier to manage. Adding the iShares MSCI World Index Fund ETF, however, would slightly increase the cost of the portfolio, considering its 0.47 percent annual expense ratio.

Mark Holmes, 45, and his wife Christina, 42, might choose a slightly different allocation. Teachers at the Shanghai United International School, they'll eventually receive a couple of partial pensions. When Mark turns 60, he'll receive income from British Airways, where he once worked as an aircraft technician. He'll also receive income from the UK's National Insurance. Unlike Ian and Bridget, Mark and Christina are unsure of where they want to retire. "Malaysia looks very attractive," says Mark, "but we also like Vancouver Island."

Mark's partial pensions represent future guaranteed income— "If we can believe the providers' promises," says Mark. The pension is much like a bond, so Mark and Christina can take slightly higher risks. Instead of matching their bond allocation with their average age (45 and 42), they could settle for 30 percent bonds and 70 percent stocks, increasing their bond allocation slightly over time. They might also consider a lower allocation to Canadian stocks if they start leaning more toward retiring in Malaysia.[15]

Table 16.5 shows how their portfolio might look.

Table 16.5 Mark and Christina's Couch Potato Model

Allocation	ETF	Symbol	Expense Ratio
30% Canadian short-term government bonds	Vanguard Canadian Short-Term Bond Index ETF	VSB	0.17%
10% Canadian stocks	iShares S&P/TSX Capped Composite Index ETF	XIC	0.05%
30% U.S. stocks	Vanguard U.S. Total Market ETF	VUN	0.15%
25% international stocks	Vanguard FTSE Developed (ex North America) Index ETF	VDU	0.28%
5% emerging market stocks	Vanguard FTSE Emerging Markets Index ETF	VEE	0.33%

SOURCES: Vanguard Canada; iShares Canada.

Alternatively, by choosing the iShares MSCI World Index Fund ETF, their portfolio would be simpler still, as shown in Table 16.6.

There's no magic formula to the allocations themselves. Mark and Christina may choose to have slightly more in international stocks, and slightly less in Canadian equities. It's no big deal. They just need to remember to be fully diversified.

Whatever allocation you choose, stick with it and rebalance as necessary. At times, international stocks will outperform Canadian stocks. It

Table 16.6 Mark and Christina's Model Choosing iShares MSCI World Fund ETF

Allocation	ETF	Symbol	Expense Ratio
30% Canadian short-term government bonds	Vanguard Canadian Short-Term Bond Index ETF	VSB	0.17%
10% Canadian stocks	iShares S&P/TSX Capped Composite Index ETF	XIC	0.05%
60% global stocks	iShares MSCI World Index Fund ETF	XWD	0.47%

SOURCES: Vanguard Canada; iShares Canada.

might happen for a few years in a row. Just follow the game plan, rebalancing your portfolio back to the original allocation once a year, or purchasing (with your monthly or quarterly savings) the underperforming index. Doing so will allow you to maintain a balanced portfolio, and in Warren Buffett–speak, you'll always be acting a bit fearfully when others are greedy, and somewhat greedily when others are fearful.

ETF Canadian Price War

Canadian ETF providers are currently trying to undercut one another's costs. While a great thing for investors, it presents certain risks. Those jumping from one ETF to another when a cheaper one gets launched risk paying plenty of money in commissions. What's more, gambling bones get tickled, blood pressures rise, and investors find themselves trading more. That's what the industry wants.

For years iShares Canada was the country's dominant ETF provider. But when Vanguard started offering ETFs on the Canadian market in late 2011, iShares began losing a tremendous amount of market share. Like Schwab in the United States, iShares initiated a price war with Vanguard.

By March 2014, iShares had undercut Vanguard in a couple of categories. Costs on its S&P/TSX Capped Composite Canadian index ETF were slashed to 0.05 percent per year, compared to Vanguard's equivalent, which charges 0.12 percent. The iShares U.S. S&P 500 index ETF charges just 0.10 percent, whereas Vanguard's equivalent index charges 0.15 percent. If the price war heats up, costs for both firms will likely drop further.

The Permanent Portfolio, Canadian Style

Recall that the Permanent Portfolio (Chapter 10) may be the world's most stable. Over a 40-year period, it averaged nearly 10 percent annually, dropping just 4.1 percent in its worst year (1981). Unlike the Couch Potato portfolio, investors don't tailor the bond component to reflect their age or risk tolerance. This portfolio blends asset classes that tend to move in opposite directions.

Table 16.7   Canadian Permanent Portfolio Model

Allocation	ETF	Symbol	Expense Ratio
25% Canadian stocks	iShares S&P/TSX Capped Composite Index ETF	XIC	0.05%
25% Canadian long-term government bonds	BMO Long Federal Bond ETF	ZFL	0.20%
25% gold	iShares Gold Bullion	CGL	0.50%
25% Canadian short-term government bonds	Vanguard Canadian Short-Term Bond Index ETF	VSB	0.15%

Canadians can build such a portfolio with ETFs domiciled in Canada. The ETF holdings are listed in Table 16.7.

The portfolio is split into quarters: 25 percent stocks, 25 percent long-term bonds, 25 percent gold, and 25 percent cash. Because savings accounts offer such paltry returns, I've replaced the cash option with Vanguard's short-term bond index. Such an option was offered in Craig Rowland and J. M. Lawson's excellent book, *The Permanent Portfolio* (John Wiley & Sons, 2012).[16]

Some investors may wish to diversify their equities globally. This makes sense, considering Canada's stock market makes up less than 5 percent of the world's total capitalization. In such a case, the portfolio may look something like the one in Table 16.8.

Table 16.8   Canadian Permanent Portfolio with Global Exposure

Allocation	ETF	Symbol	Expense Ratio
12.5% Canadian stocks	Vanguard FTSE Canada All Cap Index ETF	VCN	0.12%
12.5% global stocks	iShares MSCI World Index Fund ETF	XWD	0.47%
25% Canadian long-term government bonds	BMO Long Federal Bond ETF	ZFL	0.20%
25% gold	iShares Gold Bullion	CGL	0.50%
25% Canadian short-term government bonds	Vanguard Canadian Short-Term Bond Index ETF	VSB	0.15%

Fundamental Indexing Portfolios

Recall from Chapter 11 that fundamental indexes don't weight stocks based on capitalization, but on their respective economic footprints. Companies earning greater business profits, for example, have higher influences on a fundamental index's movements than a high-priced stock would. Stocks with high prices relative to their business earnings may be popular, but their prices may be unwarranted.

As a result, high-priced stocks have higher odds of realigning with their intrinsic business values once the market tires of their popularity. According to researchers Robert D. Arnott, Jason C. Hsu, and John M. West, fundamental indexes beat capitalization-weighted indexes by roughly 2.6 percent per year from 1984 to 2007.[17]

Table 16.9 is basically a Couch Potato portfolio model for a 30-year-old investor, but utilizing fundamental instead of cap-weighted ETFs. All of these indexes trade on the Canadian market.

Fundamental indexing's popularity is slowly gaining steam among Canadians. But cap-weighted indexes are still more common. Vanguard Canada hasn't entered the market (yet) but if it does so, that will likely drive expenses down.

So far, most of iShares' fundamental indexes are performing well. Table 16.10 shows how they compare against their own cap-weighted equivalents.

Table 16.9 Canadian-Style Fundamental Indexing

Allocation	ETF	Symbol	Expense Ratio
20% Canadian stocks	iShares Canadian Fundamental Index Fund	CRQ	0.72%
25% U.S. stocks	iShares U.S. Fundamental Index Fund	CLU	0.72%
25% international stocks	iShares International Fundamental Index Fund	CIE	0.72%
30% Canadian short-term government bonds	Vanguard Canadian Short-Term Bond Index ETF (no current fundamental equivalent)	VSB	0.15%

Sources: Vanguard Canada; iShares Canada.

Table 16.10   iShares Five-Year Annual Returns: Fundamental versus Cap-Weighted Indexes, 2009–2013

Fund Categories	iShares Fundamental Indexes	iShares Cap-Weighted Indexes
Canadian equity	+13.81% (CRQ)	+11.55% (XIC)
U.S. equity	+18.27% (CLU)	+16.62% (XSP)
International equity	+8.28% (CIE)	+9.71% (XIN)
Average return	+13.45%	+12.62%

SOURCE: iShares Canada.

Between 2009 and 2013, iShares fundamental Canadian and U.S. equities outperformed their cap-weighted products. But in the international equity category, the iShares cap-weighted index outperformed its fundamental counterpart. Would a fundamental index portfolio be the winner over your lifetime? Perhaps. So far, five-year average performances for iShares' fundamental ETFs beat their cap-weighted contemporaries: 13.45 percent versus 12.62 percent. Longer-term, back-tested historical tests also favor fundamental indexes. But without a crystal ball (one that really works!), nobody knows for sure which will win.

A portfolio of fundamental indexes should be allocated much the same way as a cap-weighted Couch Potato model. Consider your age, risk tolerances, and whether you have a guaranteed defined benefit pension on the way.

What About RRSPs and TFSAs?

Expatriate Canadians aren't eligible to invest in registered retirement savings plans (RRSPs) or tax-free savings accounts (TFSAs) while living offshore. Such tax-deferred accounts encourage residents to invest. Expats can maintain such accounts if they purchased them before leaving the country, but they can't contribute new money to them. In some cases, they may choose to sell their RRSPs, which is what I did with my portfolio in 2004.

When I had my RRSP, I was living in Canada and paying roughly 40 percent marginal income tax. If I had decided to moonlight as a cashier at 7-Eleven (for additional income), I would have paid 40 cents in tax for every dollar earned.

Because of my tax rate, I earned a 40 percent rebate from the federal government on contributions to my RRSP. The money could have compounded, tax free, until I was willing to withdraw it at retirement.

But I sold the investments in 2004. At the time, I was living in Singapore. I paid a 25 percent withholding tax to do so. I had earned a 40 percent cash rebate for adding the money in the first place, and paid just 25 percent tax to sell. If you're an expatriate Canadian with an RRSP, you may consider doing the same.

Swap-Based ETFs, the Ultimate Legal Tax Dodge

There is a third type of exchange-traded fund that Canadians could use, providing the ultimate legal tax dodge. As mentioned previously, expatriate Canadians can avoid capital gains taxes. But there's also a way to dodge dividend taxes.

Horizon Canada offers three swap-based ETFs on the Canadian market. Its HXT Horizons S&P/TSX 60 index ETF costs just 0.07 percent. It tracks Canada's 60 biggest stocks. The firm's HXS Horizon S&P 500 index ETF tracks the U.S. market. It costs 0.15 percent. And Horizon's Canadian Select Bond Universe ETF costs 0.15 percent as well. Most indexes physically hold stocks or bonds within them, but not these. Instead, they're like contracts backed by the National Bank of Canada, promising investors the full return of a given index as if all dividends or interest were reinvested. Because investors don't actually own the index's holdings directly, they aren't charged dividend taxes on the stock indexes or income taxes on the bond index.

Finance writer and money manager Dan Bortolotti does a great job describing how swap-based ETFs work in his *Canadian Couch Potato* blog post, "More Swap-Based ETFs on the Horizon."[18] They're popular in Canada, having amassed more than a billion dollars in assets, because capital gains are taxed at a lower rate than dividends.

Canadian-based investors in these products pay capital gains taxes only. In expatriate accounts, however, benefits multiply. Those not liable for capital gains taxes can legally avoid capital gains and dividend withholding taxes, as well as tax on the bond interest.

I own the aforementioned three ETFs in my personal portfolio.

But there's a higher degree of counterparty risk. If Canada's National Bank gets into trouble, there's always a chance it could default on its promise.

I've said this before, but it's worth repeating: Whether you choose the Couch Potato portfolio, Permanent Portfolio, or Fundamental Index portfolio, stick to it. If you jump from strategy to strategy based on recent performance, you'll pay the same price that plagues most emotional investors. Fortunes reverse. Don't bail on tomorrow's winner because it's underperforming today.

Choose a strategy. Rebalance. And stay the course.

Notes

1. "Global Fund Investor Experience: 2013 Report," Morningstar.com. May 15, 2013. Accessed May 20, 2014. http://corporate.morningstar.com/US/ documents/MethodologyDocuments/FactSheets/Global-Fund-Investor-Experience-Report-2013.pdf.
2. Michael Nairne, "Active Mutual Fund Managers Take Another Beating," *Financial Post*, October 11, 2013. Accessed May 19, 2014. http://business .financialpost.com/2013/10/11/active-mutual-fund-managers-take-another-beating/.
3. Andrew Hallam, "How RBC Funds Compare against Index Funds, ETFs," *Globe and Mail*, January 29, 2014. Accessed July 3, 2014. www.theglobeandmail .com/globe-investor/investment-ideas/strategy-lab/index-investing/how-rbc-funds-compare-against-index-funds-etfs/article16556141/.
4. Andrew Hallam, "Putting Fidelity's Funds to the Test," *Globe and Mail*, February 6, 2014. Accessed July 3, 2014. www.theglobeandmail.com/globe-investor/investment-ideas/strategy-lab/index-investing/putting-fidelitys-funds-to-the-test/article16738022/.
5. Andrew Hallam, "Manulife Funds vs. Index Funds: Here's How They Stack Up over 10 Years," *Globe and Mail*, April 2, 2014. Accessed July 3, 2014. www .theglobeandmail.com/globe-investor/investment-ideas/strategy-lab/index-investing/how-do-manulife-mutual-funds-measure-up-against-index-funds/ article17779903/.
6. Andrew Hallam, "How Do CIBC Mutual Funds Measure Up against Its Index Funds?" *Globe and Mail*, March 11, 2014. Accessed July 3, 2014. www.theglobe andmail.com/globe-investor/investment-ideas/strategy-lab/index-investing/ mutual-fund-success-is-predicted-by-low-fees-not-history/article17441151/.
7. Andrew Hallam, "How Do TD's Mutual Funds Stack Up against Its Index Funds?" *Globe and Mail*, February 26, 2014. Accessed July 3, 2014. www

.theglobeandmail.com/globe-investor/investment-ideas/strategy-lab/index-investing/how-do-tds-mutual-funds-stack-up-against-index-funds/article17126059/.

8. Andrew Hallam, "IA Clarington Funds vs. Indexes: How They Stack Up," *Globe and Mail*, April 29, 2014. Accessed July 3, 2014. www.theglobeandmail.com/globe-investor/investment-ideas/strategy-lab/index-investing/putting-ia-claringtons-market-beating-claims-to-the-test/article18330041/.

9. Interview with Scott Rousseu. E-mail interview by author, February 3, 2014.

10. "Trowbridge Tax Presentation Part II," YouTube. Accessed May 19, 2014. www.youtube.com/watch?v=-ZjOLywi1Hc&list=FLIvQwkfwfzGP3_H9fw1YTVQ.

11. "Commissions and Fees," TD Waterhouse. Accessed May 19, 2014. www.tdwaterhouse.ca/products-services/investing/td-direct-investing/commissions-fees/.

12. "Fees and Commissions," TD Direct Investing International. Accessed May 19, 2014. http://int.tddirectinvesting.com/en-gb/investment-products/fees-and-commissions/.

13. "Some Nonresidents with U.S. Assets Must File Estate Tax Returns," Internal Revenue Service. Accessed May 19, 2014. www.irs.gov/Individuals/International-Taxpayers/Some-Nonresidents-with-U.S.-Assets-Must-File-Estate-Tax-Returns.

14. Interview with Ian Page. Interview by author, April 20, 2014.

15. Interview with Mark Holmes. E-mail interview by author, April 21, 2014.

16. Craig Rowland and J. M. Lawson, *The Permanent Portfolio: Harry Browne's Long-Term Investment Strategy* (Hoboken, NJ: John Wiley & Sons, 2012).

17. Robert D. Arnott, Jason C. Hsu, and John M. West, *The Fundamental Index: A Better Way to Invest* (Hoboken, NJ: John Wiley & Sons, 2008), 123.

18. Dan Bortolotti, "More Swap-Based ETFs on the Horizon," *Canadian Couch Potato* RSS, October 15, 2013. Accessed July 3, 2014. http://canadiancouchpotato.com/2013/10/15/more-swap-based-etfs-on-the-horizon/.

Chapter 17

Investing for British Expats

B ritish index funds fall into two categories: cheap and expensive. Index funds are supposed to be cheap. Many UK financial firms, however, have found a way to make sizable profits from indexes—at the investor's expense. Richard Branson's Virgin Money was one of the first.

In his autobiography, *Losing My Virginity*, Sir Richard says, "After Virgin entered the financial-services industry, I can immodestly say it was never to be the same again. . . . We never employed fund managers . . . since we discovered their best-kept secret: they could never consistently beat the stock-market index."[1]

Virgin created its own index tracker funds, charging plenty in the process. The company's FTSE tracker fund costs 1 percent per year. Such a cost is low compared to portfolios of offshore pensions. But for an index fund, it's higher than one of Branson's balloons. In contrast, Vanguard UK's FTSE equity index costs just 0.15 percent.[2]

Vanguard charges low fees because, unlike Virgin, its investors (everyone who buys its funds) actually own the company. It's run much like a nonprofit firm. Tracking errors are also low because the company is an experienced index fund builder. If the stocks in the FTSE All Share Index rise by 10 percent, Vanguard's tracking index should earn roughly 9.85 percent, trailing the market by its 0.15 percent management fee. If it earned a result lower than 9.85 percent, in this case, the fund managers would be to blame. Any additional performance discrepancy would be called *tracking error*.

Expensive Firms Performing Like a Virgin

Virgin Money's equivalent product would lag the market by at least its 1 percent annual fee. Any tracking errors committed would reduce profits further. Over time, high costs and tracking errors are compounding problems.

Virgin's FTSE All Share UK index earned 19.7 percent in 2013.[3] Vanguard's FTSE UK Equity index earned 20.7 percent.[4] They each track the same market. But Vanguard's index costs 0.85 percent less. Consequently, Vanguard's index should have beaten Virgin's index by 0.85 percent. But this wasn't the case. Vanguard outperformed Virgin by a full percentage point.

Virgin, living up to its name, lacks Vanguard's experience. Accurately tracking an index requires skill that Vanguard has honed over many years. Virgin has had a few years to practice, but it is still disappointing investors. And 2013 wasn't a one-off miss.

Between 2010 and 2013, Virgin's UK stock index underperformed Vanguard's by an average of 1.2 percent per year (see Table 17.1).

Such differences look small. But over an investment lifetime, paying more for the same product has costly compounding consequences.

Virgin isn't the only UK index fund provider with high expenses and poor tracking records. Kyle Caldwell, writing for *The Telegraph*, reported that the UK stock market grew by 132 percent for the decade ending 2013.[5] But the typical UK stock market index suffered

Table 17.1   Virgin versus Vanguard, 2010–2013

Year	Virgin's FTSE All Share UK Index	Vanguard's FTSE UK Equity Index
2010	+13.0%	+14.4%
2011	−4.7%	−3.5%
2012	+11.0%	+12.2%
2013	+19.7%	+20.7%

SOURCE: Morningstar UK.

zombie-like rigor mortis. Halifax's UK FTSE All Share Index tracker grew by just 92.6 percent. It lagged the market by nearly 40 percent for the decade, as did the Scottish Widows UK tracker, which grew by just 94.8 percent.

Expatriate British investors, however, shouldn't fall foul. Many can keep their money offshore, sidestepping the United Kingdom's financial firms' misguided indexing mess. While doing so, they should stick to low-cost, experienced index providers such as Vanguard UK or iShares UK.

Couch Potato Investing for British Expatriates

Sean McHugh is a 44-year-old teacher working as a digital literacy coach at United World College in Singapore. Displeased with high-cost, inflexible investment options peddled by offshore pension sales-people, he started to do some research. "Building a low-cost portfolio of exchange-traded index funds," he says, "is a far smarter option than allowing someone else to line their own pockets with my money."[6]

He opened a trading account with Saxo Capital Markets and built a Couch Potato portfolio (see Chapter 9). Trading commissions for exchange-traded funds (ETFs) on the London Stock Exchange cost 0.2 percent or a minimum of $20 USD equivalent.

Sean earns his salary in Singapore dollars. If he allows Saxo Capital Markets to exchange Singapore dollars for British pounds before mak-ing his investment purchases, he pays the fees listed in Table 17.2.

Table 17.2   Saxo Capital Markets Commission Charges Off the London Stock Exchange

If Sean Invests . . .	Saxo Capital Markets Trading Commission 0.15% (or Minimum $20 USD Equivalent)	Saxo Capital Markets Currency Trading Commission (0.5% above Spot Rate)	Total Commission
£1,000	£12.02 ($20 USD)	£5	£17.02
£5,000	£12.02 ($20 USD)	£10	£22.02
£10,000	£15	£15	£30
£15,000	£22.50	£20	£42.50

Stamp duty of 0.5 percent on UK ETF purchases and 1 percent on Irish-domiciled ETF purchases may apply.

SOURCE: "Commissions," Saxo Capital Markets. Accessed May 20, 2014. http://sg.saxomarkets.com/prices/stocks/commissions.

A £1,000 investment would cost Sean £17.02 in commissions. A £15,000 investment would cost £42.50. This contrasts greatly with commissions often charged by offshore pensions. Alexander Beard, for example, charges 5 percent per purchase. Such a fee would cost £250 on a £5,000 investment or £750 on a £15,000 investment.

Sean, however, could also use a currency conversion service charging less than Saxo Capital Markets. In such a case, he could exchange his money with the lower-cost firm before transferring British pounds to his Saxo Capital Markets account.

Recognizing he doesn't want his heirs to pay U.S. estate taxes, Sean selects ETFs domiciled outside the United States. "I don't want to bequeath, to my heirs, a U.S. tax bill when I die."

Few non–Americans realize the risks associated with U.S.-domiciled stocks or ETFs. Whether they're buying Apple, Coca-Cola, Wal-Mart, or an ETF trading on the New York Stock Exchange, the account holder's heirs may have to pay an American estate tax.

Because Sean is 44 years old, he allocates roughly 40 percent of his portfolio to a British bond index. If his risk tolerance were greater, or if he were younger, he could choose a smaller fixed income (bond) allocation (see Table 17.3).

The iShares and Vanguard global stock ETFs carry different costs: 0.6 percent versus 0.25 percent, respectively. But the price gap could

Table 17.3   Couch Potato Portfolio

For a 44-Year-Old British Investor

Allocation	ETF	Symbol	Expense Ratio
40% British government bonds	iShares UK Gilts 0–5 yr. UCITS	IGLS	0.20%
30% British stocks	Vanguard UK FTSE 100 Stock Index	VUKE	0.10%
30% global stocks	iShares Global Stock Index ACWI UCITS	SSAC	0.60%
	or		
	Vanguard FTSE All-World ETF	VWRD	0.25%

SOURCES: Vanguard UK; iShares UK.

narrow. I listed both ETFs because iShares has a habit of trying to keep pace with Vanguard's low costs. It has slashed expenses before, and may do so with its global stock ETF in the future.

Sean plans to retire in England eventually. But what if he becomes a global vagabond? If this were the case, he wouldn't need a British stock or bond market bias. His future expenditures would come in a variety of currencies. A more globally diversified portfolio might be the answer. Table 17.4 is an example.

The global bond index comprises bonds from nearly every developed world country. The global stock index is much the same, weighting

Table 17.4   Global Nomad's Couch Potato Portfolio

Allocation	ETF	Symbol	Expense Ratio
40% global government bonds	iShares Global AAA–AA Government Bond	SAAA	0.20%
60% global stocks	iShares Global Stock Index ACWI UCITS	SSAC	0.60%
	or		
	Vanguard FTSE All-World ETF	VWRD	0.25%

SOURCES: iShares UK; Vanguard UK.

countries by global capitalization. No single currency movement would rock Sean's boat.

British Investors and the Permanent Portfolio

British investors choosing Harry Browne's Permanent Portfolio model (see Chapter 10) would need to split their money equally into stocks, long-term bonds, short-term bonds (or cash), and gold. Those of different ages or risk tolerances wouldn't make adjustments.

Such assets often move in opposite directions, providing stability. Those planning to retire in the United Kingdom might choose the following ETFs. Note that Vanguard's UK Government Bond Index isn't comprised of long-term bonds. With no such product currently available, an index of bonds maturing over a medium term (as listed in Table 17.5) is the next best option.

As of this writing, a British short-term government bond ETF didn't exist. If one becomes available (and it very likely will), investors may choose it over the cash component.

Investors wishing to diversify further may choose a global stock index and a British stock index. Their portfolios might look like the one in Table 17.6.

British investors uncertain of where they'll be retiring may consider the global index for their stock market exposure, forgoing the British index entirely.

Table 17.5   Permanent Portfolio for British Investors

Allocation	ETF	Symbol	Expense Ratio
25% British government bonds	iShares UK Gilts 0–5 yr. UCITS (medium-term bond index)	IGLS	0.20%
25% British stocks	Vanguard UK FTSE 100 Stock Index	VUKE	0.10%
25% gold	iShares Physical Gold ETC	SGLN	0.25%
25% cash	Cash		

SOURCES: iShares UK; Vanguard UK.

Table 17.6 British Permanent Portfolio with a Global Allocation

Allocation	ETF	Symbol	Expense Ratio
25% British government bonds	iShares UK Gilts 0–5 yr. UCITS	IGLS	0.20%
12.5% British stocks	Vanguard UK FTSE 100 Stock Index	VUKE	0.10%
12.5% global stocks	iShares Global Stock Index ACWI UCITS	SSAC	0.60%
	or		
	Vanguard FTSE All-World ETF	VWRD	0.25%
25% gold	iShares Physical Gold ETC	SGLN	0.25%
25% cash			

SOURCES: iShares UK; Vanguard UK.

Fundamental Indexing for the British

Chapter 11 discussed the theoretical and historical advantages of fundamental index funds over their cap-weighted equivalents. British investors can purchase Invesco PowerShares fundamental ETFs.[7] They're available from any brokerage providing access to the British stock market.

Neither the cap-weighted ETFs nor the fundamental ETFs have been available on the British market for long. But Table 17.7 presents returns for the respective categories, comparing performances with Vanguard and iShares cap-weighted ETFs when possible.

Investors, however, shouldn't determine whether to invest in fundamental indexes based on the fund performances. These time frames are short and inconsequential. If the rationale behind fundamental indexes makes sense to you (see Chapter 11), then you could build such a portfolio based on the model in Table 17.8.

History suggests that over long periods of time fundamental index models should outperform cap-weighted models. But as with anything market related, there are no promises. The only certainty is that Power-Shares ETFs will outperform most actively managed funds because they're cheaper.

Table 17.7   Four-Year Annual Returns: PowerShares/RAFI Fundamental
Indexes versus Vanguard/iShares Cap-Weighted ETFs

	2010	2011	2012	2013
British Stock Indexes				
PowerShares FTSE RAFI UK 100				
(PSRU)	+11.8%	−3.8%	+11.3%	+20.8%
iShares FTSE 100 (ISF)	+12.9%	−5.8%	+13%	+17.4%
Vanguard FTSE 100 UCITS ETF				
(VUKE)	NA	NA	NA	+18.9%
Emerging Markets Indexes				
PowerShares FTSE RAFI				
Emerging Markets ETF (PSRM)	NA	−21.1%	+6.8%	−11.9%
iShares MSCI Emerging Markets				
ETF (IEEM)	+21.9%	−20.5%	+9.5%	−7.3%
World Indexes				
PowerShares FTSE RAFI All-				
World 3000 UCITS (PSRW)	NA	−11.9%	+6.9%	+21.6%
iShares ACWI UCITS ETF (SSAC)	NA	NA	+9.3%	+21.2%

Source: Morningstar UK.

With one of the ETFs in Tables 17.7 and 17.8, however, there's a
higher potential risk. The PowerShares FTSE RAFI All-World 3000
(PSRW) is a swap-based ETF. Unlike ETFs comprising physical stocks,
swap-based ETFs don't hold physical shares. This index tracks the return
of the FTSE RAFI All-World 3000 Index and provides investors with
its total return. It's much like a promissory note backed by a financial
institution.

Unlike indexes holding physical shares, however, when this ETF
generates a return of 10 percent in a given year, British expats can earn

Table 17.8   Fundamental Index Portfolio

For a 40-Year-Old British Investor

Allocation	ETF	Symbol	Expense Ratio
40% UK bonds	iShares UK Gilts 0–5 yr. UCITS	IGLS	0.2%
30% UK stocks	PowerShares FTSE RAFI UK	PSRU	0.5%
30% global stocks	PowerShares FTSE RAFI	PSRW	0.5%
	All-World 3000 UCITS		

Sources: iShares UK; Morningstar UK.

the full 10 percent. No money gets skimmed off the top for dividend withholding taxes. For many expatriates, it's a tax-free product.

■ ■ ■

It matters little whether you invest in a Couch Potato portfolio, Permanent Portfolio, or Fundamental Index portfolio. But switching your game plan to adhere to the previous year's winning strategy is foolish. Each of these strategies will have their years in the sun. The trouble is, you'll never know which are going to shine in any given year.

If you're like most people (remember that most people are nuts), you'll be inclined to invest through the rearview mirror. If the Permanent Portfolio outperforms the others for three or five years, you might be tempted to switch. If the fundamental indexes start outperforming, you might want to jump on the bandwagon. Resist the temptation.

Choose one of the three horses and stick to it. It won't earn scorching returns every year. But each of these portfolios was born to run over an investment lifetime.

Notes

1. Richard Branson, *Losing My Virginity: How I've Survived, Had Fun, and Made a Fortune Doing Business My Way* (New York: Times Business, 1998), 405.
2. "Vanguard FTSE UK Equity Index Fund," Vanguard UK. Accessed May 20, 2014. https%3A%2F%2Fwww.vanguard.co.uk%2Fuk%2Fmvc%2FloadPDF%3FdocId%3D2034.
3. "Virgin UK Index Tracking Trust Inc.," Morningstar UK. Accessed May 20, 2014. www.morningstar.co.uk/uk/funds/snapshot/snapshot.aspx?id=F0GBR04RWI.
4. "Vanguard FTSE U.K. Equity Index Acc," Morningstar UK. Accessed May 20, 2014. www.morningstar.co.uk/uk/funds/snapshot/snapshot.aspx?id=F00000 3YCZ.
5. Kyle Caldwell, "The 500,000 Fund Investors Failed by Trackers," *The Telegraph*, July 13, 2013. Accessed May 20, 2014. www.telegraph.co.uk/finance/personalfinance/investing/10580063/The-500000-fund-investors-failed-by-trackers.html.
6. Interview with Sean McHugh. E-mail interview, May 1, 2014.
7. Invesco PowerShares Professional Clients. Accessed May 20, 2014. www.invescopowershares.co.uk/portal/site/ukprops/ouretfs/fullrange.

Chapter 18

Investing for Australian Expats

Many Australians equate investing with a single asset class: real estate. And while Australian property values have certainly soared, the stock market hasn't been too shabby, either.

According to Philip Soos, a research Masters student at Deakin University's School of Humanities and Social Sciences, Australian property prices rose 400 times faster than inflation between 1900 and 2012. He sourced such data from the Australian Bureau of Statistics.[1]

This means if your great-grandfather had a typical residential property in 1900 and you sold it in 2012, you could buy 400 times what he could have bought had he sold the property in 1900. Purchasing a decade ago would have reaped decent returns as well. According to Global Property Guide,[2] Australian property prices increased by 89.23 percent for the decade ending in 2013.

How would you have done if your great-grandfather had purchased a broad selection of Australian stocks instead? If sold today, you could buy 2,408 times what he could have purchased with the proceeds in 1900. Stock prices outpaced real estate during the decade ending 2013 as well. Vanguard's Australian stock market index increased roughly 125 percent[3] while Australian residential properties grew 89.23 percent.

I'm not suggesting properties aren't great investments. They are, especially if purchased when they're unpopular, after a particularly dismal run. But many Australians are property-mad—rarely diversifying across different asset classes. Two asset classes they could add are global stock and bond indexes.

Lawson Dixon, based in Saigon, is the CEO of Harley-Davidson Vietnam. Business is booming. But the 47-year-old Australian wants to diversify some of his net earnings into stock and bond investments. "Over the years, I've looked at all sorts of investment options: property, pension schemes, savings plans, insurance products, and the stock market. And it's fair to say there's a lot of 'snake oil' salesmen out there."

Lawson, 47, and his wife Hanh have two children, Huey, 7, and newborn Maggie. He left Australia in 2000 and recognizes the high cost of investment products, both in Australia and abroad.

"Most of these so-called experts," he says, "are only after one thing: your hard-earned money. I even had one tell me: 'I'm a Wall Street banker; my word is my bond.'"[4]

Lawson could open an account with any number of offshore brokerages, including TD Direct Investing International or Saxo Capital Markets. Each provides access to the Australian stock market.

According to Singapore's Saxo Capital Markets senior manager, Eoh You Loong, dividend withholding tax on Australian ETFs is 30 percent.[5] If Lawson earned a 10 percent return, with 8 percent coming from capital gains and 2 percent from dividends, the capital gains would be tax-free, but he would pay 30 percent tax on his dividends. If he earned a 10 percent pretax investment return, dividend taxes (assuming a 2 percent dividend yield) would deduct 0.6 percent from the total growth (0.02 dividend × 0.3 tax = 0.006).

After-tax returns on a portfolio averaging a 10 percent return would therefore be 9.4 percent. The brokerage would deduct such taxes at the source.

Fancy an Australian Couch Potato?

Vanguard and iShares have a solid selection of low-cost exchange-traded funds (ETFs) available on the Australian market. The Dixons could build a couch potato portfolio costing less than 0.15 percent. As is the case with most global ETFs, fees are falling.

Lawson's wife, Hanh, is younger than he is, so she may outlive him. Considering this, the portfolio could be geared toward a smaller bond allocation than Lawson would have if he were single. Table 18.1 shows how the portfolio might look.

The Dixons may also want exposure to Vietnamese stocks. But they shouldn't go overboard. The Vietnamese stock market is small.

Including Vietnamese exposure, the Dixons' Couch Potato portfolio could look something like Table 18.2.

If Lawson and Hanh plan to remain in Vietnam, they wouldn't require such a strong Australian stock and bond market bias. They could create a globally balanced portfolio instead.

A sample is shown in Table 18.3.

As with any Couch Potato model, the Dixons would stick to their goal allocation, incrementally increasing the bond allocations as they age. They would also rebalance their portfolio once a year, selling pieces of their winners to buy pieces of their losers. Or they could purchase the underperforming asset class with their savings each month.

Table 18.1   Australian Couch Potato Portfolio Model

Allocation	ETF	Symbol	Expense Ratio
30% Australian government bonds	Vanguard Australian Government Bond Index	VGB	0.20%
35% Australian stocks	Vanguard Australian Shares Index	VAS	0.15%
17.5% U.S. stocks	Vanguard U.S. Total Stock Index	VTS	0.05%
17.5% global stocks	Vanguard All-World (ex U.S.) Stock Index	VEU	0.15%

SOURCE: Vanguard Australia.

Table 18.2   An Australian Couch Potato Portfolio Hooks Up with Vietnam

Allocation	ETF	Symbol	Expense Ratio
30% Australian government bonds	Vanguard Australian Government Bond Index	VGB	0.20%
35% Australian stocks	Vanguard Australian Shares Index	VAS	0.15%
15% U.S. stocks	Vanguard U.S. Total Stock Index	VTS	0.05%
15% global stocks	Vanguard All-World (ex U.S.) Stock Index	VEU	0.15%
5% Vietnamese stocks	db X-trackers FTSE Vietnam	3087.HK (Hong Kong exchange)	0.85%

SOURCES: Vanguard Australia; Bloomberg.

How About an Australian Permanent Portfolio?

Recall the advantages of Harry Browne's Permanent Portfolio model (Chapter 10). Asset classes often move in different directions. Therefore, splitting assets evenly among stocks, bonds, cash, and gold tends to smooth long-term returns.

Table 18.3   An Australian's Global Couch Potato Portfolio

Allocation	ETF	Symbol	Expense Ratio
10% Australian government bonds	Vanguard Australian Government Bond Index	VGB (Australian exchange)	0.20%
20% global government bonds	iShares Global Government Bond Index	IGLO (UK exchange)	0.20%
5% Australian stocks	Vanguard Australian Shares Index	VAS (Australian exchange)	0.15%
30% U.S. stocks	Vanguard U.S. Total Stock Index	VTS (Australian exchange)	0.05%
30% global stocks	Vanguard All-World (ex U.S.) Stock Index	VEU (Australian exchange)	0.15%
5% Vietnamese stocks	db X-trackers FTSE Vietnam	3087.HK (Hong Kong exchange)	0.85%

Table 18.4   Permanent Portfolio—Australian Style

Allocation	ETF	Symbol	Expense Ratio
25% Australian government bonds	Vanguard Australian Government Bond Index	VGB (Australian exchange)	0.20%
8.33% Australian stocks	Vanguard Australian Shares Index	VAS (Australian exchange)	0.15%
8.33% U.S. stocks	Vanguard U.S. Total Stock Index	VTS (Australian exchange)	0.05%
8.33% global stocks	Vanguard All-World (ex U.S.) Stock Index	VEU (Australian exchange)	0.15%
25% gold	BetaShares Gold Bullion ETF	QAU (Australian exchange)	0.49%
25% cash			

Historical results speak for themselves. The model has never crashed, despite some horrendous stock market drops. When stocks drop, gold often rises. When bonds fall, stocks often rise. When everything falls (which is rare), cash holds steady.

The model shown in Table 18.4 splits money evenly into the four different asset classes. It would suit Australian investors planning to re-patriate at some point in the future, based on its bias toward Australian bonds and its Aussie stock exposure. The cash component could sit in an Australian dollar savings account.

The decimal places depicting how much the investor should have in Australian and U.S. stocks (8.33 percent allocated to each) take things a bit far. Rounding up or down is fine. If any given sector is out by a percentage point or two, it's not going to make much difference.

Australians not planning to repatriate may consider a more globally diversified Permanent Portfolio. Table 18.5 shows how it could look.

Fundamental Indexing for Australians

Just one fundamental index is available on the Australian stock exchange: the BetaShares FTSE RAFI Australia 200 ETF.[6]

Table 18.5   Globally Diversified Permanent Portfolio

Allocation	ETF	Symbol	Expense Ratio
25% global government bonds	iShares Global Government Bond Index	IGLO (UK exchange)	0.20%
12.5% U.S. stocks	Vanguard U.S. Total Stock Index	VTS (Australian exchange)	0.05%
12.5% global stocks	Vanguard All-World (ex U.S.) Stock Index	VEU (Australian domiciled)	0.15%
25% gold	BetaShares Gold Bullion ETF	QAU (Australian exchange)	0.49%
25% cash			

Introduced in late 2013, it carries an expense ratio of 0.3 percent, which is low for a fundamental index. It comprises 200 Australian companies, weighted based on fundamental elements like business earnings and dividends, instead of market capitalization. Australians wishing to build portfolios with a fundamental indexing component could choose this index over their Vanguard or iShares cap-weighted counterparts.

No fundamental index exists for the bond allocation, but Australians can purchase a fundamental global stock index off the British exchange. The RAFI All-World Index (PSRW) has an expense ratio of 0.5 percent.[7] It's a swap-based ETF. Such products carry slightly higher risks. Unlike ETFs comprising physical stocks, swap-based ETFs don't hold physical shares. Instead, they track the return of the index, providing investors with its total return. It's much like a promissory note backed by a financial institution.

Unlike indexes holding physical shares, however, when this ETF generates a return of 10 percent in a given year, investors can earn the full 10 percent. Dividend withholding taxes aren't charged. As such, for many expats, it's a tax-free product.

Table 18.6 shows how an Australian's fundamental index portfolio might look.

Regardless of whether you choose the standard Couch Potato, Permanent Portfolio, or Fundamental Indexing model, don't switch your game plan. Some years, the Permanent Portfolio will crush the others. Other

Table 18.6   Fundamental Portfolio Sample

For a 40-Year-Old Australian Investor

Allocation	ETF	Symbol	Expense Ratio
35% Australian government bonds	Vanguard Australian Government Bond Index	VGB (Australian exchange)	0.20%
30% Australian stocks	BetaShares FTSE RAFI Australia 200	QOZ (Australian exchange)	0.30%
35% global stocks	PowerShares FTSE RAFI All-World 3000	PSRW (UK exchange)	0.50%

years, the Couch Potato portfolio will outperform. Still other times, you may find the Fundamental Index portfolio beating the other two.

If you want to be like everyone else, chase the strategy that's performing best. But by continuing to do so, your money will run like a car on flat tires. One year's winner may be the next year's loser. Invest intelligently, consistently, and follow a solid game plan. Over time, each of these models will perform well for the patient.

Notes

1. "The History of Australian Property Values," MacroBusiness, February 13, 2013. Accessed May 20, 2014. www.macrobusiness.com.au/2013/02/the-history-of-australian-property-values/.
2. "Global Property Guide House Price Changes," Global Property Guide. Accessed May 20, 2014. www.globalpropertyguide.com/Pacific/Australia/price-change-10-years.
3. Vanguard Australia—Retail Managed Funds ($5,000 Min.). Accessed May 20, 2014. https://www.vanguardinvestments.com.au/adviser/jsp/investments/managed-funds-retail.jsp#grossperformancetab.
4. Interview with Lawson Dixon. E-mail interview by author, May 14, 2014.
5. Interview with Eoh You Loong. Telephone interview by author, March 20, 2014.
6. BetaShares Exchange Traded Funds. Accessed July 3, 2014. http%3A%2F%2Fwww.betashares.com.au%2Fproducts%2Fname%2Fftse-rafi-australia-200-etf%2F%23each-performance.
7. "PowerShares FTSE RAFI All-World 3000 UCITS ETF (GBP) | PSRW," Morningstar UK. Accessed July 3, 2014. www.morningstar.co.uk/uk/etf/snapshot/snapshot.aspx?id=0P0000NHSB.

Chapter 19

Investing for New Zealand Expats

Many people who aren't from New Zealand would be shocked to learn the country is home to just 4.5 million people. After all, Kiwis are everywhere—or so it seems. *The Telegraph* reported in 2010 that roughly a quarter of New Zealand's skilled workforce had fled the country.[1] No other developed nation has a poorer record retaining skilled workers.

Higher wages abroad might be the reason. According to *The Telegraph*, highly skilled Kiwis abroad earn 78 percent more than they can in their home country.[2] If you're reading this, you're likely one of them— or thinking about taking the plunge.

Those living overseas can open accounts at any of the offshore brokerages listed in Chapter 13.

New Zealanders who wish to repatriate one day may want exposure to their home country stock market. But options are limited from offshore brokerages, without choosing a New Zealand stock index do-miciled in the United States. The iShares MSCI New Zealand Capped ETF[3] comprises 30 publicly traded Kiwi shares. The five largest com-panies make up roughly 30 percent of the index's market capitalization. They are the Telecom Corporation of New Zealand, Auckland Interna-tional Airport, Ryman HealthCare Ltd., Sky Network Television, and Skycity Network.

The index's annual expense ratio is 0.51 percent. From January 2010 to January 2014, its total return was +98 percent, measured in U.S. dollars.[4] In previous chapters, I warned against purchasing stocks or exchange-traded funds (ETFs) off the U.S. market. Expatriates who own more than $60,000 in U.S.-domiciled investment products may end up triggering U.S. estate taxes upon death. It hardly seems fair. The index, after all, comprises New Zealand–based stocks, not American ones. But because it trades on the New York Stock Exchange, the U.S. government takes its portion upon the investor's death.

Kiwis Chilling Out with the Couch Potato

Expatriate Kiwis, however, could still build a Couch Potato portfo-lio with exposure to the New Zealand market—as long as the index doesn't exceed a $60,000 USD value. Table 19.1 is a model portfolio for a 30-year-old investor. The global government bond and global stock

Table 19.1   Couch Potato Model for a 30-Year-Old New Zealand Investor

Allocation	ETF	Symbol	Expense Ratio
30% global bonds	iShares Global AAA-AA Government Bond	SAAA (UK market)	0.20%
10% New Zealand stocks	iShares MSCI New Zealand Capped ETF	ENZL (U.S. market)★	0.51%
60% global stocks	iShares Global Stock Index ACWI UCITS or	SSAC (UK market)	0.60%
	Vanguard FTSE All-World ETF	VWRD (UK market)	0.25%

★Maintain less than $60,000 USD in this index.

indexes trade on the British exchange, while the New Zealand stock index trades on the U.S. market.

Vanguard's FTSE All-World Index provides cheaper exposure to global markets than its iShares equivalent. But I've listed both because these ETF companies are in a price war. It's entirely possible that by the time you read this, iShares could have undercut Vanguard in the fee department. Unlike the practice among actively managed mutual fund providers, ETF firms tend to lower their fees.

Older investors or others who prefer a lower risk portfolio may choose a higher bond allocation than presented in Table 19.1. Younger investors or others with a higher tolerance for risk could choose fewer bonds.

New Zealanders not planning to repatriate may skip their home country exposure entirely. In such cases, they could choose just two indexes: the global stock index and the global government bond index, both available on the British exchange.

Permanent Portfolio for Kiwis

As mentioned in Chapter 10, investors interested in Harry Browne's Permanent Portfolio needn't worry about their bond allocations reflecting their age or risk tolerance. Such a portfolio has fixed percentages. Investors occasionally rebalance (see Chapter 10) back to the original allocation. Or, as with the Couch Potato portfolio, they would purchase the lagging ETF each time they invest. The strategy ensures that investors stick close to the goal allocation: 25 percent gold, 25 percent bonds, 25 percent stocks, and 25 percent cash (see Table 19.2).

Fundamental Indexing for New Zealanders

As detailed in Chapter 11, back-tested comparisons between fundamental indexes and their cap-weighted equivalents usually give fundamental indexes the edge. As of this writing, no fundamental index for the Kiwi market exists. But New Zealanders could build a Couch Potato portfolio and then replace a cap-weighted global stock index with one that's fundamentally weighted.

Table 19.2   Global Permanent Portfolio for New Zealanders

Allocation	ETF	Symbol	Expense Ratio
25% gold	iShares Physical Gold ETC	SGLN (UK market)	0.25%
25% global bonds	iShares Global AAA–AA Government Bond	SAAA (UK market)	0.20%
15% global stocks	iShares Global Stock Index ACWI UCITS or	SSAC (UK market)	0.60%
	Vanguard FTSE All-World ETF	VWRL (UK market)	0.25%
10% New Zealand stocks	iShares MSCI New Zealand Capped ETF	ENZL (U.S. market)*	0.51%
25% cash			

*Maintain less than $60,000 USD in this index.

The PowerShares FTSE RAFI All-World Index (PSRW) fits the bill.[5] It's swap-based, which has advantages and potential disadvantages. On the plus side, it doesn't generate dividend withholding taxes. The risk is that the ETF doesn't hold physical shares. Instead, it tracks the return of the FTSE RAFI All-World 3000 Index and provides investors with its total return. It's much like a promissory note backed by a financial institution.

Table 19.3 shows what a Fundamental Index portfolio could look like for a 30-year-old investor.

Table 19.3   Global Fundamental Portfolio for New Zealanders

Allocation	ETF	Symbol	Expense Ratio
30% global bonds	iShares Global AAA–AA Government Bond	SAAA (UK market)	0.20%
10% New Zealand stocks	iShares MSCI New Zealand Capped ETF	ENZL (U.S. market)*	0.51%
60% global stocks	PowerShares FTSE RAFI All-World Index	PSRW (UK market)	0.50%

*Maintain less than $60,000 USD in this index.

I've mentioned this before, but it's worth repeating. Choose an investment strategy you're comfortable with. Don't jump from strategy to strategy. People who track performances of the three portfolio types and then jump onto the most recent winning formula are investing like kids playing musical chairs. As a result, they miss out on the point of intelligent investing. This year's or this decade's top-performing strategy will almost certainly not be the next year's or the next decade's best. Jumping around to invest in yesterday's winner is a path to mediocrity.

Each of the three strategies should work well if you're patient. So choose a method and stick to the game plan.

Notes

1. Sean O'Hare, "New Zealand Brain-Drain Worst in World," *The Telegraph*, September 2, 2010. Accessed July 3, 2014. www.telegraph.co.uk/expat/ expatnews/7973220/New-Zealand-brain-drain-worst-in-world.html.
2. Ibid.
3. "IShares MSCI New Zealand Capped ETF | ENZL," BlackRock. Accessed July 3, 2014. https://www.ishares.com/us/products/239672/ishares-msci-new-zealand-capped-etf.
4. Ibid.
5. "PowerShares FTSE RAFI All-World 3000 UCITS ETF (GBP) | PSRW," Morningstar UK. Accessed July 3, 2014. www.morningstar.co.uk/uk/etf/ snapshot/snapshot.aspx?id=0P0000NHSB.

Chapter 20

Investing for South African and South American Expats

South African Investors

South Africans are quickly becoming some of the world's most educated investors. Years ago, they began recognizing the futility of actively managed products. As a result, the country's firms started offering an array of stock market indexes and exchange-traded funds (ETFs).[1]

Such offerings are a godsend to South African expats looking for offshore investment solutions. Saxo Capital Markets offers trading on the Johannesburg Stock Exchange. Trading commissions are 0.25 percent of the invested total or 100 ZAR, whichever is higher. According to Saxo's website, the Johannesburg Stock Exchange applies an additional Securities Transfer Tax (STT) of 0.25 percent when someone opens a stock position.[2]

As a result, a purchase valued at $10,000 USD would cost the equivalent of $25 USD. Or, if it were a newly opened position, it would cost $50 USD.

An iShares South African stock index does trade on the U.S. market, but such a product could attract unwanted estate tax when the account holder dies so it isn't worth purchasing.

Thirty-nine-year-old Wayne Richmond doesn't wish to toss such headaches to his two children. Married to a New Zealand–born schoolteacher, he works as a manager at a South African–owned printing company based in Sushou, China. He uses the firm Interactive Brokers for his investments.[3]

Unfortunately, Interactive Brokers doesn't offer trading on South Africa's Johannesburg Stock Exchange so he may consider switching to Saxo Capital Markets. What's more, unlike Interactive Brokers, Saxo's funds aren't held in the United States, offering further distance from any possible U.S. estate taxes.

South Africans Fry Up the Couch Potato

Table 20.1 shows how Wayne's investments could look with a Couch Potato portfolio (see Chapter 9 for a full explanation of the strategy).

Vanguard's FTSE All-World ETF trades on the UK market. It has lower expense ratio and trading commission costs than global ETFs trading on the South African exchange.

Table 20.1   A South African's Couch Potato Portfolio

Allocation	ETF	Symbol	Expense Ratio
35% South African bonds	NewFunds Govi SA Government Bond Total Return Index	NFGOVIJ (Johannesburg exchange)	0.28%
20% South African stocks	Satrix 40	STX40 (Johannesburg exchange)	0.45%
45% global stocks	Vanguard FTSE All-World ETF	VWRL (UK market)	0.25%

SOURCES: Absa Bank (www.etfabsa.co.za); Satrix (www.satrix.co.za); Vanguard UK.

Table 20.2   New Zealander/South African Couch Potato Hybrid

Allocation	ETF	Symbol	Expense Ratio
17.5% global government bonds	iShares Global AAA-AA Government Bond	SAAA (UK market)	0.20%
17.5% South African government bonds	NewFunds Govi SA Government Bond Total Return Index	NFGOVIJ (Johannesburg exchange)	0.28%
10% South African stocks	Satrix 40	STX40 (Johannesburg exchange)	0.45%
10% New Zealand stocks	iShares MSCI New Zealand Capped ETF	ENZL (U.S. market)*	0.51%
45% global stocks	Vanguard FTSE All-World ETF	VWRL (UK market)	0.25%

*Maintain less than $60,000 USD in the iShares New Zealand index, considering the risk of U.S. estate taxes.

SOURCES: Absa Bank (www.etfabsa.co.za); Satrix (www.satrix.co.za); Vanguard UK; iShares USA.

The Couch Potato portfolio model in Table 20.1 allocates 20 percent exposure to South African stocks and 45 percent to global stocks. Nobody knows whether South African stocks will outperform global markets over the years ahead, so allocations shouldn't reflect speculation. But expats wanting to eventually repatriate to South Africa may consider an even larger percentage to their home country market.

Whatever allocation you choose, be consistent. As always, avoid chasing the asset class or geographic sector that has recently made the most money. Stick to your allocation, year in and year out.

Because Wayne is married to a New Zealander, they could repatriate to either country. Consequently, they might balance their portfolio between two markets. Table 20.2 is a sample portfolio.

South African Writer Likes the Permanent Portfolio

South African Troy Blacklaws prefers the long-term stability of the Permanent Portfolio (see Chapter 10). "I dream of one day having a *pondok* (Malay for *shack*) by the sea in Cape Town, living by the pen," says the 48-year-old Luxembourg-based teacher and author of *Blood Orange*,

Table 20.3   A South African's Permanent Portfolio

Allocation	ETF	Symbol	Expense Ratio
25% South African government bonds	NewFunds Govi SA Government Bond Total Return Index	NFGOVIJ (Johannesburg exchange)	0.28%
12.5% global stocks	Vanguard FTSE All-World ETF	VWRL (UK market)	0.25%
12.5% South African stocks	Satrix 40	STX40 (Johannesburg exchange)	0.45%
25% gold	iShares Physical Gold ETC	SGLN (UK market)	0.25%
25% cash			

SOURCES: Absa Bank (www.etfabsa.co.za); Satrix (www.satrix.co.za); Vanguard UK.

Karoo Boy, and *Cruel Crazy Beautiful World*. "Earnings from writing are mercurial and fickle. If I am to fulfill this dream I need to see to it that the money I have will out-foot bank rates, yet not jump around like some kind of crazed jackrabbit."[4]

Permanent Portfolio gains have exceeded 9 percent per year since 1972. No annual loss has been greater than 4.1 percent. So the Permanent Portfolio could be the writer's perfect match.

Table 20.3 shows how Troy's portfolio could look with some South African exposure.

South Africans who do not intend to repatriate to their home country may choose a more global Permanent Portfolio, such as the one shown in Table 20.4.

Table 20.4   Global Permanent Portfolio Model

Allocation	ETF	Symbol	Expense Ratio
25% global bonds	iShares Global Government Bond Index	IGLO (UK market)	0.20%
25% global stocks	Vanguard FTSE All-World ETF	VWRD	0.25%
25% gold	iShares Physical Gold ETC	SGLN	0.25%
25% cash			

SOURCES: Absa Bank (www.etfabsa.co.za); Satrix (www.satrix.co.za); Vanguard UK; iShares UK.

South Africans Preferring Fundamental Platforms

Thanks to the plethora of ETFs trading on the Johannesburg exchange, South Africans can also build portfolios with fundamental indexes (see Chapter 11). The eRAFI Overall SA index is fundamentally weighted. Academic studies suggest such indexes are superior, and this one has done well. Between its June 30, 2008, inception and May 12, 2014, it gained 110 percent (measured in South African rand) compared to 61.97 percent for the cap-weighted JSE All Shares Index.[5]

Will it continue to outperform? I don't know, nor does anyone else. But if you like the idea of fundamental indexing, you could build a portfolio such as the one in Table 20.5, which has a bond allocation suitable for investors between 35 and 45 years of age. The allocation of bonds would be lower or higher for investors with different risk tolerances.

South Africans unsure of whether they'll return to their home country may prefer a more globally balanced portfolio. A sample is presented in Table 20.6.

South American Investors

Vanessa Marisa Calunho Lopes Hardinge grew up in Santos, Brazil. She and her husband, New Zealander Michael Hardinge, met while he worked as a teacher in Campinas, Brazil. "I thought about keeping some of our investments in Brazil," says Vanessa. "I know it's volatile, and

Table 20.5   Global Fundamental Index Portfolio with South African Exposure

Allocation	ETF	Symbol	Expense Ratio
35% global bonds	iShares Global AAA–AA Government Bond	SAAA (UK market)	0.2%
25% South African stocks	eRAFI Overall SA	RAFISA.J	0.1%
40% global stocks	PowerShares FTSE RAFI All-World 3000 Global Fundamental Stock Index	PSRW (UK market)	0.5%

Sources: iShares UK; Invesco PowerShares; Absa Bank (www.etfabsa.co.za); Satrix (www.satrix.co.za).

Table 20.6   Global Fundamental Index Portfolio

Allocation	ETF	Symbol	Expense Ratio
35% government bonds	iShares Global AAA-AA Government Bond	SAAA (UK market)	0.2%
65% global stocks	PowerShares FTSE RAFI All-World 3000	PSRW (UK market)	0.5%

SOURCES: Invesco PowerShares; iShares UK.

I am concerned about the way Brazil is selling out its natural resources to countries such as China. But there's no denying how rapidly South American economies are developing."[6]

Vanessa is right. Economic output growth for most South American economies exceeded that of Canada, the United States, and Mexico from 2010 to 2013.[7]

Latin American stocks, however, haven't kept pace. And that's a good thing—if you're thinking like a contrarian. The iShares Canada Latin American index dropped 3.3 percent between late 2010 and mid-2014.[8] Those who prefer to chase rising asset classes (remember, this isn't a smart thing to do) would avoid such an index because Latin American stocks didn't profit in the three years up to 2014. But avoiding this market could be a mistake.

Most investors perform poorly because they prefer investing with strong recent performers. But the worst-performing markets in a given period often star in the years that follow. Investments du jour change all the time. By diversifying and rebalancing, disciplined investors ensure that they buy more when prices are cheap.

The same Latin American index also trades on the UK exchange through iShares UK. But the Canadian-domiciled ETF has an expense ratio costing 0.07 percent less than its UK-domiciled equivalent.

Brazilian Investing Models

Vanessa, however, may never return to Brazil, so she might choose a lighter allocation to Latin American stocks. If she also wants exposure to her husband's New Zealand market, Table 20.7 is how the Singapore-based couple's couch potato portfolio might look.

Table 20.7   When a Latin American Picks a Kiwi with a Couch Potato Model

Allocation	ETF	Symbol	Expense Ratio
35% global bonds	iShares Global AAA–AA Government Bond	SAAA (UK market)	0.20%
20% Latin American or Brazilian stocks	iShares Canada Latin American Index	XLA (Canadian market)	0.67%
	or		
	iShares MSCI Brazil Index ETF	XBZ (Canadian market)	0.75%
5% New Zealand stocks	iShares MSCI New Zealand Capped ETF	ENZL (U.S. market)*	0.51%
40% Global stocks	iShares Global Stock Index ACWI UCITS	SSAC (UK market)	0.60%
	or		
	Vanguard FTSE All-World ETF	VWRL (UK market)	0.25%

*Maintain less than $60,000 USD in this index.

If Vanessa and Mike want more stability, they could choose the Permanent Portfolio (see Chapter 10) with exposure to each of their home country markets (see Table 20.8).

And if the couple wanted a Couch Potato portfolio with a fundamental twist, they could add the PowerShares FTSE RAFI All-World 3000. By doing so, they could have a portfolio that looks something like the one in Table 20.9.

Regardless of which portfolio combination Wayne, Troy, and Vanessa choose, they need to stick to their plan. Over the next five years, the Permanent Portfolio may outperform the others. Or the winner could be the Fundamental Index model. The worst thing an investor can do is jump ship. Investors need to stick to their game plan and keep costs low. By rebalancing their portfolios, they'll remain diversified. Investors will also remain a little bit greedy when others are fearful, and fearful when others are greedy.

Each of these portfolios should perform well over an investment lifetime. But investors need to be patient.

Table 20.8   Vanessa and Mike's Permanent Portfolio

Allocation	ETF	Symbol	Expense Ratio
25% global government bonds	iShares Global Government Bond Index	IGLO (UK market)	0.20%
15% global stocks	iShares Global Stock Index ACWI UCITS	SSAC	0.60%
	or		
	Vanguard FTSE All-World ETF	VWRL	0.25%
7% Latin American or Brazilian stocks	iShares Canada Latin American Index	XLA (Canadian market)	0.67%
	or		
	iShares MSCI Brazil Index ETF	XBZ (Canadian market)	0.75%
3% New Zealand stocks	iShares MSCI New Zealand Capped ETF	ENZL (U.S. market)*	0.51%
25% Gold	iShares Physical Gold ETC	SGLN	0.25%
25% cash			

*Maintain less than $60,000 USD in this index.

Table 20.9   Vanessa and Mike's Fundamental Index Portfolio

Allocation	ETF	Symbol	Expense Ratio
35% global government bonds	iShares Global AAA-AA Government Bond	SAAA (UK market)	0.20%
20% Latin American or Brazilian stocks	iShares Canada Latin American Index	XLA (Canadian market)	0.67%
	or		
	iShares MSCI Brazil Index ETF	XBZ (Canadian market)	0.75%
5% New Zealand stocks	iShares MSCI New Zealand Capped ETF	ENZL (U.S. market)*	0.51%
40% global stocks	PowerShares FTSE RAFI All-World 3000	PSRW (UK market)	0.50%

*Maintain less than $60,000 USD in this index.

Notes

1. Reitumetse Pitso, "Six More SA Indices from S&P Dow Jones," BusinessDay Live, May 5, 2014. Accessed May 10, 2014. www.bdlive.co.za/markets/2014/05/05/six-more-sa-indices-from-sp-dow-jones.
2. "Stock Trading Conditions," Saxo Capital Markets. Accessed July 3, 2014. http://sg.saxomarkets.com/prices/stocks/trading-conditions.
3. Interview with Wayne Richmond. E-mail interview by author, May 13, 2014.
4. Interview with Troy Blacklaws. E-mail interview by author, May 12, 2014.
5. "NewFunds eRAFI™ Overall SA Index," Absa Capital. Accessed July 3, 2014. http://etf.absacapital.com/Fund%20Documents/eRafi%20Overall%20Data sheet%2031%20March%202014.pdf.
6. *Regional Economic Outlook* (Washington, DC: International Monetary Fund, 2013). Accessed July 3, 2014. www.imf.org/external/pubs/ft/reo/2013/whd/eng/pdf/wreo0513.pdf.
7. "iShares Latin America," Morningstar. Accessed July 3, 2014. http://quote.morningstar.ca/QuickTakes/ETF/etf_performance.aspx?t=XLA®ion=CAN&culture=en-CA.

Chapter 21

Investing for European Expats

S paniard Urko Masse enjoys salsa dancing, soccer, and spending time with his wife and kids. What the 39-year-old doesn't enjoy is giving a pound of flesh to the financial services industry. So he opened a brokerage account with Saxo Capital Markets and built a portfolio of low-cost index funds.

Country-Specific European ETFs

What's odd is that country-specific European stock exchange-traded funds (ETFs) appear to be more popular among Americans than they are among Europeans. The giant ETF provider iShares offers U.S.-domiciled indexes for the European countries listed in Table 21.1.

Table 21.1   European ETFs Trading on U.S. Exchanges

ETF	Symbol	Expense Ratio	Five-Year Total Gain Ending April 2014*
iShares MSCI Germany	EWG	0.51%	+93.6%
iShares MSCI Germany Small Cap stocks	EWGS	0.59%	NA†
iShares MSCI Spain	EWP	0.51%	+48.6%
iShares MSCI Italy	EWI	0.50%	+24.5%
iShares MSCI Switzerland	EWL	0.51%	+123.3%
iShares MSCI Sweden	EWD	0.51%	+124%
iShares MSCI Turkey	TUR	0.61%	+81.6%
iShares MSCI France	EWQ	0.51%	+66.8%
iShares MSCI Poland	EPOL	0.61%	NA†
iShares MSCI Russia	ERUS	0.61%	NA†
iShares MSCI Netherlands	EWN	0.50%	+87%
iShares MSCI Ireland	EIRL	0.50%	NA†
iShares MSCI Belgium	EWK	0.50%	+107%
iShares MSCI Austria	EWO	0.51%	+47.8%
iShares MSCI Denmark	EDEN	0.53%	NA†
iShares MSCI Finland	EFNL	0.53%	NA†
iShares MSCI Norway	ENOR	0.53%	NA†

*All returns in USD.

†Funds haven't been available for five years.

Source: iShares U.S.

Europeans have no such variety on their stock exchanges. It might tempt some to build portfolios using the ETFs in Table 21.1. But those doing so must be aware of keeping such exposure below $60,000. Otherwise, their heirs may have to pay Uncle Sam's dreaded death tax when the original investor dies.[1] It doesn't matter whether such funds hold Spanish, Belgian, Russian, or French stocks. It doesn't matter whether the investor has never set foot on U.S. soil. The American government wants your money. And as a non-U.S. voter, there's nothing you can do about it.

That said, Europeans have a couple of options. They could purchase a straight European index off the UK exchange, or they could do the same while adding a smidgen of a U.S.-domiciled ETF to reflect their home country market.

In the list of ETFs in Table 21.1, I provided five-year total returns, where available, in U.S. dollars. I did it to distract you. Historical returns mean nothing. The best-performing index during one time period can be the worst-performing index in another. Can you guess what the typical American investor in European stock indexes was probably doing in 2014? He was buying Swiss, Swedish, and Belgian indexes, after they returned 123.3 percent, 124 percent, and 107 percent, respectively, over the past five years. Such a reaction is natural. But chasing yesterday's winners is a recipe for mediocrity—at best. Instead, as always, investors are wise to diversify and rebalance.

European Indexes That Investors Will Like

Provider iShares offers two MSCI European indexes, one including UK stocks and one without. Because they trade on the UK market, neither would attract the dreaded American estate tax. Vanguard offers a third European index. As of this writing, it's also the cheapest.

Investors bypassing British stocks can gain more exposure to their home country market by purchasing the iShares MSCI Europe (ex UK) index. Such would be the case with Urko Masse if he wanted greater exposure to Spanish stocks. As you can see in Table 21.2, the iShares MSCI Europe index comprises 5.25 percent Spanish stocks; the iShares MSCI Europe (ex UK) index comprises 7.75 percent Spanish equities, and Vanguard's FTSE Developed Europe index comprises 5.3 percent Spanish equities.

Table 21.3 shows how Urko Masse could build a Couch Potato portfolio without a Spanish-specific ETF.

Choosing the lowest-cost options, this portfolio's average expense ratio would be 0.186 percent per year.

When choosing between two ETFs tracking the same index, such as Vanguard's FTSE Developed Europe and iShares' MSCI Developed Europe, choose the index with the lower expense ratio. Forget about trying to figure out which has beaten the other over the previous year or five. It's irrelevant. Over time, if they track the same index (as these

Table 21.2   Weighting Emphasis In Three European Indexes

Market	iShares MSCI Europe Symbol: IMEU	iShares MSCI Europe (ex UK) Symbol: IEUX	Vanguard FTSE Developed Europe Symbol: VEUR
United Kingdom	26.91%	0.00%	31.5%
France	15.33%	22.61%	14.6%
Switzerland	14.23%	19.72%	13.8%
Germany	13.49%	19.89%	13.9%
Netherlands	6.96%	5.99%	4.4%
Spain	5.25%	7.75%	5.3%
Sweden	4.68%	6.89%	4.8%
Italy	3.64%	5.36%	3.9%
Denmark	1.94%	2.87%	2.3%
Belgium	1.82%	2.67%	1.8%
Finland	1.31%	1.93%	
Norway	1.24%	1.82%	
Other	2.15%	2.49%	3.7%

SOURCES: iShares UK; Vanguard UK, May 11, 2014.

Table 21.3   Couch Potato Portfolio Model without a Spanish Index

Allocation	ETF	Symbol	Expense Ratio
35% European bonds	iShares Euro Government Bond 1–3 yr. UCITS	IBGS (UK exchange)	0.20%
25% European stocks	iShares MSCI Europe or	IMEU (UK exchange)	0.35%
	iShares MSCI Europe (ex UK) or	IEUX (UK exchange)	0.40%
	Vanguard FTSE Developed Europe	VEUR (UK exchange)	0.15%
20% U.S. stocks	iShares S&P 500 U.S.	CSPX (UK exchange)	0.07%
5% developed Asia stocks, excluding Japan	Vanguard FTSE Developed Asia (ex Japan)	VAPX (UK exchange)	0.22%
10% Japanese stocks	Vanguard FTSE Japan	VJPN (UK exchange)	0.19%
5% emerging market stocks	Vanguard FTSE Emerging Markets	VFEM (UK exchange)	0.29%

SOURCES: iShares UK; Vanguard UK.

roughly do), the better long-term performer will be the one with the lower expense ratio. Considering that Vanguard's expenses are lower, it's currently the better option.

Having said this, iShares is battling Vanguard in a price war. Before selecting your European index, take a peek at the iShares MSCI Europe's expense ratio. If it's lower than Vanguard's, go for it.

But stay true to your selection. Brokerages love it when there's an ETF price war. Investors jumping ship to lower-cost products generate trading commissions.. Keep expenses in perspective. If an ETF charges 0.15 percent, this means investors are paying €15 in fees for every €10,000 invested. An expense ratio of 0.3 percent costs €30 for the year. If you're jumping from one ETF to the next with a large sum of money, it could cost more in commissions than you would be saving with the lower-cost index.

If Urko wanted a portfolio that was even simpler than the one in Table 21.3, he could use a total world index for his stock market exposure. Such an index has exposure to European, American, developed international, and emerging market stocks in proportion to their market capitalization.

It would contain nearly the same respective country exposure that is represented in Urko's model portfolio in Table 21.3. Investors choosing it would have exposure to European stocks. But if they want similar European exposure to my previous portfolio model, they could add a European index as well.

Vanguard's FTSE All-World UCITS ETF[2] comprises the following geographic market exposures:

48.4%	United States
7.9%	United Kingdom
7.8%	Japan
3.6%	France
3.5%	Switzerland
3.4%	Germany
3.3%	Canada
3.0%	Australia
1.9%	China
1.6%	South Korea
15.7%	Others

Table 21.4   Couch Potato Portfolio Using a Global Index (No Spanish Index)

Allocation	ETF	Symbol	Expense Ratio
35% European bonds	iShares Euro Government Bond 1–3 yr. UCITS	IBGS (UK exchange)	0.20%
40% global stocks	Vanguard's FTSE All-World UCITS ETF	VWRD (UK exchange)	0.25%
25% European stocks	iShares MSCI Europe or	IMEU (UK exchange)	0.35%
	iShares MSCI Europe (ex UK) or	IEUX (UK exchange)	0.40%
	Vanguard FTSE Developed Europe	VEUR (UK exchange)	0.15%

Sources: iShares UK; Vanguard UK.

You may be wondering why China's exposure is so low. Despite much of what you read in the media about the Chinese taking over the world, they're currently far from it. Each of the breakdowns reflects the respective countries' global capitalization. This means if you sold every stock in the world, roughly 48.4 percent of the proceeds would come from U.S. stocks, 7.9 percent from UK stocks, 7.8 percent from Japanese stocks, and so on. The Chinese stock market is a pebble, valued at just 1.9 percent of global capitalization. For this reason, exposing a greater amount to Chinese stocks is an unnecessary risk.

Table 21.4 is how Urko's Couch Potato portfolio could look if he utilized Vanguard's global stock ETF.

Why Not Choose the Simpler Option?

The portfolio shown in Table 21.4 would be easy to maintain. And it's cheap, costing just 0.2 percent per year (if selecting Vanguard's index for the European component).

If Urko wanted to add more Spanish stock market exposure, he could build a portfolio like the one in Table 21.5.

Table 21.5   Couch Potato Portfolio with Spanish Stock Market Exposure

Allocation	ETF	Symbol	Expense Ratio
35% European bonds	iShares Euro Government Bond 1–3 yr. UCITS	IBGS (UK exchange)	0.20%
5% Spanish stocks	iShares MSCI Spain	EWP (U.S. exchange)*	0.51%
40% global stocks	Vanguard FTSE All-World UCITS ETF	VWRL (UK exchange)	0.25%
20% European stocks	iShares MSCI Europe or	IMEU (UK exchange)	0.35%
	iShares MSCI Europe (ex UK) or	IEUX (UK exchange)	0.40%
	Vanguard FTSE Developed Europe	VEUR (UK exchange)	0.15%

*Maintain less than $60,000 USD in this index.

SOURCES: iShares UK; Vanguard UK; iShares US.

Europeans of other nationalities could do much the same, replacing the Spanish stock index with one representing their home country market. See Table 21.1 for a complete list of U.S.-domiciled European ETFs.

But keep such exposure below U.S. $60,000. Otherwise, when you float to your ultimate exchange, your heirs may get an American tax bill.

Calling Italians and the Swiss

Expatriate investors from Italy or Switzerland may not need a U.S.-domiciled index to gain specific exposure to their home country stock markets. For some bizarre reason, iShares UK offers an Italian stock index: the iShares FTSE MIB UCITS ETF.[3] I don't know what mob boss pulled the strings for this one. But it's the only non-UK country-specific European ETF trading on the UK market. As such, Italians wouldn't have to worry about capping their domestic stock exposure to just U.S. $60,000. Comprising 40 Italian stocks, the index costs a respectable 0.35 percent per year. A 35- to 40-year-old Italian investor's portfolio might look like the one shown in Table 21.6.

Table 21.6   Viva L'Italia: Global Couch Potato Portfolio with Italian Stock Exposure

Allocation	ETF	Symbol	Expense Ratio
35% European bonds	iShares Euro Government Bond 1–3 yr. UCITS	IBGS (UK exchange)	0.20%
25% Italian stocks	iShares FTSE MIB UCITS ETF (Italy)	IMIB (UK exchange)	0.35%
40% global stocks	Vanguard FTSE All-World UCITS ETF	VWRL (UK exchange)	0.25%

SOURCES: iShares UK; Vanguard UK.

Swiss investors with access to Switzerland's exchange (check your international broker's market availability) can purchase an index reflecting their domestic stock market. The iShares SMI[4] tracks the largest 20 stocks in Switzerland for 0.39 percent per year.

A 35- to 40-year-old Swiss investor could build the global portfolio shown in Table 21.7.

The European's Permanent Portfolio

Some investors freak out when their money gyrates. While panicking, they risk selling at a loss or giving up on investing completely. Neither reaction makes sense. Such investors may find solace in the Permanent Portfolio.

Table 21.7   Global Couch Potato Portfolio with Swiss Stock Exposure

Allocation	ETF	Symbol	Expense Ratio
35% European bonds	iShares Euro Government Bond 1–3 yr. UCITS	IBGS (UK exchange)	0.20%
25% Swiss stocks	iShares SMI (Switzerland)	CH (Swiss exchange)	0.39%
40% global stocks	Vanguard FTSE All-World UCITS ETF	VWRL (UK exchange)	0.25%

SOURCES: iShares UK; iShares SMI.

Table 21.8 The European Permanent Portfolio

Allocation	ETF	Symbol	Expense Ratio
25% European bonds	iShares Euro Government Bond 7–10 yr.	IBGM (UK exchange)	0.20%
12.5% global stocks	Vanguard's FTSE All-World UCITS ETF	VWRL (UK exchange)	0.25%
12.5% European stocks)	Vanguard FTSE Developed Europe	VEUR (UK exchange)	0.15%
25% gold	iShares Physical Gold ETC	SGLN (UK market)	0.25%
25% cash			

SOURCES: iShares UK; Vanguard UK.

Detailed in Chapter 10, it's an equal split among stocks, bonds, gold, and cash. It won't ever soar like a pure stock index during a roaring bull market. But neither will it crash when markets plunge. Between 1972 and 2012, it had only three losing years—the worst of which was 1981, when it dropped 4.1 percent. During the 40-year period, it averaged more than 9 percent annually. Note that the government bond index, as per Harry Browne's original recommendation, comprises long-term bonds.

Such a global portfolio, with a European lean, could look like the one shown in Table 21.8.

Investors who wish to add their home country stock indexes could do so. But they would need to ensure that their total stock allocation didn't exceed 25 percent of the portfolio's total value. And, of course, if any of their stock exposure comes from a U.S.-domiciled ETF, it should be kept to a maximum of U.S. $60,000. Table 21.9 is a sample for a French investor, adding further exposure to the French stock market.

In either case, some investors may prefer to replace their cash with a short-term government bond index, such as the iShares Euro Government Bond 1–3 yr. UCITS.[5]

Fundamental Indexing for Europeans

The fundamental index, as outlined in Chapter 11, weights businesses based on book values, cash flow, dividends, and profits. Simply put,

Table 21.9   The European Permanent Portfolio with French Stock Exposure

Allocation	ETF	Symbol	Expense Ratio
25% European bonds	iShares Euro Government Bond 7–10 yr.	IBGM (UK exchange)	0.20%
10% global stocks	Vanguard FTSE All-World UCITS ETF	VWRL (UK exchange)	0.25%
10% European stocks	Vanguard FTSE Developed Europe	VEUR (UK exchange)	0.15%
5% French stocks	iShares MSCI France	EWQ (U.S. exchange)*	0.51%
25% gold	iShares Physical Gold ETC	SGLN (UK market)	0.25%
25% cash			

*Maintain less than $60,000 USD in this index.

SOURCES: iShares UK; Vanguard UK; iShares US

businesses with the greatest profits take up the largest part of the index. Back-tested studies reveal that fundamental indexes outperform their cap-weighted equivalents—not every year, but during most three-year rolling periods.

Although slightly more expensive, they still cost less than actively managed funds. For Europeans, Invesco PowerShares[6] offers two such indexes for a fundamentally juiced Couch Potato portfolio.

One thing to consider, however, is that the PowerShares indexes are swap-based. Investors don't receive dividends. Instead, the index earns the full return of the market, as if dividends were reinvested. Unlike the indexes I've listed so far, the PowerShares products in Table 21.10 don't own the securities within the indexes themselves. Instead, they're more like a promissory note providing investors with the total return of the index, as if all dividends were reinvested. Table 21.10 is a sample portfolio for a 35- to 40-year-old European investor.

Investors wishing to add a country-specific cap-weighted index could do so. But as mentioned before, if the index is domiciled in the U.S. market, keep its value below $60,000. When it approaches this threshold, sell off some proceeds to add to another index.

Table 21.10 The European Fundamental Index Portfolio

Allocation	ETF	Symbol	Expense Ratio
35% European bonds	iShares Euro Government Bond 1–3 yr. UCITS	IBGS (UK exchange)	0.20%
35% global stocks	PowerShares FTSE RAFI All-World 3000	PSRW (UK exchange)	0.50%
30% European stocks	PowerShares FTSE RAFI Europe	PSRE (UK exchange)	0.50%

SOURCE: iShares UK; Invesco PowerShares UK

So What's It Going to Be—Couch Potato, Permanent, or Fundamentally Indexed?

Each of the portfolios presented in this chapter should outperform the vast majority of actively managed portfolios. But you'll never know which of the three models will be best during the next year, five years, or 10 years. Choose your portfolio and stick to it. Don't bother back-testing to see which has performed better during the past few years. Nor should you abandon a strategy if you notice one of the other portfolios is outperforming it. The first-place portfolio during the next five years could be the third-place portfolio during the following five. By jumping into different strategies, one thing's for sure: Over time, you'll underperform all three.

Don't let that happen.

Notes

1. "Some Nonresidents with U.S. Assets Must File Estate Tax Returns," Internal Revenue Service. Accessed July 4, 2014. www.irs.gov/Individuals/International-Taxpayers/Some-Nonresidents-with-U.S.-Assets-Must-File-Estate-Tax-Returns.
2. "Vanguard FTSE All-World UCITS ETF," Vanguard UK. Accessed July 4, 2014. https%3A%2F%2Fwww.vanguard.co.uk%2Fuk%2Fportal%2FloadPDF%3FdocId%3D1011.
3. "IShares FTSE MIB UCITS ETF," iShares UK. Accessed July 4, 2014. www.ishares.com/uk/individual/en/products/251805/ishares-ftse-mib-ucits-etf-inc-fund.

4. "IShares SMI," BlackRock. Accessed July 4, 2014. www.ishares.com/ch/individual/en/products/261154/CSSMI?locale=en_CH.

5. "IShares Euro Government Bond," BlackRock. Accessed July 4, 2014. www.ishares.com/uk/individual/en/products/251733/ishares-euro-government-bond-13yr-ucits-etf.

6. "Invesco PowerShares," Invesco. Accessed July 4, 2014. https://www.invesco.com/portal/site/us/psgateway.

Chapter 22

Investing for
Asian Expats

Two stock exchanges come to mind when Asians consider exchange-traded funds (ETFs): Singapore and Hong Kong. Shirlene Tsui, Dow Jones investment banker, reported in 2011 that the Hong Kong market was valued at $2.7 trillion. Singapore's market trailed, at just $840 billion.[1] Hong Kong's stock exchange also has much higher trading volume each day. What does this mean for you?

Think of two airport currency exchange booths side by side. In some Asian airports, they hustle you a bit for business. Which booth do you pick? Assume neither attendant has mossy teeth or knock-me-over breath. So you look at the currency rates and spreads on the electronic board behind them.

One of the booths has a wider spread between each currency's listed buy and sell prices. You want a decent deal when selling a currency and a decent deal when buying. So you select the booth with the narrower spreads. When investing, most Asians would select the Hong Kong over the Singapore exchange for the same reason. Hong Kong's market offers narrower bid/ask spreads on its stocks and ETFs because daily business volume is higher than it is in Singapore.

Some Asians bypass both exchanges, purchasing ETFs and individual shares off U.S. exchanges. But doing so adds risk: Their heirs may have to pay American estate taxes if their U.S.-domiciled holdings exceed $60,000.[2] It doesn't matter whether or not such products are purchased from a non-U.S. brokerage.

An Indian National Divulges Her Plan

Indian citizen Shabari Karumbaya doesn't want to bequeath her son an estate tax bill from a country he may never set foot in. Wanting a Couch Potato portfolio (see Chapter 9) with some home country exposure, she chose an iShares MSCI India stock ETF off the Canadian exchange for two reasons: First, the equivalent product on the Singapore exchange trades thinly, whereas its Canadian counterpart doesn't. Second, Deutsche Bank AG offers an Indian stock ETF on the Hong Kong exchange, but it's a synthetic (swap-based) product.

Exchange-traded funds either hold genuine shares within them or they don't. A synthetic ETF, like Hong Kong–traded XIE Shares India, doesn't actually contain Indian stocks. Instead, another institution promises to provide the ETF investor with the total return of the Indian stock market. It's like a promissory note backed by a financial institution. Although the ETF doesn't hold physical shares, it behaves identically to an index that would hold physical Indian shares, rising and falling with the market it tracks.

The added risk is also small. The other party is Deutsche Bank AG, which carries an A+ credit rating from Standard & Poor's and an Aa3 rating from Moody's Investors Service.[3]

Shabari, however, wants her money to be as risk-averse as possible. So she buys the Canadian-domiciled iShares product, which holds physical Indian shares. Table 22.1 shows how her Couch Potato portfolio looks.

Table 22.1   Couch Potato Portfolio for a 35-Year-Old Indian Investor

Allocation	ETF	Symbol	Expense Ratio
15% Indian stocks	iShares India Index	XID (Toronto exchange)	0.99%
35% global government bonds	iShares AAA-AA Government Bond UCITS ETF	SAAA (UK exchange)	0.20%
50% global stocks	Vanguard FTSE All-World UCITS	VWRD (UK exchange)	0.25%

Shabari allocates 35 percent of her portfolio to bonds because it's an allocation closely aligned with her age. She uses the iShares AAA-AA Government Bond index, offering international fixed income exposure. It trades on the British stock exchange. As with the other ETFs in her portfolio, she could purchase it through firms such as Saxo Capital Markets, TD Direct Investing International, or Interactive Brokers.

For global stock market exposure, Vanguard UK offers a perfect solution: the FTSE All-World UCITS index comprising 2,709 international stocks.[4] Here's the ETF's breakdown of global market exposure:

48.4%   United States
 7.9%   United Kingdom
 7.8%   Japan
 3.6%   France
 3.5%   Switzerland
 3.4%   Germany
 3.3%   Canada
 3.0%   Australia
 1.9%   China
 1.6%   South Korea
15.7%   Others

You may wonder why China's exposure is so low. Based on market capitalization, Chinese stocks comprise less than 2 percent of the world's stock market value. In other words, if you sold every one of the world's stocks, collecting all the proceeds, less than 2 percent of the money would come from Chinese businesses. In contrast, roughly

48 percent of the proceeds would come from the United States. The most heavily weighted stocks in the global index, in descending order, are Apple, Exxon Mobil, Google, Microsoft, Johnson & Johnson, and General Electric.

Investors of different Asian nationalities can follow a similar Couch Potato portfolio concept, emphasizing a blend between a global stock index and one representing their home country.

Some investors may choose to allocate half their stock exposure to their home market and half to global stocks. Others—especially those from developing countries—may prefer lighter exposure to their home country market. Such markets tend to be volatile. And if their currencies get hammered, diversification saves those who have spread their eggs across multiple global baskets.

What's important, however, is that investors don't speculate. Don't adjust your portfolio based on your gut or what a stock market media expert suggests. Choose your allocation and stick to it. Most investors don't, which leads to their downfall. Even if they build responsibly diversified portfolios, they chase the winning index with fresh cash, shunning the underperformer.

But the winning market during one period is often the losing market during the next. Chasing recent outperformers leads to buying high and selling low. Whether you choose to divide your stocks 50–50 between a global index and a home country index or to give your home country market higher exposure means little. Over the long term, the key to success will be discipline. Marry a suitable allocation of ETFs and rebalance annually. Or you could purchase the lagging index each month, maintaining a close alignment with your goal allocation.

Asians Embracing the Couch Potato

Table 22.2 shows examples of ETFs from which Asians could build a Couch Potato portfolio. Note that for Singaporean expats, I've included home country stock and bond ETFs trading on the Singaporean market. No such product exists in Hong Kong (at the time of writing), and the trading volume for these Singapore ETFs is more than sufficient.

Table 22.2   Bond and Stock Market Exposure for Asian Markets

Bond ETFs	Symbol	Expense Ratio	Exchange
iBoxx ABF Hong Kong Index	2819.HK	0.15%	Hong Kong
ABF Pan Asia Bond Index	2821.HK	0.19%	Hong Kong
CSOP China 5 Year Treasury [Government] Bond	3199.HK	0.49%	Hong Kong
ABF Singapore Bond Index Fund	A35.SI	0.26%	Singapore

Stock ETFs	Symbol	Expense Ratio	Exchange
Tracker Fund of Hong Kong	2800.HK	0.15%	Hong Kong
SPDR Straits Times (Singapore) Index	ES3.SI	0.30%	Singapore
Vanguard FTSE Japan	VJPN/VDJP	0.19%	UK
Horizon MSCI China	2823.HK	0.25%	Hong Kong
Polaris Taiwan Top 50	4363.HK	0.61%	Hong Kong
XIE Shares Malaysia*	3029.HK	0.39%	Hong Kong
XIE Shares Indonesia*	3031.HK	0.39%	Hong Kong
XIE Shares Philippines*	3037.HK	0.39%	Hong Kong
XIE Shares Thailand*	3069.HK	0.39%	Hong Kong
XIE Shares Korea*	3090.HK	0.39%	Hong Kong
XIE Shares India*	3091.HK	0.39%	Hong Kong
iShares India	XID	0.99%	Canada
db X-trackers FTSE Vietnam	3087.HK	0.85%	Hong Kong
Vanguard FTSE Asia (a blend of Asian stock markets, excluding Japan)	3085.HK	0.45%	Hong Kong

*Synthetic ETF.

Sources: SPDR State Street Global Advisors; Bloomberg.

Investors finding a bond market ETF representing their home country may want to divide their fixed income exposure between a global bond and a home country bond index. Doing so provides greater bond market diversification. Those unable to find a home country bond index may choose to split bond exposure between a Pan Asia Index[5] and a global index. The Pan Asia Bond Index includes government bonds from China, Hong Kong, South Korea, Malaysia, Indonesia, the Philippines, Singapore, and Thailand.

Table 22.3   Couch Potato Portfolio for a 40- to 50-Year-Old South Korean Investor

Allocation	ETF	Symbol	Expense Ratio
30% South Korean stocks	XIE Shares Korea	3090.HK (Hong Kong exchange)	0.39%
30% global stocks	Vanguard FTSE All-World UCITS	VWRD (UK exchange)	0.25%
40% global government bonds	iShares AAA-AA Government Bond UCITS ETF	SAAA (UK exchange)	0.20%

Table 22.3 is a sample Couch Potato portfolio for a 40- to 50-year-old South Korean investor.

A 40- to 50-year-old South Korean wanting to increase Asian bond market exposure (at the expense of global bonds) may choose the allocations listed in Table 22.4.

Younger investors or others with a higher tolerance for risk would have a smaller allocation to bonds.

Table 22.5 is a similar model for a 40- to 50-year-old Malaysian investor.

Table 22.4   Couch Potato Portfolio for a 40- to 50-Year-Old South Korean Investor with Global and Asian Bond Exposure

Allocation	ETF	Symbol	Expense Ratio
30% South Korean stocks	XIE Shares Korea	3090.HK (Hong Kong exchange)	0.39%
30% global stocks	Vanguard FTSE All-World UCITS	VWRD (UK exchange)	0.25%
20% global bonds	iShares AAA-AA Government Bond UCITS ETF	SAAA (UK exchange)	0.20%
20% Asian government bonds	ABF Pan Asia Bond Index	2821.HK (Hong Kong exchange)	0.19%

Table 22.5   Couch Potato Portfolio for a 40- to 50-Year-Old Malaysian Investor

Allocation	ETF	Symbol	Expense Ratio
30% Malaysian stocks	XIE Shares Malaysia	3029.HK (Hong Kong exchange)	0.39%
30% global stocks	Vanguard FTSE All-World UCITS	VWRD (UK exchange)	0.25%
20% global government bonds	iShares AAA-AA Government Bond UCITS ETF	SAAA (UK exchange)	0.20%
20% Asian government bonds	ABF Pan Asia Bond Index	2821.HK (Hong Kong exchange)	0.19%

Asians Choosing the Permanent Portfolio

Many Asian cultures have a love affair with gold. And it makes sense. When inflation and currencies plunge, gold offers stability. Coupling it in ETF form with bonds and equities creates what may be the most stable portfolio in the world. This is the magic of the Permanent Portfolio (see Chapter 10). It rarely falls in value, and has averaged more than 9 percent per year since 1972.

It comprises stocks, bonds, gold, and cash (or short-term government bonds) in equal proportions. And as mentioned in Chapter 10, it must be properly rebalanced when needed.

Table 22.6 is a sample portfolio for a Hong Kong citizen wanting global stock market exposure.

Table 22.6   Permanent Portfolio for a Hong Kong Citizen

Allocation	ETF	Symbol	Expense Ratio
25% gold	Hang Seng RMB Gold ETF	83168.HK (Hong Kong exchange)	1.00%
25% Hong Kong bonds	iBoxx ABF Hong Kong Index (Bond Index)	2819.HK (Hong Kong exchange)	0.15%
12.5% global stocks	Vanguard FTSE All-World UCITS	VWRD (UK exchange)	0.25%
12.5% Hong Kong stocks	Tracker Fund of Hong Kong (Stock Index)	2800.HK (Hong Kong exchange)	0.15%
25% cash			

Table 22.7   Permanent Portfolio for a Chinese Citizen

Allocation	ETF	Symbol	Expense Ratio
25% gold	Hang Seng RMB Gold ETF	83168.HK (Hong Kong exchange)	1.00%
25% Chinese government bonds	CSOP China 5 Year Treasury [Government] Bond	3199.HK (Hong Kong exchange)	0.49%
12.5% global stocks	Vanguard FTSE All-World UCITS	VWRD (UK exchange)	0.25%
12.5% Chinese stocks	Horizon MSCI China	2823.HK (Hong Kong exchange)	0.25%
25% cash			

As with any Permanent Portfolio model, the allocation doesn't adjust over time. Unlike the Couch Potato portfolio, investors wouldn't increase their exposure to bonds as they age.

Table 22.7 is a Permanent Portfolio sample for a Chinese citizen.

Fundamental Portfolio for Asians

Based on back-tested studies, fundamental indexes outperform their cap-weighted equivalents (see Chapter 11). But such products haven't caught on in Asia yet. Those wishing for a fundamental lean, however, could choose the RAFI All-World Index (PSRW) trading on the UK market. Unlike ETFs comprising physical stocks, swap-based ETFs don't hold physical shares. This index tracks the return of the FTSE RAFI All-World 3000 Index and provides investors with its total return. It's much like a promissory note backed by a financial institution.

Unlike indexes holding physical shares, however, when this ETF generates a return of 10 percent in a given year, expats can earn the full 10 percent. No money gets skimmed off the top for dividend withholding taxes. For many expatriates, it's a tax-free product.

Table 22.8 Fundamental Index Portfolio for a 40-Year-Old Thai Investor

Allocation	ETF	Symbol	Expense Ratio
35% Asian government bonds	ABF Pan Asia Bond Index	2821.HK (Hong Kong exchange)	0.19%
32.5% Thai stocks	XIE Shares Thailand	3069.HK (Hong Kong exchange)	0.39%
32.5% global stocks	PowerShares FTSE RAFI All-World 3000	PSRW (UK exchange)	0.50%

Table 22.8 shows how a 40-year-old Thai expatriate could build a portfolio with a global fundamental stock index.

As I've repeated for each of the past few chapters, investors should choose a portfolio model and stick to it. Switching your game plan to adhere to the previous year's winning strategy is foolish. Each of these strategies will have their years in the sun. The trouble is, you'll never know which are going to shine in any given year.

If you're like most people (remember that most people are crazy), you'll emphasize yesterday's winners. If the Permanent Portfolio outperforms the others for one year, three years, or five years, you might be tempted to switch. If the fundamental indexes start outperforming, you might join the bandwagon. But resist the temptation.

Choose one of the three trains and stick to it. They won't all earn scorching returns every year. But each of these portfolios was born to run over an investment lifetime.

Notes

1. Shirlene Tsui, "SGX—A Prescription for Growth," *Exchange* RSS, *Wall Street Journal*, March 14, 2011. Accessed July 4, 2014. http://blogs.wsj.com/exchange/2011/03/14/sgx-a-prescription-for-growth/.
2. "Some Nonresidents with U.S. Assets Must File Estate Tax Returns," Internal Revenue Service. Accessed July 4, 2014. www.irs.gov/Individuals/International-Taxpayers/Some-Nonresidents-with-U.S.-Assets-Must-File-Estate-Tax-Returns.

3. "Deutsche Bank db X-trackers." Accessed July 4, 2014. www.etf.db.com/ GBR/ENG/Download/Brochure/143d4562-8d4f-449d-9361-bb38c f14a24c/db-X-trackers-ETF-Brosch-Microscope-5c-en-web.pdf.

4. "Vanguard FTSE All-World UCITS," Vanguard UK. Accessed July 4, 2014. https://www.vanguard.co.uk/documents/portal/factsheets/ftse-all-world-etf.pdf.

5. "Pan Asia Index," Bloomberg.com. Accessed July 4, 2014. www.bloomberg .com/quote/2821%3AHK.

Conclusion

This book has one financial lesson worth more than any other. Is it choosing the right financial planner? For those wanting one, this comes a close second. Most offshore pension sellers flog bubonic plagues. Avoid those chumps. Choose an advisor based on Chapter 12's guidelines, and your savings shouldn't suffer.

If you're a do-it-yourself investor, is the biggest lesson the choice of an exchange-traded fund (ETF) charging 0.15 percent instead of 0.20 percent? No way. Don't sweat the microscopic.

What about commissions and foreign exchange costs? Nope, those are negligible.

How about fretting over whether your portfolio comprises 36.5 percent in bonds instead of 41 percent bonds? No again—such a difference *won't* change your life.

Investment behaviors? Getting warmer now. I beat this concept silly, hoping you realize that rebalancing a low-cost, diversified portfolio will be worth more to you than all the schizophrenic economic forecasts combined. But as important as it is, there's one thing even greater: your ability to save.

Varied international and cultural experiences enrich expat lives. But by living abroad, you'll reduce payments to your home country social programs. As a result, your government retirement payouts will get trimmed or chopped.

Those suffering from expatitis will giggle in delight . . . until there's nothing left to laugh at. But immunization isn't tough. Find a free, expense-tracking app for a smartphone. Document everything you spend. You'll think twice before booking the higher-priced hotel, choosing business-class tickets, or purchasing a brand-new car. You'll see how much you're spending at the pub, and will opt to socialize more with friends at home. You'll become more conscious of grocery bills, choosing lower-cost brands when possible. And you'll taper the coffee-shop trips when you're forced to enter each croissant or muffin into your iPhone.

Document your costs. They'll start dropping. You won't have to strain yourself with a household budget. But set a monthly savings goal. As soon as you get paid, put money aside for a revenue-generating rental property or for your stock and bond market account. Whether you choose the stock and bond markets, real estate, or a combination of both, increasing financial assets should be a top priority. As I mentioned in Chapter 1, you need to build a pension.

Whether you choose to repatriate, vagabond, or reside in a foreign oasis, your older self will thank you. After all, you're a custodian for a senior. So do yourself a favor. Plan for your retirement.

About the Author

Andrew Hallam is the author of the international best seller, *Millionaire Teacher*. He taught personal finance and English at Singapore American School. A columnist for the *Globe and Mail* (Toronto) and *AssetBuilder*, he has also been published in *Canadian Business, MoneySense,* and *Reader's Digest.* Currently, he and his wife travel internationally, speaking to expatriates about the importance of intelligent saving and investing.

Index

Actively managed mutual funds, 46–47, 52–65, 69, 147, 150, 163–164
Admiral Shares, 209, 211
The Adventurer's Guide to Early Retirement (Kaderlis), 4
The Alexander Beard Company, 1 16–117
Alfred, Mike, 114
American expats:
　index advisors for, 154–165
　investing for, 205–218
American retirees, average spent by, 2
Annual fees, 45–50, 52–53, 71, 201
Annual income:
　estimated in retirement, 2
　postinflation adjustment, 6, 10
Apple, 143
Arnott, Robert D., 144–147, 229
Asia, stock markets in, 37–38
Asian expats, investing for, 281–289
AssetBuilder, 115–117, 158–159, 169
Australian expats:
　index advisors for, 166–167
　investing for, 245–251

Australian real estate, 245
Australian retirees, average spent by, 3

Back-end loads, 221
Bangladesh, 178
Banking costs, 192–193
Barber, Brad M., 107, 177–178
Barsky, Neil, 160
Basu, Anup K., 144
Batchelor, Steve, 75–76, 87–89
Bengen, Bill, 14
Bernanke, Ben, 164–165
BetaShares, 153
BetaShares FTSE RAFI Australia 200 ETF, 249–250
Blacklaws, Tony, 261–262
Boerma, Ties, 14
Bogle, John, 98, 103, 144
Bond indexes, 41, 58–59, 62–64
Bonds/bond indexes, 13, 38–41, 57, 62, 63, 89–92, 137–138, 200, 240, 255
　in Couch Potato portfolio, 119–126, 129
　relative to age and risk, 124–125, 213
Bortolotti, Dan, 190, 231

Branson, Richard, 235
Brazil, retiring in, 129
Brazilian investors, 263–266
Brierly, Shane, 5
British expats:
    index advisors for, 167–168
    investing for, 235–243
British index funds, 235–237
British Isles, 188
British retirees, average spent by, 2
Brokerage firms:
    for Canadian expats, 221–223
    fee comparisons, 179–184
    making trades with, 196–200
    minimum monthly investments with,
        201–202
    for non-Americans, 173–184
    offshore, 173–185
    opening account with, 195–196
Browne, Harry, 132–133, 240
Buffett, Warren, 34, 36, 47, 54–55, 57, 58,
    96–98, 162, 178
Burns, Scott, 119–120, 158
Burridge, Nicky, 82–83
Burton, Scott, 166–167

Caldwell, Kyle, 236
Cambodia, 6
Canada Pension Plan and Old Age
    Security, 21
Canadian Couch Potato portfolio, 122–124
Canadian ETFs, 223–230
Canadian expats:
    brokerage options for, 221–223
    index advisors for, 165–166
    investing for, 219–233
Canadian funds, 164, 220–221
Canadian Imperial Bank of Commerce
    (CIBC), 221
Canadian Pension Plan (CPP), 224
Canadian retirees, average spent by, 2
Canadian stock index, 123–124, 127
Canadian stock market, 175
Capital appreciation, 32–35
Capital gains taxes, 53–54, 70, 188, 231, 246
Cap-weighted indexes, 142–146, 229–230
Cash, 137–138

Cayman Islands, 188
Certified Financial Planners, 86
Charles Schwab, 153, 164, 212–215
Chen, Madeline, 174
Chile, 6
China, 37, 274, 283–284
    market returns in, 128
    retiring in, 129
Chung-yan, Leung, 84
Cities, cost of living in, 2
Cognitive dissonance, 96
Commissions, 201–202
    charged by financial advisors, 71–74, 79,
        151–153
    on ETFs, 188
    on offshore pensions, 71–74, 79
Corporate bonds, 41, 64, 120
Corporations, stocks of largest, 104–105
Corruption, 38
Cost of living:
    increases, 14
    inflation and, 6
Couch Potato portfolio, 119–130, 158
    for American expats, 207–210, 212–214
    for Asian expats, 282–287
    for Australian expats, 247–248
    for British expats, 237–240
    for Canadian expats, 223–227
    for European expats, 271–275
    for New Zealand expats, 254–255
    for South African expats, 260–261
    for South American expats, 264–265
Counterparty risk, 232
Courtney, Tim, 60
Cramer, Jim, 100
Creveling, Chad and Peggy, 70, 155
Creveling & Creveling, 155, 169
Currency conversions, 192–193, 238
Currency-hedged funds, 189–190, 223
Currency risks, 193
CXO Advisory, 162

Dahlgren-Ferrell, Annika, 18–22
Datwani, Meena, 80
DBS Vickers Securities, 174–176, 179–184
Deflation, 137–138
Devens, Jeff and Nanette, 8–9

DeVere Group, 79, 84
Dickson, Joel, 54
Dimensional Fund Advisors (DFA), 153
Discount brokerage accounts, 173–185,
    195–200
Diversification, 61–63, 86–90, 152–153
Dividends, 32–35
    reinvesting, 35, 187, 188
    taxes on, 191–192, 231–232, 256
Dixon, Lawson, 246
Dollar cost averaging, 26, 28–29, 102–103,
    194, 211
Downsizing, 4

E★Trade Financial, 176
Economic growth, stock market growth
    and, 37–38
Emerging markets:
    fundamental indexes in, 146–147
    funds from, 90–91, 103
    investing in, 128–129, 213
    retirement in, 129–130
    stock returns from, 37–38
Employer-based plans, 111–118
eRAFI Overall SA index, 263
Estate taxes, 175, 176, 188, 189, 223, 238,
    254, 260, 282
ETFs. See Exchange-traded funds (ETFs)
European ETFs, 269–271
European expats, investing for, 269–280
European indexes, 271–274
Exchange rate fees, 201
Exchange-traded funds (ETFs), 153, 157,
    175, 221, 291
    for Asian expats, 281–289
    for Australian expats, 247–251
    bonds, 200
    for Canadian expats, 223–230
    currency risks and, 193
    European, 269–271
    expense ratios, 194, 271
    fundamental, 241–243
    vs. index funds, 187–188
    moving between, 201
    for New Zealand expats, 254–256
    purchasing, 196–200
    Schwab, 212–214

sector-specific, 188–189
    for South African expats, 260–263
    swap-based, 231–232, 250, 256, 278
    unit prices of, 194
Expatitis, 3, 292
Expense ratios, 194, 271
Exxon Mobil, 143

Facebook, 105
Fama, Eugene, 157
Family-owned businesses, 37
Fastenal, 106
Ferrell, Keith, 18–22
Fidelity, 164, 206–207
Fidelity Canada, 220
Financial advisors:
    for American expats, 154–165
    for Australian expats, 166–167
    for British expats, 167–168
    for Canadian expats, 165–166
    commissions earned by, 71–74, 79,
        151–153
    company-based, 111–113
    to manage index portfolios, 149–171
    mutual funds and, 45–50, 51–52, 54–58,
        59–65
    qualities of great, 151–153
    recommendations for, 153–170
    as salesmen, 72–73
    selling offshore pension, 70–75
    stock picking by, 152–153
Financial freedom, 1–2, 7
Financial services industry, 45–50, 54–58
Fisher, Kenneth, 35
Forbes, Brigitte, 144
Forecasting, market, 97–100, 129, 153, 162,
    164–165, 202–203
Foreign earned income exclusion, 215, 216
Fosher, Ken, 98
401(k)s, 113–115
French, Kenneth, 157
Friends Provident, 74, 75–77, 87
Fundamental Index portfolio, 141–148
    for American expats, 212, 214–215
    for Asian expats, 288–289
    for Australian expats, 249–250
    for British expats, 241–243

Fundamental Index portfolio (*continued*)
  for Canadian expats, 229–230
  for European expats, 277–279
  global, 264
  for New Zealand expats, 255–256
  for South African expats, 263
  for South American expats, 266
Fund costs, 201, 220–221
Fund managers, 47, 52–53
Furness, Frank, 72–73
Fursova, Erica Holt, 111

Galbraith, John Kenneth, 162
Global bond index, 239, 255
Global capitalization, 126–129
Global fundamental indexes, 146, 264
Global Index Investment Company,
      166–167, 169
Global stock indexes, 91, 126–129,
      239–240, 255, 273, 283–284
Gold, 131–133, 135–139
Google, 65, 106
Government bonds, 120
Government pension benefits, 21–23,
      224, 292
GOV.UK, 21
Green, Kelly, 114
Grose, Kennon, 117, 158

Hardinge, Vanessa and Michael, 263–265
Haskins, Suzan, 4–5
Haslam, Penny, 79
Health care costs, 4, 5, 9
Heath, Jason, 165–166, 169
Hebner, Mark, 157
Hedge funds, 57–62
Hilbert, Mark, 54
Holding periods, 178
Home country market, 127–129
Hong Kong, 188, 222, 281–282
Horizon, 153
Horizon Canada, 231
Hsu, Jason C., 144, 145, 146, 147, 229

IA Clarington, 221
Index Fund Advisors (IFA), 60, 150,
      156–157, 169

Index funds, 51–65, 71, 77, 115–117, 141
  British, 235–237
  Canadian, 164, 220–221
  cap-weighted, 142–146, 229–230
  commission-free, 188
  vs. ETFs, 187–188
  European, 271–274
  financial advisors for, 149–171
  fundamental index, 141–148
  hedged, 189–190, 223
  high-cost, 153
  holding, 178
  rebalancing, 151
  South African, 260
  tracking errors, 236
  Vanguard, 115, 126–127, 143, 153, 164,
      205–210
Indian expats, 282–284
Individual investors:
  discipline needed by, 210
  emotions of, 149–150
  fees paid by, 45–50
  questions asked by, 187–203
  speculation by, 210–211
  underperformance by, 150, 210–211
Individual retirement accounts (IRAs),
      215–217
  illegal contributions to, 215
  Roth, 216–217
  traditional, 216
Indonesia, 177
Inflation, 2, 6, 7, 14
  gold and, 138
  stocks and, 30–31
Initial public offerings (IPOs), 105–107
Institutional investors, 46
Insured death benefit, 77–78
Interactive Brokers, 184, 260
Interest rates, 14
Internal Revenue Service (IRS), 69, 175,
      188, 215
International brokerage firms, 173–185
International funds, 102
*The International Living Guide to Retiring
      Overseas on a Budget* (Haskins and
      Prescher), 4
International stocks, 30, 31

Invesco PowerShares fundamental
    ETFs, 241
Investing strategies:
    for American expats, 205–218
    for Australian expats, 245–251
    for British expats, 235–243
    for Canadian expats, 219–233
    for European expats, 269–280
    for New Zealand expats, 253–257
    for South African expats, 259–263
    for South American expats, 263–266
Investment clubs, 107
Investment-linked assurance schemes
    (ILASs), 69–94
Investment portfolio, diversification, 87–90
Investment portfolios:
    for Asian expats, 281–289
    building own, 173–174
    choosing type, 147–148
    Couch Potato portfolio, 119–130, 158,
        207–210, 212–214, 223–227, 237–
        240, 247–248, 254–255, 260–261,
        264–265, 271–275, 282–287
    diversification, 61–62, 63, 86, 152–153
    Fundamental Index portfolio, 141–148,
        212, 214–215, 229–230, 241–243,
        249–250, 255–256, 263, 266,
        277–279, 288–289
    Permanent Portfolio, 131–140, 212, 214,
        227–228, 240–241, 248–249, 250,
        255–256, 261–262, 266, 276–278,
        287–288
    rebalancing, 121, 123, 125–128, 135–136,
        137, 151, 291
    switching between, 215, 232, 243,
        250–251, 257, 265, 279, 289
    withdrawals from, 14–17
Investments:
    401(k)s, 113–115
    bonds (see Bonds/bond indexes)
    consistent monthly investments in,
        102–103
    employer-based, 111–118
    fees paid on, 45–50, 52–53, 70–74,
        112–115
    gold, 131–133, 135–139
    hedge funds, 57–62

    with lump sums, 194
    minimum monthly, 201–202
    offshore pensions, 69–94
    real estate, 13, 19–20, 245
    returns on, 21, 71, 92–93, 121–124, 150,
        210–211, 245–246
    selling, at a loss, 195
    speculation and, 90–91, 153, 164,
        210–212, 284
    stocks (see Stocks)
    timing, 202–203
    underperforming, 62–65, 92–93,
        104–105
IRAs. See Individual retirement accounts
    (IRAs)
iShares, 147, 153, 247–248, 255, 260, 273,
    282
    Euro Government Bond 1-3 yr. UCITS,
        277
    FTSE MIB UCITS ETF, 275
    MSCI Europe, 271, 272
    MSCI New Zealand Capped ETF, 254
    MSCI World Index Fund ETF, 226
    S&P 500 ETF, 187
    SMI, 276
iShares Canada, 227
IShares Canada Latin American index, 264
iShares UK, 237
Italian investors, 275–276

Japan, 178
Jenkinson, Janet, 116
Johannesburg Stock Exchange, 259–260
JSE All Shares Index, 263

Kaderlis, Billy and Akaisha, 4–5
Kahneman, Daniel, 55–56
Karumbaya, Shabari, 282–284
Kelly, Bruce, 160
Kennon, Joshua, 35
Kerzerho, Raymond, 190
Kimball, Chip, 74
Knight, John R., 194
Kritzman, Mark, 54

Lack, Simon, 58
Laos, 6

Latin American indexes, 264
Lawson, J. M., 135
Lewis, Malcom, 166–167
Life expectancy, 14
Living expenses:
    documenting your, 293
    estimating future, 2
    low, 4
Lock-in periods, 81
Long-term bonds, 120
Long-term capital gains, 53
Loong, Eoh You, 179, 246
Lowenstein, Louis, 160
Loyalty bonuses, 79–80
Lucy, Lindell, 16–18
Lump sum investing, 194
Luxembourg, 176–177, 188, 222

Malaysia, retiring in, 129
Malkiel, Burton, 152
Mandell, Lewis, 194
Manulife Financial, 220–221
Market capitalization, 142–143
Market forecasts, 97–100, 129, 153, 162,
        164–165, 202–203
Market orders, 199–200
Market timing, 97–98
Markowitz, Harry, 157, 158
MASECO Private Wealth, 155–156, 169
Masse, Urko, 269
Materialism, 5
Matthews, Josh, 156
McGugan, Ian, 122
McHugh, Sean, 237–240
Medicare, 9
Mensa Investment Club, 107
Mercer, Rick, 168
Meyer, Jack, 48
MFS Meridian funds, 113–115
Microsoft, 106
Miller, Merton, 56
Ming, Tsang Sau, 83–84
Minimum monthly investments, 201–202
Moneychimp.com, 6, 7
Money managers, 45–52, 59–65, 70–71.
        See also Financial advisors
Morningstar ratings, 59–60, 102, 220

Mutual fund companies, 206–207
Mutual funds:
    actively managed, 46–47, 52–65, 69, 147,
        150, 163–164
    currency-hedged, 189–190
    emerging market, 90–91, 103
    fees charged buy, 58–59
    holding, 178
    index funds (see Index funds)
    international, 102
    past performance of, 59–62, 103
    ratings of, 59–60
    returns on, 102–103
    sales loads, 78
    switching between, 78

Nagratha, Arun, 221
Nairne, Michael, 220
National Bank of Canada, 231, 232
New Zealand expats, investing for, 253–257
New Zealand stock indexes, 254
Non-Americans:
    brokerage firms for, 173–184
    estate taxes and, 188
    withholding taxes for, 191–192
Noto, Tony, 71–72, 154
Noto Financial Planning, 154, 169

Objective Financial Partners Inc., 165–166,
        169
Odean, Terrance, 107, 178
Offshore brokerage firms, choosing,
        173–185
Offshore pensions, 69–94, 221, 291
    abuses of, 73
    average performance of, 92
    complaints about, 83–84
    early redemption penalties on, 74, 75, 81,
        84–85
    fees and charges of, 70–77, 79, 81–82, 85,
        112–113, 115, 238
    fund switching and, 78
    vs. index funds, 71
    insured death benefit, 77–78
    lack of diversification in, 86–90
    lock-in periods, 81
    loyalty bonuses, 79–80

regulation of, 80–83
sales loads, 78
sales pitches for, 82–83, 87
withholding taxes on, 192
in the workplace, 74–75
Overseas retirement, 4–6

Pan Asia Bond Index, 285
Pan Asia Index, 285
Pensions, 63–65
building your, 13–24
employer-based, 111–118
fees on, 112–115
government benefits, 21–23, 224, 292
offshore, 69–94, 221, 291
Permanent Portfolio, 130–140
for American expats, 212, 214
for Asian expats, 287–288
for Australian expats, 248–249, 250
for British expats, 240–241
for Canadian expats, 227–228
for European expats, 276–278
for New Zealand expats, 255–256
for South African expats, 261–262
for South American expats, 266
Postinflation income adjustment, 6–8, 10
PowerShares, 153, 278
PowerShares FTSE RAFI All-World Index
(PSRW), 250, 256, 265, 288
Prescher, Dan, 4–5
Proctor, Susan, 90–91
Prosperity, 137
Protected Asset TEP Fund (PATF), 87
Protégé Partners, 58
PS FTSE RAFI All-World 3000 index, 146

Quantitative Analysis of Investor Behavior, 62

Randall, David, 164
Rao, Alla, 75
Raymond James Financial Services, 116,
159–165, 169
Real estate:
Australian, 245
rental, 13, 19–20
Real returns, on stocks, 31
Recessions, 138

Registered retirement savings plans
(RRSPs), 230–231
Reinvestment, of dividends, 35, 187, 188
Rekenthaler, John, 60
Rental property, 13, 19–20
Retail investors, 46–47
Retire Early Lifestyle, 4
Retirement:
overseas, 4–5
planning, 1–11
rules, cheating conventional, 3–5
Retirement savings:
estimated amount needed for, 6–10,
16–24
setting target for, 1–3
withdrawals from, 14–16, 17
Richmond, Wayne, 260
Risk taking, 125
Robertson, Benjamin, 72
Rothery, Norman, 210
Roth IRAs, 216–217
Rousseu, Scott, 221
Rowland, Craig, 135, 214, 228
Royal Bank of Canada (RBC), 220
Russell Investments, 147
RW Investment Strategies, 157–158, 169

S&P/Dow Jones Indices vs. Active Funds
(SPIVA), 220
Sales loads, 78
Samuelson, Paul, 207
Sandler, Ron, 53
Satis Asset Management, 167–169
Saunders, Laura, 206
Saving ability, 292–293
Saxo Capital Markets, 174, 177–184,
237–238, 246, 259, 260, 269
Schwab, 153, 164, 212–215
Schwed, Fred, 51
Sector-specific ETFs, 188–189
Securities Transfer Tax (STT), 259
Sharpe, William F., 46, 55, 71, 114, 158
Shearon, Ben and Chiho, 6–7
Sherwood, Ben, 167–168
"Shorting the market, 57
Short-term bonds, 120
Short-term capital gains, 53

Shoven, John, 54
Siegel, Jeremy, 100–101, 106, 132
Sinclair, Upton, 70
Singapore, 174–176, 188, 222, 281–282
Smith, Jeff and Cheryl, 22–24
Social Security, 9, 21–23
Soos, Philip, 245
South African expats, investing for, 259–263
South American expats, investing for, 263–266
Southeast Asia, 5–6
Speculation, 90–91, 153, 164, 210–212, 284
Standard & Poor's (S&P) 500 index, 26–29, 101, 104, 121–122, 143, 144, 189
Stewart, Jon, 100
Stock brokers, 47
Stock markets:
　average U.S. returns, 101–102
　crash of 2008–2009, 125–126
　investing in down market, 96–97
　predictions, 95–107, 129, 162, 164–165, 202–203
　timing, 97–98, 202–203
Stocks, 13, 24, 137–138
　business earnings and, 35–37
　buying in down market, 125–126
　dividends, 32–35, 187, 188
　in emerging economies, 37–38
　holding, 178
　inflation and, 30–31
　international, 30, 31
　investing in falling, 96–97
　IPOs, 105–107
　of largest companies, 104–105
　picking individual, 98–102, 104–105, 107, 152–153
　returns on, 25–38, 63, 92–93, 246
　S&P 500 index, 26–29, 101, 104, 121–122, 143, 144, 189
　underperforming, 104–105
Swap-based ETFs, 231–232, 250, 256, 278
Swedroe, Larry, 152
Swensen, David, 47
Swiss investors, 275–276

Target Retirement funds, 207–209, 210
Target setting, 1–3

Taxes, 155–156
　capital gains, 53–54, 70, 188, 231, 246
　on dividends, 191–192, 231–232, 256
　estate, 175, 176, 188, 189, 223, 238, 254, 260, 282
　on foreign investment income, 70, 173–174
　IRAs and, 215–217
　swap-based ETFs and, 231–232
　withholding, 176, 191–192, 231, 246, 256
Tax evasion, 69
Tax-free savings accounts (TFSAs), 230–231
Tax havens, 188, 222
TD Direct Investing International, 174, 176–177, 179–184, 222
TD Waterhouse, 221, 222
Thailand, retiring in, 129
Tie Care International, 152, 161, 163–164
Toronto-Dominion Bank, 221
Tracking errors, 236
Trading costs, 201
T. Rowe Price, 153, 164
TrustedHousesitters.com, 4
Tucker, Doug, 73

Unemployment, 98, 99
Unit trusts, 46
U.S. stock market, 26, 29, 32, 37, 57–58, 60–63, 84, 87, 101–102, 127, 132, 175, 238

Vanguard funds, 115, 126–127, 143, 153, 164, 205–210
　Admiral Shares, 209, 211
　in Canada, 227
　ETFs, 247–248
　fees charged by, 236, 273
　FTSE All-World ETF, 260
　FTSE All-World Index, 255
　FTSE All-World UCITS ETF, 273–274, 283
　FTSE Developed Europe, 271, 272
　FTSE UK Equity index, 236
　Short-Term Treasury Index, 211
　Target Retirement funds, 207–209, 210

Total International Stock Market
    Index, 211
Total Stock Market Index, 211
Total World Stock Index, 211–212, 213
Vanguard S&P 500 index, 26–29, 187
    vs.Virgin Money, 236–237
Vanguard UK, 237
Vietnam, 5–6
Virgin Money, 235–237
    FTSE All Share UK index, 236

Wal-Mart, 142–143
Wasilewski, Robert, 157–158

West, John M., 144, 145, 146, 147, 229
WIlliams, Jon, 74–75
Withdrawal rate, 14–16, 17
Withholding taxes, 176, 191–192, 231,
    246, 256
Wong, Shawn, 86

Yahoo! Finance, 197
Yates, Lara, 160, 162
Young, Steve, 72–73

Zargar, Adam, 61–62
Zweig, Jason, 55, 96, 162